The Little Seagull Handbook

The Little Seagull Handbook

Richard Bullock
WRIGHT STATE UNIVERSITY

Francine Weinberg

WRITE

RESEARCH

EDIT

W. W. NORTON & COMPANY
New York • London

W. W. Norton & Company has been independent since its founding in 1923, when William Warder Norton and Mary D. Herter Norton first published lectures delivered at the People's Institute, the adult education division of New York City's Cooper Union. The firm soon expanded its program beyond the Institute, publishing books by celebrated academics from America and abroad. By mid-century, the two major pillars of our publishing program—trade books and college texts—were firmly established. In the 1950s, the Norton family transferred control of the company to its employees, and today—with a staff of 400 and a comparable number of trade, college, and professional titles published each year—W. W. Norton stands as the largest and oldest publishing house owned wholly by its employees.

Editor: Marilyn Moller
Associate editor: Ana Cooke
Project editor: Rebecca Homiski
Editorial assistant: Betsye Mullaney
Production manager: Benjamin Reynolds
Design director: Rubina Yeh
Designers: Lisa Buckley/Anna Palchik/Carole Desnoes
Photo editor: Stephanie Romeo
Marketing manager: Scott Berzon
Emedia editor: Peter Lesser
Composition: Matrix Publishing Services
Page layout: Carole Desnoes
Manufacturing: QuadGraphics—Leominster, MA

Library of Congress Cataloging-in-Publication Data

Bullock, Richard.
    The Little Seagull handbook / Richard Bullock, Francine Weinberg.
— 1st ed.
        p.   cm.
    Includes bibliographical references and index.
    ISBN 978-0-393-91151-0 (pbk.)
    1. English language—Rhetoric—Handbooks, manuals, etc.   2. English
        language—Grammar—Handbooks, manuals, etc.   3. Report
        writing—Handbooks, manuals, etc.   I. Weinberg, Francine.   II. Title.
    PE1408.B883823 2011
    808'.042—dc22   2010031651

W. W. Norton & Company, Inc., 500 Fifth Avenue, New York, N.Y. 10110
www.wwnorton.com

W. W. Norton & Company Ltd., Castle House, 75/76 Wells Street, London
    W1T 3QT

7 8 9

Preface

The Little Seagull Handbook began as an attempt to create a pocket-sized handbook that would provide the help students need with the kinds of writing they are most often assigned to do. There are any number of little handbooks that cover grammar, punctuation, documentation, and the writing process; and a couple that offer some guidance in the basic elements of argument. But none offer help with other kinds of writing that students are routinely assigned—or, too often, just expected to be able to do: analyses, reports, narratives, annotated bibliographies, and such. *The Little Seagull* provides that help.

I had one other goal: to make the book as brief and easy to use as possible. From my own experience as a teacher and writing program administrator, I've seen how much students prefer smaller books, and so to paraphrase Elmore Leonard, I've tried to give the information college writers need—and to leave out the details they skip. I've also seen how important it is that a handbook be easy to use. To that end, the book is organized around the familiar categories of writing, researching, and editing—and includes menus, directories, a glossary/index, and more to help students find the help they need.

Highlights

Help with the kinds of writing students are assigned—arguments, analyses, reports, narratives, and more. Brief chapters cover seven common genres, with models demonstrating each genre on the companion website. An index of common writing assignments leads students to places in the book where they'll find some help on most of the kinds of writing they need to do.

Easy to use. Menus, directories, a glossary/index, and color-coded parts help students find the information they need. And a simple three-part organization—Write, Research, and Edit—will make it easy for them to know where to look. Even the cover flaps are useful, with an index of writing assignments on the front flap and a checklist for revising and editing on the back.

Just enough detail, but with color-coded links that refer students to the glossary/index for more information if they need it.

User-friendly documentation guidelines—on MLA, APA, *Chicago,* and CSE styles. Documentation directories lead students to the examples they need, color-coded templates show what information to include, and documentation maps show where to find the required detail. Model papers demonstrate each style, with brief examples in the book and complete papers on the companion website.

A full chapter on paragraphs, a subject neglected in all other pocket handbooks. But students write in paragraphs, and can use help doing so. They'll find the help they need in *The Little Seagull.*

It takes a big team to write even a small handbook, starting with my coauthor Francine Weinberg and not one but two superb developmental editors, Ana Cooke and Judy Voss—and a magnificent project editor, Rebecca Homiski. A deep bow as well to Ben Reynolds for producing this book in record time. And a special shout out to Carole Desnoes for her deft and speedy layout work. Thanks also to Marian Johnson, Betsye Mullaney, Steve Dunn, Elizabeth Audley, Leah Clark, and especially Scott Berzon; I've always appreciated the fact that Norton is employee-owned, but who knew that meant both the managing editor and the director of marketing would read page proofs *on a weekend?* I thank Peter Lesser, Jack Lamb, and Kristin Bowen for creating the digital versions; and Debra Morton Hoyt and Carin Berger for the fabulous cover design. Marilyn Moller, the guiding intelligence behind all my textbooks, deserves special thanks. Finally come my students and colleagues at Wright State: most of what I know about teaching and writing I've learned from them. And as always, my wife Barb keeps me honest, keeps me whole. Hats off to you all.

Richard Bullock

How to Use This Book

Write. Research. Edit. Perhaps you've been assigned to write a paper that makes a case for why parking on campus should be free. Maybe you need to find sources for a report on organic farming in your state. Or you may just want to make sure that the punctuation in your cover letter is perfect before you apply for a new job. Whether you need to write, research, edit — or all three — *The Little Seagull Handbook* can help.

Ways of Using the Book

Menus. If you are looking for a specific chapter, start with the Brief Menu on the inside front cover; if you are looking for a specific section in a chapter, start with the Detailed Menu on the inside back cover.

Glossary / index. If you're looking for definitions of key terms and concepts, turn to the combined glossary and index at the back of the book. Be aware also that words highlighted in TAN throughout the book are defined in the glossary/index. Check the glossary/index when you aren't sure which chapter covers a topic you're looking for—for instance, guidance on when to use *a* and when to use *the*.

Color-coded organization. The parts of this book are color-coded for easy reference: red for WRITE, blue for RESEARCH, and yellow for EDITING.

Index of common writing assignments. The front flap lists many of the kinds of writing you will need to do. Whether you have a specific assignment or are simply trying to figure out what kind of writing will work best for a particular topic or purpose, this index can lead you to places in the book where you'll find help. And you'll find model papers demonstrating most of these kinds of writing on the companion website: **wwnorton.com/write/little-seagull-handbook**.

Checklist for revising and editing. On the back flap is a list of prompts to guide you as you revise and edit a draft—and that lead you to pages in the book where you'll find help.

MLA, APA, *Chicago*, and CSE guidelines. Color-coded chapters cover each style, with directories in the back of the book that lead to the specific examples you need. Color-coded templates show what information to include, and documentation maps show you where to find the information required. You'll find model papers demonstrating each style on the companion website: **wwnorton.com/write/ little-seagull-handbook**.

Scanning for information. Sometimes you may simply turn to a part of the book where you know that information you're looking for is located. You could scan the red headings to find where the topic is explained. Or if you just want to find an example showing you what to do, you'll find that examples are all marked by little blue pointers (▶) to make them easy to spot.

Write

I think I did pretty well, considering
I started out with nothing but a bunch
of blank paper.

—STEVE MARTIN

W-1 Writing Contexts

Whenever we write, whether it's an email to a friend, a toast at a wedding, or an essay, we do so within some kind of context—a rhetorical situation that helps shape our choices as writers. Whatever our topic, we have a purpose, a certain audience, a particular stance, a genre, and a medium to consider—and often as not a design. This chapter discusses each of these elements and provides some questions that can help you think about some of the choices you have as you write.

W-1a Purpose

All writing has a purpose. We write to explore our thoughts, express ourselves, and entertain; to record words and events; to communicate with others; to persuade others to think or behave in certain ways. Here are some questions to help you think about your purpose(s) as you write:

- What is the primary purpose of the writing task: to entertain? to inform? to persuade? to demonstrate knowledge? something else?

- What are your own goals?

- What do you want your audience to do, think, or feel? How will they use what you tell them?

- What does this writing task call on you to do? Do you have an assignment that specifies a certain GENRE or strategy—to argue a position? to report on an event? to compare two texts?

- What are the best ways to achieve your purpose? Should you take a particular STANCE? Write in a particular MEDIUM? Use certain DESIGN elements?

W-1b Audience

What you write, how much you write, and how you phrase it are all influenced by the AUDIENCE you envision. For example, as a student writing an essay for an instructor, you will be expected to produce a text with few or no errors, something you may worry less about in an email to a friend.

- Whom do you want to reach? What expectations does your audience have from you? What's your relationship with them, and how does it affect your TONE?

- What is your audience's background — their education and life experiences?

- What are their interests? What motivates them? Do they have any political attitudes or interests that may affect the way they read your piece?

- Is there any demographic information that you should keep in mind, such as race, gender, sexual orientation, religious beliefs, or economic status?

- What does your audience already know—or believe—about your topic? What do you need to tell them?

- What kind of response do you want from your audience? Do you want them to do or believe something? Accept what you say? Something else?

- How can you best appeal to your audience? What kind of information will they find interesting or persuasive? Are there any design elements that will appeal to them?

W-1c Genre

Genres are kinds of writing. Reports, position papers, poems, letters, instructions—even jokes—are genres. Each one has certain features and follows particular conventions of style and presentation. Academic assignments generally specify the GENRE, but if it isn't clear, ask your instructor. Then consider these issues:

- What is your genre, and what are its key elements and conventions? How do they affect what content you should include?

- Does your genre require a certain organization or **MEDIUM**? Does it have any **DESIGN** requirements?
- How does your genre affect your **TONE**, if at all?
- Does the genre require formal (or informal) language?

W-1d Topic

An important part of any writing context is the topic—what you are writing about. As you choose a topic, keep in mind your rhetorical situation and any requirements specified by your assignments.

- If your topic is assigned, what do the verbs in the assignment ask you to do: **ANALYZE**? **COMPARE**? **SUMMARIZE**? something else?
- Does the assignment offer a broad subject area (such as the environment) that allows you to choose a limited topic within it (such as a particular environmental issue)?
- What do you need to do to complete the assignment? Do you need to do research? Find illustrations?
- If you can choose a topic, think about what you are interested in. What do you want to learn more about? What topics from your courses have you found intriguing? What community, national, or global issues do you care about?
- Do you need to limit your topic to fit a specified time or length?

W-1e Stance and Tone

Whenever you write, you have a certain stance, an attitude toward your topic. For example, you might be objective, critical, passionate, or indifferent. You express that stance through the words you use and the way you approach your subject and audience—in other words, your tone. Just as you likely alter what you say depending on whether you're speaking to a boss or a good friend, so you need to make similar adjustments as a writer. Ask yourself these questions:

- What is your stance, and how can you best present it to achieve your purpose? Be sure that your language and even your typeface are appropriate to your purpose.

- What TONE will best convey your stance? Do you want to be seen as reasonable? Angry? Thoughtful? Ironic? Check your writing for words that reflect that tone—and for ones that do not.

- How is your stance likely to be received by your AUDIENCE?

W-1f Media / Design

We communicate through many media, both verbal and nonverbal: our bodies (we wave), our voices (we shout), and various technologies (we write with a pencil, send email, tweet). No matter the MEDIUM, a text's DESIGN affects the way it is received and understood. To identify your media and design needs, consider these questions:

- Does your assignment call for a certain medium? A printed essay? An oral report with visual aids? A website?

- How does your medium affect the way you will write and organize your text? For example, long paragraphs may be fine on paper, but bulleted phrases or key words work better on PowerPoint slides.

- How does your medium affect your language? Do you need to be more formal or informal?

- Are there any elements that need to be designed? Anything you would like to highlight by putting it in a box?

- Should you include headings? Would they help you organize your material and help readers follow the text?

- Will your audience expect or need any illustrations? Is there any information that would be easier to understand as a chart?

W-2 Writing Processes

To create anything, we generally break the work down into a series of steps. We follow a recipe (or the directions on a box) to bake a cake; we divide a piece of music into various singing parts to arrange it for a choir. So it is when we write. We rely on various processes to get from a blank page to a finished product. This chapter offers advice on some of these processes—from generating ideas to drafting to revising and editing.

W-2a Generating Ideas

The activities that follow can help you explore a topic—what you already know about it, or how you might look at it in new ways.

- **Brainstorming.** Jot down everything that comes to mind about your topic, working either alone or with others. Look over your list, and try to identify connections or patterns.

- **Freewriting.** Write as quickly as you can without stopping for 5–10 minutes. Then underline interesting passages. Write more, using an underlined passage as your new topic.

- **Looping.** Write for 5–10 minutes, jotting down whatever you know about your subject. Then write a one-sentence summary of the most important idea. Use this summary to start another loop. Keep looping until you have a tentative focus.

- **Clustering.** Clustering is a way of connecting ideas visually. Write your topic in the middle of a page, and write subtopics and other ideas around it. Circle each item and draw lines to connect related ideas.

- **Questioning.** You might start by asking *What? Who? When? Where? How?* and *Why?* You could also ask questions as if the topic were a play: What happens? Who are the participants? When does the action take place? How? Where? Why does this happen?

- *Keeping a journal.* Jotting down ideas, feelings, or the events of your day in a journal is a good way to generate ideas—and a journal is a good place to explore why you think as you do.

- *Starting some research.* Depending on your topic and purpose, you might do a little preliminary research to get basic information and help you see paths you might follow.

W-2b Coming Up with a Tentative Thesis

A **THESIS** is a statement that indicates your main point, identifying your topic and the **CLAIM** you are making about it. Here are some steps for developing a tentative thesis statement:

1. **State your topic as a question.** You may have a topic, such as "gasoline prices." But that doesn't make a statement. To move from a topic to a thesis statement, start by turning your topic into a question: *What causes fluctuations in gasoline prices?*

2. **Then turn your question into a position.** A thesis statement is an assertion—it takes a stand or makes a claim. One way to establish a thesis is to answer your own question: *Gasoline prices fluctuate for several reasons.*

3. **Narrow your thesis.** A good thesis is specific, telling your audience exactly what your essay will cover: *Gasoline prices fluctuate because of production procedures, consumer demand, international politics, and oil companies' policies.* A good way to narrow a thesis is to ask and answer questions about it: *Why do gasoline prices fluctuate?* The answer will help you craft a narrow, focused thesis.

4. **Qualify your thesis.** Though you may sometimes want to state your thesis strongly and bluntly, often you need to acknowledge that your assertion may not be unconditionally true. In such cases, consider adding such terms as *may*, *very likely*, and *often* to qualify your statement: *Gasoline prices very likely fluctuate because of production procedures, consumer demand, international politics, and oil companies' policies.*

Whatever tentative thesis you start out with, keep in mind that you may want to modify it as you proceed.

W-2c Organizing and Drafting

Organizing. You may want to use an outline to help you organize your ideas before you begin to draft. You can create an informal outline by simply listing your ideas in the order in which you want to write about them.

> Thesis statement
>
> First main idea
> > Supporting evidence or detail
> > Supporting evidence or detail
>
> Second main idea
> > Supporting evidence or detail
> > Supporting evidence or detail

An outline can help you organize your thoughts and see where more research is needed. As you draft and revise, though, stay flexible—and ready to change direction as your topic develops.

Drafting. At some point, you need to write out a draft. As you draft, you may need to get more information, rethink your thesis, or explore some new ideas. But first, you just need to get started.

- *Write quickly in spurts.* Try to write a complete draft, or a complete section of a longer draft, in one sitting. If you need to stop in the middle, jot down some notes about where you're headed so that you can pick up your train of thought when you begin again.

- *Expect surprises.* Writing is a form of thinking; you may end up somewhere you didn't anticipate. That can be a good thing—but if not, it's okay to double back or follow a new path.

- *Expect to write more than one draft.* Parts of your first draft may not achieve your goals. That's okay—as you revise, you can fill in gaps and improve your writing.

- *Don't worry about correctness.* You can check words, dates, and spelling at a later stage. For now, just write.

W-2d Getting Response

As writers, we need to be able to look at our work with a critical eye, to see if our writing is doing what we want it to. We also need to get feedback from other readers. Here is a list of questions for reading a draft closely and considering how it should or could be revised:

- Will the beginning grab readers' attention? If so, how does it do so? If not, how else might the piece begin?

- What is the THESIS? Is it stated directly? If not, should it be?

- Are there good REASONS and sufficient EVIDENCE to support the thesis? Is there anywhere you'd like to have more detail?

- Are all QUOTATIONS introduced with a SIGNAL PHRASE and documented? Are they accurately quoted, and have any changes and omissions been indicated with brackets and ellipses?

- Is there a clear pattern of organization? Does each part relate to the thesis? Are there appropriate TRANSITIONS to help readers follow your train of thought? Are there headings that make the structure of the text clear—and if not, should there be?

- Are there any VISUALS —tables, charts, photos? If so, are they clearly labeled with captions? If you did not create them yourself, have you cited your sources?

- Will the text meet the needs and expectations of its AUDIENCE? Where might readers need more information or guidance?

- Is your STANCE on the topic clear and consistent throughout? Is the TONE appropriate for your audience and purpose?

- Is the ending satisfying? What does it leave readers thinking? How else might the text end?

- Is the title one that will attract interest? Does it announce your topic and give some sense of what you have to say?

W-2e Revising

Once you've studied your draft with a critical eye and gotten response from other readers, it's time to revise. Start with global (whole-text) issues, and gradually move to smaller, sentence-level details.

- *Give yourself time to revise.* Set deadlines that will give you plenty of time to work on your **REVISION**. Try to get some distance. If you can, get away from your writing for a while and think about something else.

- *Revise to sharpen your focus.* Examine your **THESIS** to make sure it matches your purpose and clearly articulates your main point. Does each paragraph contribute to your main point? Does your beginning introduce your topic and provide any necessary contextual information? Does your ending provide a satisfying conclusion?

- *Revise to strengthen the argument.* Make sure that all your key ideas are fully explained. If readers find some of your **CLAIMS** unconvincing, you may need to qualify them—or to provide more **REASONS** or **EVIDENCE**. If you need to provide additional evidence, you may need to do additional research. Make sure that all quotations, paraphrases, summaries, and visuals support your point and include any needed documentation.

- *Revise to improve the organization.* You may find it helpful to outline your draft to help you see all the parts. If anything seems out of place, move it, or if need be cut it completely. Check to see if you've included appropriate **TRANSITIONS** or headings.

- *Revise to be sure readers will understand what you're saying.* Make sure that you've defined any terms they may not know. If you don't state a thesis directly, consider whether you should. Look closely at your title to be sure it gives a sense of what your text is about.

W-2f Editing and Proofreading

Your ability to produce clear, error-free writing shows something about your ability as a writer, so you should be sure to edit and proofread your work carefully. Editing is the stage when you work on the details of your paragraphs, sentences, language, and punctuation to make your writing as clear, precise, and correct as possible. The following guidelines can help you check the paragraphs, sentences, and words in your drafts.

Editing paragraphs

- Does each paragraph focus on one point and have a **TOPIC SENTENCE** that announces that point? Does every sentence in the paragraph relate to that point?

- Where is the most important information—at the beginning? the end? in the middle?

- Check to see how your paragraphs fit together. Does each one follow smoothly from the one before it? Do you need to add **TRANSITIONS**?

- How does the first paragraph catch readers' attention? How else might you begin?

- Does the final paragraph provide a satisfactory ending? How else might you conclude?

For more help with paragraphs, see **W-3**.

Editing sentences

- Check to see that each sentence is complete, with a **SUBJECT** and a **VERB**, and that it begins with a capital letter and ends with a period, question mark, or exclamation point.

- Are your sentences varied? If they all start with a subject or are all the same length, try varying them by adding transitions or introductory phrases—or by combining some sentences.

- Be sure that lists or series are parallel in form—all nouns (*lions, tigers, bears*), all verbs (*hop, skip, jump*), and so on.

- Do many of your sentences begin with *It* or *There*? Sometimes these words help introduce a topic, but often they make a text vague.

For more help with sentences, see **S-1** through **S-9**.

Editing language

- Are you sure of the meaning of every word?

- Do your words all convey the appropriate **TONE**?

- Is any of your language too general? For example, do you need to replace verbs like *be* or *do* with more specific verbs?

- Check all **PRONOUNS** to see that they have clear **ANTECEDENTS**.

- Have you used any **CLICHÉS**? Your writing will almost always be better without such predictable expressions.

- Be careful with language that refers to others. Edit out language that might be considered sexist or would otherwise stereotype any individual or group.

- Check for it's and its. Use *it's* to mean "it is" and *its* to mean "belonging to it."

For more help with language, see **L-1** through **L-7**.

Proofreading

This is the final stage of the writing process, the point when you check for misspelled words, mixed-up fonts, missing pages, and so on.

- Use your computer's grammar and spelling checkers, but be aware that they're not very reliable. Computer programs rely on formulas and banks of words—so what they flag (or not) as mistakes may not be accurate. For example, if you were to write "Sea you soon," the word *Sea* would not be flagged as misspelled.

- Place a ruler or piece of paper under each line as you read. Use your finger or a pencil as a pointer.

- Try beginning with the last sentence and working backward.
- Read your text out loud to yourself—or better, to others. Ask someone else to read your text.

W-2g Collaborating

Even if you do much of your writing alone at your computer, you probably spend a lot of time working with others. Here are some guidelines for collaborating successfully with other writers.

Working in a group

- For face-to-face meetings, make sure everyone is facing one another and is physically part of the group.
- Be respectful and tactful.
- Each meeting needs an agenda—and careful attention to the clock. Appoint one person as timekeeper and another person as group leader; a third member should keep a record of the discussion and write a summary afterward.

Working on a group writing project

- Define the overall project as clearly as possible, and divide the work into parts.
- Assign each group member specific tasks with deadlines.
- Try to accommodate everyone's style of working, but make sure everyone performs.
- Work for consensus, if not necessarily total agreement.

W-3 Developing Paragraphs

If you've opened to this chapter, chances are that you have some questions about paragraphs. Here one writer recalls when he first understood what a paragraph does.

> I can remember picking up my father's books before I could read. The words themselves were mostly foreign, but I still remember the exact moment when I first understood, with a sudden clarity, the purpose of a paragraph. I didn't have the vocabulary to say "paragraph," but I realized that a paragraph was a fence that held words. The words inside a paragraph worked together for a common purpose. They had some specific reason for being inside the same fence. . . .
> —Sherman Alexie, "The Joy of Reading and Writing"

This chapter will help you build "fences" around words that work together on a common topic. It offers tips and examples for composing strong paragraphs.

W-3a Focusing on the Main Point

All the sentences in a paragraph should focus on one main idea, as they do in this paragraph from an article about the Mall of America.

> There is, of course, nothing naturally abhorrent in the human impulse to dwell in marketplaces or the urge to buy, sell, and trade. Rural Americans traditionally looked forward to the excitement and sensuality of market day; Native Americans traveled long distances to barter and trade at sprawling, festive encampments. In Persian bazaars and in the ancient Greek agoras the very soul of the community was preserved and could be seen, felt, heard, and smelled as it might be nowhere else. All over the planet the humblest of people have always gone to market with hope in their hearts and in expectation of something beyond mere goods—seeking a place where humanity is temporarily in ascendance, a palette for the senses, one another. —David Guterson, "Enclosed. Encyclopedic. Endured: The Mall of America"

Topic sentences. To help you focus a paragraph on one main point, state that point in a TOPIC SENTENCE. Often, but not always, you might start a paragraph with a topic sentence, as in this example from an essay about legalizing the sale of human kidneys.

> Dialysis is harsh, expensive, and, worst of all, only temporary. Acting as an artificial kidney, dialysis mechanically filters the blood of a patient. It works, but not well. With treatment sessions lasting three hours, several times a week, those dependent on dialysis are, in a sense, shackled to a machine for the rest of their lives. Adding excessive stress to the body, dialysis causes patients to feel increasingly faint and tired, usually keeping them from work and other normal activities.
>
> —Joanna MacKay, "Organ Sales Will Save Lives"

Sometimes you may choose to put the topic sentence at the end of the paragraph. See how this strategy works in another paragraph in the essay about kidneys.

> In a legal kidney transplant, everybody gains except the donor. The doctors and nurses are paid for the operation, the patient receives a new kidney, but the donor receives nothing. Sure, the donor will have the warm, uplifting feeling associated with helping a fellow human being, but this is not enough reward for most people to part with a piece of themselves. In an ideal world, the average person would be altruistic enough to donate a kidney with nothing expected in return. The real world, however, is run by money. We pay men for donating sperm, and we pay women for donating ova, yet we expect others to give away an entire organ with no compensation. If the sale of organs were allowed, people would have a greater incentive to help save the life of a stranger.

Occasionally the main point is so obvious that you don't need a topic sentence. Especially in NARRATIVE writing, you may choose only to imply—not state—the main idea, as in this paragraph from an essay about one Latina writer's difficulty in learning Spanish.

> I came to the United States in 1963 at age 3 with my family and immediately stopped speaking Spanish. College-educated and

> seamlessly bilingual when they settled in west Texas, my parents
> (a psychology professor and an artist) wholeheartedly embraced
> the notion of the American melting pot. They declared that their
> two children would speak nothing but *inglés*. They'd read in Eng-
> lish, write in English, and fit into Anglo society beautifully.
> —Tanya Barrientos, "Se Habla Español"

Sticking to the main point. Whether or not you announce the
main point in a topic sentence, be sure that every sentence in a
paragraph relates to that point. Edit out any sentences that stray off
topic, such as those crossed out below.

> In "Se Habla Español," Tanya Barrientos notes some of the
> difficulties she encounters *has* ~~encounters~~ *ed* as a Latina who is not fluent in Spanish.
> ~~Previous generations of immigrants were encouraged to speak
> only English.~~ When someone poses a question to her in Spanish,
> she often has to respond in English. In other instances, she tries
> to speak Spanish but falters over the past and future tenses. Situ-
> ations like these embarrass Barrientos and make her feel left out
> of ~~the Latino~~ *a* community she want*s*~~ed~~ to be part of. ~~Native Guate-
> malans who are bilingual do not have such problems.~~

W-3b Strategies for Developing the Main Point

A good paragraph provides enough good details to develop its main
point—to fill out and support that point. Following are some common strategies for fleshing out and organizing paragraphs—and
sometimes even for organizing an entire essay.

Analyzing cause and effect. Sometimes you can develop a paragraph on a topic by analyzing what CAUSES it—or what its EFFECTS
might be. The following paragraph about air turbulence identifies
some of its causes.

> A variety of factors can cause turbulence, which is essentially
> a disturbance in the movement of air. Thunderstorms, the jet

stream, and mountains are some of the more common natural culprits, while what is known as wake turbulence is created by another plane. "Clear air turbulence" is the kind that comes up unexpectedly; it is difficult to detect because there is no moisture or particles to reveal the movement of air.

—Susan Stellin, "The Inevitability of Bumps"

Classifying and dividing. When we **CLASSIFY** something, we group it with things that share similar characteristics. See how David Brooks uses classification to tell us how one marketing firm views potential customers.

The most famous of these precision marketing firms is Claritas, which breaks down the U.S. population into sixty-two psycho-demographic clusters, based on such factors as how much money people make, what they like to read and watch, and what products they have bought in the past. For example, the "suburban sprawl" cluster is composed of young families making about $41,000 a year and living in fast-growing places such as Burnsville, Minnesota, and Bensalem, Pennsylvania. These people are almost twice as likely as other Americans to have three-way calling. They are two and a half times as likely to buy Light n' Lively Kid Yogurt. Members of the "towns & gowns" cluster are recent college graduates in places such as Berkeley, California, and Gainesville, Florida. They are big consumers of Dove Bars and *Saturday Night Live*. They tend to drive small foreign cars and to read *Rolling Stone* and *Scientific American*.   —David Brooks, "People Like Us"

As a writing strategy, **DIVISION** is a way of separating something into parts. See how the following paragraph divides the concept of pressure into four kinds.

I see four kinds of pressure working on college students today: economic pressure, parental pressure, peer pressure, and self-induced pressure. It is easy to look around for villains—to blame the colleges for charging too much money, the professors for assigning too much work, the parents for pushing their children too far, the students for driving themselves too hard. But there are no villains; only victims.

—William Zinsser, "College Pressures"

Comparing and contrasting. Comparing things looks at their similarities; contrasting them focuses on their differences—though often we use the word *comparison* to refer to both strategies. You can structure a paragraph that COMPARES AND CONTRASTS two ways. One is to shift back and forth between each item, as in this paragraph contrasting the attention given to a football team and to academic teams.

> The football team from Mountain View High School won the Arizona state championship last year. Again. Unbeknownst to the vast majority of the school's student body, so did the Science Bowl Team, the Speech and Debate Team, and the Academic Decathlon team. The football players enjoyed the attentions of an enthralled school, complete with banners, assemblies, and even video announcements in their honor, a virtual barrage of praise and downright deification. As for the three champion academic teams, they received a combined total of around ten minutes of recognition, tacked onto the beginning of a sports assembly. Nearly all of the graduating seniors will remember the name and escapades of their star quarterback; nearly none of them will ever even realize that their class produced Arizona's first national champion in Lincoln-Douglas Debate. After all, why should they? He and his teammates were "just the nerds."   —Grant Penrod,
> "Anti-Intellectualism: Why We Hate the Smart Kids"

Another way to compare and contrast two items is to cover all the details about one and then all the details about the other. See how this approach works in the following example, which contrasts photographs of President Clinton and Hillary Clinton on the opening day of the 1994 baseball season.

> The next day photos of the Clintons in action appeared in newspapers around the country. Many papers, including the *New York Times* and the *Washington Post*, chose the same two photos to run. The one of Bill Clinton showed him wearing an Indians cap and warm-up jacket. The President, throwing lefty, had turned his shoulders sideways to the plate in preparation for delivery. He was bringing the ball forward from behind his head in a clean-looking throwing action as the photo was snapped. Hillary Clinton was pictured wearing a dark jacket, a scarf, and an oversized Cubs hat. In preparation for her throw she was standing directly facing the plate. A right-hander, she had the elbow of her throwing arm

pointed out in front of her. Her forearm was tilted back, toward her shoulder. The ball rested on her upturned palm. As the picture was taken, she was in the middle of an action that can only be described as throwing like a girl.
                                  —James Fallows, "Throwing Like a Girl"

Another way to make a comparison is with an **ANALOGY**, explaining something unfamiliar by comparing it with something familiar. See how one writer uses analogy to explain the way DNA encodes genetic information.

Although the complexity of cells, tissues, and whole organisms is breathtaking, the way in which the basic DNA instructions are written is astonishingly simple. Like more familiar instruction systems such as language, numbers, or computer binary code, what matters is not so much the symbols themselves but the order in which they appear. Anagrams, for example, "derail" and "redial," contain exactly the same letters but in a different order, and so the words they spell out have completely different meanings. . . . In exactly the same way the order of the four chemical symbols in DNA embodies the message. "ACGGTA" and "GACAGT" are DNA anagrams that mean completely different things to a cell, just as "derail" and "redial" have different meanings for us.
                         —Bryan Sykes, "So, What Is DNA and What Does It Do?"

Defining. When you **DEFINE** something, you put it in a general category and then add characteristics that distinguish it from others in that group. The following paragraph provides brief definitions of three tropical fruits.

My grandfather died some years ago and, as is natural, my memories of our childhood spitting games receded from memory until this May, when I visited a friend's house in Mérida, in the Yucatán peninsula of Mexico. I walked onto a patio speckled with dark stains, as if the heavens had been spitting down on it. I looked up; there were the two trees responsible. One was a lollipop mango tree. Lollipop mangos are little heart-shaped mangos that you eat not by peeling and slicing the flesh, but by biting off their heads and sucking out the juices. The other was a nispero tree. A nispero (called a loquat in English) is a golf-ball-sized tropical fruit, with a thin rind the color of a deer's coat and sweet golden flesh. Beyond the patio, I saw a mammee tree, which bears large, football-shaped fruit. The fruit's flesh is just as sweet as the nispero's, but it's much more suggestive—with its carmine hues and its ominous single black seed. My friend's black-spotted patio would have made my grandmother pull out all three of her mop buckets.

—Ernesto Mestre-Reed, "A Spitting Image of Cuba"

Describing. A DESCRIPTIVE paragraph provides specific details to show what something looks like—and perhaps how it sounds, feels, smells, and tastes. Here, a paragraph weaves together details of background, appearance, and speech to create a vivid impression of Chuck Yeager, the first pilot to break the sound barrier.

Yeager grew up in Hamlin, West Virginia, a town on the Mud River not far from Nitro, Hurricane, Whirlwind, Salt Rock, Mud, Sod, Crum, Leet, Dollie, Ruth, and Alum Creek. His father was a gas driller (drilling for natural gas in the coalfields), his older brother was a gas driller, and he would have been a gas driller had he not enlisted in the Army Air Force in 1941 at the age of eighteen. In 1943, at twenty, he became a flight officer, i.e., a non-com who was allowed to fly, and went to England to fly fighter planes over France and Germany. Even in the tumult of the war Yeager was somewhat puzzling to a lot of other pilots. He was a short, wiry, but muscular little guy with dark curly hair and a tough-looking face that seemed (to strangers) to be saying: "You best not be lookin' me in the eye, you peckerwood, or I'll put four more holes in your nose." But that wasn't what was puzzling. What was puzzling was the way Yeager talked. He seemed to talk with some older forms of English elocution, syntax, and conjugation that had been preserved uphollow in the Appalachians. There were people up there who never said they disapproved of anything, they said: "I don't hold with it." In the present tense they were willing to *help* out, like anyone else; but in the past tense they only *holped.* "H'it weren't nothin' I hold with, but I holped him out with it, anyways."

—Tom Wolfe, *The Right Stuff*

Explaining a process. Sometimes you might write a paragraph that explains a process—telling someone how to do something, such as how to parallel park—or how something is done, such as how bees make honey. Cookbooks explain many processes step-by-step, as in this explanation of how to pit a mango.

> The simplest method for pitting a mango is to hold it horizontally, then cut it in two lengthwise, slightly off-center, so the knife just misses the pit. Repeat the cut on the other side so a thin layer of flesh remains around the flat pit. Holding a half, flesh-side up, in the palm of your hand, slash the flesh into a lattice, cutting down to, but not through, the peel. Carefully push the center of the peel upward with your thumbs to turn it inside out, opening the cuts of the flesh. Then cut the mango cubes from the peel. —Paulette Mitchell, *Vegetarian Appetizers*

Narrating. When you write a NARRATIVE paragraph in an essay, you tell a story to support a point. In the following paragraph, one author tells about being mistaken for a waitress and how that incident of stereotyping served "as a challenge" that provoked her to read her poetry with new confidence.

> One such incident that has stayed with me, though I recognize it as a minor offense, happened on the day of my first public poetry reading. It took place in Miami in a boat-restaurant where we were having lunch before the event. I was nervous and excited as I walked in with my notebook in my hand. An older woman motioned me to her table. Thinking (foolish me) that she wanted me to autograph a copy of my brand-new slender volume of verse, I went over. She ordered a cup of coffee from me, assuming that I was the waitress. Easy enough to mistake my poems for menus, I suppose. I know that it wasn't an intentional act of cruelty, yet of all the good things that happened that day, I remember that scene most clearly, because it reminded me of what I had to overcome before anyone would take me seriously. In retrospect, I understand that my anger gave my reading fire, that I have almost always taken doubts in my abilities as a challenge—and that the result is, most times, a feeling of satisfaction at having won a convert when I see the cold, appraising eyes warm to my words, the body language change, the smile that indicates that I have opened some avenue for communication. That day I read to that woman and her lowered eyes told me that she was embarrassed at her little faux pas, and when I willed her to look up at me, it was my victory, and she graciously allowed me to punish her with

my full attention. We shook hands at the end of the reading, and
I never saw her again. She has probably forgotten the whole thing
but maybe not.   —Judith Ortiz Cofer, *The Latin Deli*

Using examples. Illustrating a point with one or more examples
is a common way to develop a paragraph, like the following one,
which uses lyrics as examples to make a point about the similarities
between two types of music.

> On a happier note, both rap and [country-and-western] fea-
> ture strong female voices as well. Women rappers are strong, con-
> fident, and raunchy: "I want a man, not a boy/to approach me/
> Your lame game really insults me. . . . I've got to sit on my feet to
> come down to your level," taunt lady rappers Entice and Barbie
> at Too Short in their duet/duel, "Don't Fight the Feeling." Like-
> wise, Loretta Lynn rose to C&W fame with defiant songs like "Don't
> Come Home a-Drinkin' with Lovin' on Your Mind" and "Your
> Squaw Is on the Warpath Tonight."
> —Denise Noe, "Parallel Worlds: The Surprising Similarities
> (and Differences) of Country-and-Western and Rap"

W-3c Making Paragraphs Flow

There are several ways to make your paragraphs COHERENT so that
readers can follow your train of thought. Repetition, parallelism, and
transitions are three strategies for making paragraphs flow.

Repetition. One way to help readers follow your train of thought
is to repeat key words and phrases, and pronouns referring to those
keywords.

> Not that long ago, blogs were one of those annoying
> buzz words that you could safely get away with ignoring. The
> word *blog*—it works as both noun and verb—is short for
> *Web log*. It was coined in 1997 to describe a website where
> you could post daily scribblings, journal-style, about whatever
> you like—mostly critiquing and linking to other articles online
> that may have sparked your thinking. Unlike a big media out-
> let, bloggers focus their efforts on narrow topics, often rising to

> become de facto watchdogs and self-proclaimed experts. Blogs can be about anything: politics, sex, baseball, haiku, car repair. There are blogs about blogs.   —Lev Grossman, "Meet Joe Blog"

Instead of repeating one word, you can use synonyms.

> Predictably, the love of cinema has waned. People still like going to the movies, and some people still care about and expect something special, necessary from a film. And wonderful films are still being made.... But one hardly finds anymore, at least among the young, the distinctive cinephilic love of movies, which is not simply love of but a certain *taste* in films.
> —Susan Sontag, "A Century of Cinema"

Parallel structures. Putting similar items into the same grammatical structure helps readers see the connection between those elements and follow your sentences—and your thoughts.

> The disease was bubonic plague, present in two forms: one that infected the bloodstream, causing the buboes and internal bleeding and was spread by contact; and a second, more virulent pneumonic type that infected the lungs and was spread by respiratory infection. The presence of both at once caused the high mortality and speed of contagion. So lethal was the disease that cases were known of persons going to bed well and dying before they woke, of doctors catching the illness at a bedside and dying before the patient. So rapidly did it spread from one to another that to a French physician, Simon de Covino, it seemed as if one sick person "could infect the whole world."
> —Barbara Tuchman, "This Is the End of the World: The Black Death"

Transitions help readers follow your train of thought—and move from sentence to sentence, paragraph to paragraph. Here are some common ones:

- *To show causes and effects:* accordingly, as a result, because, consequently, hence, so, then, therefore, thus
- *To show comparison:* along the same lines, also, in the same way, like, likewise, similarly

- *To show contrasts or exceptions:* although, but, even though, however, in contrast, instead, nevertheless, nonetheless, on the contrary, on the one hand . . . on the other hand, still, yet

- *To show examples:* for example, for instance, indeed, in fact, of course, such as

- *To show place or position:* above, adjacent to, below, beyond, elsewhere, here, inside, near, outside, there

- *To show sequence:* again, also, and, and then, besides, finally, first, furthermore, last, moreover, next, too

- *To show time:* after, as soon as, at first, at last, at the same time, before, eventually, finally, immediately, later, meanwhile, next, simultaneously, so far, soon, then, thereafter

- *To signal a summary or conclusion:* as a result, as we have seen, finally, in a word, in any event, in brief, in conclusion, in other words, in short, in the end, in the final analysis, on the whole, therefore, thus, to summarize

See how Julia Alvarez uses several transitions to show time and to move her ideas along.

> Yolanda, the third of the four girls, became a schoolteacher but not on purpose. For years after graduate school, she wrote down *poet* under profession in questionnaires and income tax forms, and later amended it to *writer*-slash-*teacher*. Finally, acknowledging that she had not written much of anything in years, she announced to her family that she was not a poet anymore.   —Julia Alvarez, *How the Garcia Girls Lost Their Accents*

Transitions can also help readers move from paragraph to paragraph, and signal any connections between paragraphs.

> Today the used-book market is exceedingly well organized and efficient. Campus bookstores buy back not only the books that will be used at their university the next semester but also those that will not. Those that are no longer on their lists of required books they resell to national wholesalers, which in turn sell them to college bookstores on campuses where they will be required. This means that even if a text is being adopted for the first time at a particular college, there is almost certain to be an ample supply of used copies.

As a result, publishers have the chance to sell a book to only one of the multiple students who eventually use it. Hence, publishers must cover their costs and make their profit in the first semester their books are sold—before used copies swamp the market. That's why the prices are so high.

—Michael Granof, "Course Requirement: Extortion"

W-3d When to Start a New Paragraph

Paragraphs may be long or short, and there are no strict rules about how many sentences are necessary for a well-developed paragraph. But while a brief, one- or two-sentence paragraph can be used to set off an idea you want to emphasize, too many short paragraphs can make your writing choppy. Here are some reasons for beginning a new paragraph:

- to introduce a new subject or idea
- to signal a new speaker (in dialogue)
- to emphasize an idea
- to give readers a needed pause

W-3e Opening and Closing Paragraphs

A good opening engages readers and provides some indication of what's to come; a good closing leaves them feeling satisfied—that the story is complete, the questions have been answered, the argument has been made.

Opening paragraphs. Sometimes you may begin with a general statement that provides context or background for your topic, and then proceed to state your THESIS. In the following opening paragraph, the writer begins with a generalization about academic architecture, then ends with a specific thesis stating what the rest of the essay will argue.

Academic architecture invariably projects an identity about campus and community to building users and to the world beyond. Some institutions desire new buildings to be stand-alone statements, with ultramodern exteriors to symbolize the cutting-edge research to be conducted within. Yet in other cases, the architectural language established in surrounding precedents may be more appropriate, even for high-tech facilities. Simon Hall, a new $46.6 million interdisciplinary science building on the Indiana University campus, designed by Flad Architects of Madison, Wisconsin, inserts state-of-the-art research infrastructure in a building mass and exterior crafted to respond to their surroundings in the established vernacular of the historic Bloomington campus.

—Gregory Hoadley, "Classic Nuance:
Simon Hall at Indiana University"

OTHER WAYS OF OPENING AN ESSAY

- with an **ANECDOTE**
- with a quotation
- with a question
- with a startling fact or opinion

Closing paragraphs. One approach is to conclude by summarizing the text's argument. The following paragraph reiterates the writer's main point ("the bottom line") and then issues a call for action.

The bottom line is that drastically reducing both crime rates and the number of people behind bars is technically feasible. Whether it is politically and organizationally feasible to achieve this remains an open question. It would be tragic if the politics proved prohibitive, but it would be genuinely criminal if we didn't even try.   —Mark A. R. Kleiman, "The Outpatient Prison"

OTHER WAYS OF CONCLUDING AN ESSAY

- by discussing the implications of your argument
- by asking a question
- by referring to something discussed at the beginning
- by proposing action

≫ **SEE W-2f** for help editing paragraphs.

W-4   Designing What You Write

Tables, photos, graphs, charts, headings: these are just some of the visuals that can help you get readers' attention—and help them understand what you say. Even when you choose a typeface, you are designing what you write. This chapter offers advice on designing texts to suit your purpose, audience, GENRE, and topic. If you are writing an academic paper, you may be expected to use a specific format and style common in your discipline; if you're unsure what specific style is required, check with your instructor. This book includes guidelines for MLA, APA, *Chicago*, and CSE styles.

W-4a Some Elements of Design

Whatever your text, you have various design decisions to make. The following guidelines will help you make those decisions.

Fonts. The fonts you choose will affect how well readers can read your text. For most academic writing, you'll want to use 10- or 11- or 12-point type. It's usually a good idea to use a serif font (such as Times New Roman or Bookman) for your main text, reserving sans serif (such as Calibri, Verdana, or Century Gothic) for headings and parts you want to highlight. Decorative fonts (such as Chiller) should be used sparingly. If you use more than one font, use each one consistently: one for headings, one for captions, one for the main body of your text. You won't often need more than two or three fonts in any one text.

Every common font has regular, **bold,** and *italic* options. In general, use regular for the main text, bold for major headings, and italic for titles of books and other long works. If, however, you are following a specific discipline's style, be sure you conform to its requirements.

Layout. Layout is the way text is arranged on a page. An academic essay, for example, will usually have a title centered at the top and one-inch margins all around. Items such as lists, tables, headings, and images should be arranged consistently.

Line spacing. Generally, academic writing is double-spaced, whereas letters and résumés are usually single-spaced. In addition, you'll often need to add an extra space to set off parts of a text—lists, for instance, or headings.

Paragraphs. In general, indent paragraphs five spaces when your text is double-spaced; either indent or skip a line between paragraphs that are single-spaced. When preparing a text intended for online use, single-space your document, skip a line between paragraphs, and begin each paragraph flush left (no indent).

Lists. Use a list format for information that you want to set off and make easily accessible. Number the items when the sequence matters (in instructions, for example); use bullets when the order is not important. Set off lists with an extra line of space above and below, and add extra space between the items on a list if necessary for legibility.

White space and margins. To make your text attractive and readable, use white space to separate its various parts. In general, use one-inch margins for the text of an essay or report. Unless you're following a format that has specific guidelines (such as APA), include space above headings, above and below lists, and around photos, graphs, and other visuals.

Headings. Headings make the structure of a text easier to follow and help readers find specific information. Some academic styles require standard headings—announcing a list of **WORKS CITED**, for example, to follow MLA format. Whenever you include headings, you need to decide how to phrase them, what fonts to use, and where to position them.

Phrase headings consistently. Make your headings succinct and parallel in structure. For example, you might make all the headings nouns (*Mushrooms*), noun phrases (*Kinds of Mushrooms*), gerund phrases (*Recognizing Kinds of Mushrooms*), or questions (*How Do I Identify Mushrooms?*). Whatever form you decide on, use it consistently.

Make headings visible. Consider setting headings in bold or italics, or with an underline—or in a different, or slightly larger, font. When you have several levels of headings, use capitalization, bold, and italics to distinguish among the various levels:

> **First-Level Head**
> *Second-Level Head*
> Third-level head

Be aware that some academic fields have specific requirements about how to format headings; see the **MLA**, **APA**, *Chicago*, and **CSE** chapters for details.

Position headings appropriately. If you're following APA or MLA format, center first-level headings. If you are not following a prescribed format, you get to decide where to position your headings: centered, flush with the left margin, or even alongside the text, in a wide left-hand margin. Position each level of head consistently.

W-4b Visuals

If you include visuals, be sure they contribute to your point and are appropriate for your purpose and audience. The following guidelines will help you use photos, graphs, charts, tables, and diagrams effectively. Also see the examples on page 31, along with advice for using each one.

- *Choose visuals that relate directly to your subject,* support your assertions, and add information that words alone can't provide as clearly or easily. Avoid clip art, which is primarily intended as decoration.

- *Number all visuals,* using a separate sequence for figures (photos, graphs, and drawings) and tables: *Figure* 1, *Table* 1.

- *Position visuals as close as possible* to the relevant discussion.

- *Refer to the visual before it appears,* identifying it and summarizing its main point. For example: "As Figure 1 shows, Japan's economy grew dramatically between 1965 and 1980."

- *Provide an informative title or caption* for each visual. Here's an example shown in MLA style: "Table 1. Japanese Economic Output, 1965–80."

- DOCUMENT any visuals you found or adapted from another source. Here's an example shown in APA style: "*Note.* Adapted from 'Creating False Memories: Remembering Words Not Presented in Lists,' by H. Roediger and K. McDermott, 1995, *Journal of Experimental Psychology: Learning, Memory, and Cognition, 21*(4), p. 812."

- *Obtain permission* to use any visuals you found in another source if you publish in any form outside a course.

- *Label visuals clearly* so readers understand what they show. For example, label each section of a pie chart to show what it represents. Check the documentation system you are using to be sure you label visuals correctly.

If you crop a photograph (cutting it to show only part) or alter it in some other way (such as darkening it), be sure the image represents the subject accurately. Tell readers how you have changed the image, and provide relevant information about the source.

Be careful with charts and graphs as well. Changing the scale on a bar graph, for example, can change the visual effect of a comparison and may mislead readers.

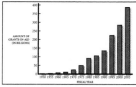

Photographs can support an argument, illustrate events and processes, present other points of view, and help readers "place" your information in time and space.

Line graphs are a good way of showing changes in data over time. Each line here shows a different set of data; plotting the two lines together allows readers to compare the data at different points in time.

Bar graphs are useful for comparing quantitative data, measurements of how much or how many. The bars can be horizontal or vertical.

Pie charts can be used for showing how a whole is divided into parts or how something is apportioned.

Tables are useful for displaying information concisely, especially when several items are being compared.

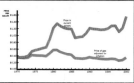

Diagrams, flowcharts, and drawings are helpful for showing relationships and processes.

W-5 Arguments

Everything we say or do presents some kind of argument, takes some kind of position. Often we take overt positions: "Everyone in the United States is entitled to affordable health care." "Barack Obama shouldn't have compromised on the single-payer plan." In college course work, you are constantly called on to argue positions: in an English class, you may argue for a certain interpretation of a poem; in a business course, you may argue for the merits of a flat tax. All of those positions are arguable—people of goodwill can agree or disagree with them. This chapter provides a description of the key elements of an essay that argues a position and tips for writing one.

W-5a Key Elements of an Argument

A clear and arguable position. At the heart of every argument is a claim with which people may reasonably disagree. Some claims are not arguable because they're matters of taste or opinion ("I hate sauerkraut"), because they are a matter of fact ("The first *Star Wars* movie came out in 1977"), or because they are based on belief or faith ("There is life after death"). To be arguable, a position must reflect one of at least two points of view, making reasoned argument necessary: Internet file sharing should (or should not) be considered fair use; selling human organs should be legal (or illegal). In college writing, you will often argue not that a position is correct but that it is plausible—that it is reasonable, supportable, and worthy of being taken seriously.

Necessary background information. Sometimes we need to provide some background on a topic so that readers can understand what is being argued. To argue that file sharing should be considered fair use, for example, you might begin by describing the rise in file sharing and explaining fair-use laws.

Good reasons. By itself, a position does not make an argument; the argument comes when a writer offers reasons to support the position.

There are many kinds of good REASONS. You might argue that file sharing should be fair use by comparing, showing many examples of so-called piracy in other media. You might base an argument in favor of legalizing the sale of human organs on the fact that transplants save lives and that regulation would protect impoverished people who currently sell their organs on the black market.

Convincing evidence. It's one thing to give reasons for your position. You then need to offer EVIDENCE for your reasons: facts, statistics, expert testimony, anecdotal evidence, case studies, textual evidence. Often you'll use a mix of these types of evidence. For example, to support your position that fast food should be taxed, you might cite a nutrition expert who links obesity to fast food, offer facts that demonstrate the effects of widespread obesity on health-care costs, and provide statistics that show how taxation affects behavior.

Appeals to readers' values. Effective arguments appeal to readers' values and emotions. For example, arguing that legalizing organ sales will save the lives of those in need of transplants appeals to the value of compassion—a deeply held value that we may not think about very much, and as a result may see as common ground. To appeal to readers' emotions, you might describe the plight of those who are dying in want of a transplant. Keep in mind, however, that emotional appeals can make readers feel manipulated—and so less likely to accept an argument.

A trustworthy TONE. Readers need to trust the person who's making the argument. There are many ways of establishing yourself (and your argument) as trustworthy: by providing facts that demonstrate your knowledge of the subject, by showing that you have some experience with it, and by showing that you're fair and honest.

Careful consideration of other positions. No matter how reasonable we are in arguing our positions, others may disagree or hold other positions. We need to acknowledge any COUNTERARGUMENTS and, if possible, refute them in our written arguments. For example, you might acknowledge that some object to file sharing because they think "piracy" is inherently wrong, but counter that some types of content piracy have historically been productive for industry—and then give examples.

W-5b Tips for Writing an Argument

Choosing a topic. A fully developed argument requires significant work and time, so choosing a topic in which you're interested is very important. Widely debated topics such as "animal rights" or "gun control" can be difficult to write on if you have no personal connection to them. Better topics include those that interest you right now, are focused, and have some personal connection to your life. Here's one good way to **GENERATE IDEAS** for a topic that meets those three criteria:

Start with your roles in life. On a piece of paper, make four columns with the headings "Personal," "Family," "Public," and "School." Then list the roles you play in life that relate to each heading. Under school, for example, your list might include *college student, dorm resident, chemistry major,* and *work-study employee.*

Identify issues that interest you. Pick two or three of the roles you list and identify the issues that interest or concern you. Try wording each issue as a question starting with *should: Should college cost less than it does? Should on-campus housing be made available to students for all four years, rather than for only the first two?*

Try framing your topic as a problem: *Why has college tuition risen so rapidly in recent years? Why is it so difficult to get into required courses?* This will help you think about the issue and find a clear focus for your essay.

Choose one issue to write about. It is a preliminary choice; if you have trouble writing about it, you'll be able to go back to your list and choose another.

Generating ideas and text

Explore the issue. Write out whatever you know about the issue, perhaps by **FREEWRITING** or making an **OUTLINE**. Consider what interests you about the topic, and what more you may need to learn in order to write about it. It may help to do some preliminary research; start with one general source of information (a national weekly news-magazine or an encyclopedia, for example) to find out the main questions raised about your issue and to get some ideas about how you might argue it. You'll want to make sure your issue is arguable—and worth arguing about.

Draft a THESIS. Once you've explored the issue thoroughly, decide your position on it, and write it out as a complete sentence. For example, "Pete Rose should not be eligible for the Hall of Fame." In most cases you'll then want to qualify your thesis—not only to acknowledge that your position is not the only plausible one, but also to help limit your topic and make it manageable. There are various ways to qualify your thesis: in certain circumstances, with certain conditions, with these limitations, and so on. For example, "Pete Rose should not be elected to the Hall of Fame, though his achievements and records should be noted there in other ways."

Come up with good REASONS. You need to convince your readers that your thesis is plausible. Start by stating your position and then answering the question *why?*

> **THESIS:** Pete Rose should not be eligible for the Hall of Fame. *Why?*
> **REASON:** He illegally bet on professional baseball games. *Why?*

Keep in mind that you will likely have a further reason, a principle that underlies the reason you give for your **CLAIM**.

> **UNDERLYING REASON:** If players bet on the games they play, they may unfairly affect the outcome. *Why?*
> **UNDERLYING REASON:** Betting on outcomes may tempt players to bend or undermine the rules of the game. *Why?*
> **UNDERLYING REASON:** Sports are defined by their rules, and adherence to those rules is the essence of fair play.

This exercise can continue indefinitely as the underlying reasons grow more and more general and abstract. When you've listed several reasons, consider which are the most persuasive and best suit your **PURPOSE** and **AUDIENCE**.

Find EVIDENCE to support your reasons. Here are some kinds of evidence you can offer as support: facts; statistics; testimony by authorities and experts; **ANECDOTAL** evidence; case studies and observation; and **TEXTUAL EVIDENCE**.

Identify other positions. Think about positions that differ from yours and about the reasons that might be given for those positions. Even if you can't refute them, you need to acknowledge potential doubts, concerns, and objections to show that you've considered other perspectives. To refute other positions, state them as clearly and as fairly as you can, and then show why you believe they are wrong. Perhaps the reasoning is faulty, or the supporting evidence is inadequate. Acknowledge their merits, if any, but emphasize their shortcomings.

Ways of organizing an argument. Sometimes you'll want to give all the reasons for your argument first, followed by discussion of any other positions. Alternatively, you might discuss each reason and any counterargument together. And be sure to consider the order in which you discuss your reasons. Usually what comes last is the most emphatic and what comes in the middle is the least emphatic.

[Reasons to support your argument, followed by counterarguments]

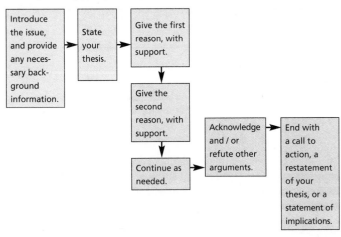

[Reason / counterargument, reason / counterargument]

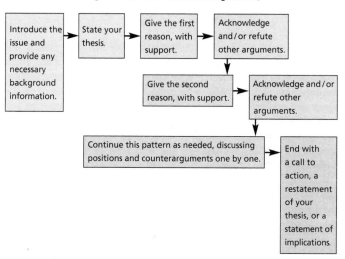

>> **SEE W-1** for help analyzing your writing context. See **W-2** for
guidelines on drafting, revising, editing, and proofreading your
argument. See **W-12b** for guidelines on analyzing an argument.
To read an example argument essay, go to **wwnorton.com/write/
little-seagull-handbook**.

W-6 Textual Analyses

Both *Time* and *U.S. News and World Report* cover the same events, but each magazine interprets them differently. All toothpaste ads claim to make teeth "the whitest." Those are just a couple of examples that demonstrate why we need to be careful, analytical readers of magazines and newspapers, ads, political documents, even textbooks—to understand not only what texts say but also how they say it. Assignments in many disciplines ask you to analyze texts: you may be asked to analyze the use of color and space in Edward Hopper's painting *Nighthawks* for an art history course, or to analyze a set of data to find the standard deviation in a statistics course. This chapter describes the key elements of an essay that analyzes a text and provides tips for writing one.

W-6a Key Elements of a Textual Analysis

A summary of the text. Your readers may not know the text you are analyzing, so you need to include it or tell them about it before you can analyze it. A well-known text such as the Gettysburg Address may require only a brief description, but less well-known texts require a more detailed **SUMMARY**. For an analysis of several advertisements, for example, you'd likely show several ads and also describe them in some detail.

Attention to the context. All texts are part of ongoing conversations, controversies, or debates, so to understand the text, you need to understand the larger context. To analyze the lyrics of a new hip-hop song, you might need to introduce other artists that the lyrics refer to or explain how the lyrics relate to aspects of hip-hop culture.

A clear interpretation or judgment. Your goal is to lead readers through careful examination of the text to some kind of interpretation or reasoned judgment, generally announced clearly in a thesis statement. When you interpret something, you explain what you think it means. If you're analyzing the TV show *Family Guy*, you might argue that a particular episode is actually a parody of the controversy over health care. In an analysis of a cologne advertisement, you might explain how the ad encourages consumers to objectify themselves.

Reasonable support for your conclusions. You'll need to support your analysis with EVIDENCE from the text itself and sometimes from other sources. You might support your interpretation by quoting passages from a written text or referring to images in a visual text. To argue that Barack Obama's inaugural speech aligns him with specific historic predecessors, you might trace allusions to historic events or describe how his wording echoes that of previous presidents' speeches, for example. Note that the support you offer need only be "reasonable"—there is never any one way to interpret something.

W-6b Tips for Writing a Textual Analysis

Choosing a text to analyze. Most of the time, you will be assigned a text or a type of text to analyze: the work of a political philosopher in a political science class, a speech in a history or communications course, a painting or sculpture in an art class, and so on. If you must choose a text to analyze, look for one that suits the assignment—one that is neither too large or complex to analyze thoroughly nor too brief or limited to generate sufficient material. You might also analyze three or four texts by examining elements common to all.

Generating ideas and text. In analyzing a text, your goal is to understand what it says, how it works, and what it means. To do so, you may find it helpful to follow a certain sequence for your analysis: read, respond, summarize, analyze, and draw conclusions.

Read to see what the text says. Start by reading carefully, noting the main ideas, key words and phrases, and anything that seems noteworthy or questionable.

Once you have a sense of what the text says, consider your initial response. What's your reaction to the argument, the tone, the language, the images? Do you find the text difficult? puzzling? Do you agree with what the writer says? Whatever your reaction, think about how you react—and why.

Then consolidate your understanding of the text by SUMMARIZING or DESCRIBING it in your own words.

Decide what you want to analyze. Think about what you find most interesting about the text and why. Does the language interest you? The imagery? The larger context? Something else? You might begin your analysis by exploring what attracted your notice.

Study how the text works. Texts are made up of several components—words, sentences, images, punctuation. Visual texts might be made up of images, lines, angles, color, light and shadow, and sometimes words. To analyze these elements, look for patterns in the way they're used. Write a sentence or two describing the patterns you discover and how they contribute to what the text says.

Analyze the argument. An important part of understanding any text is to recognize its ARGUMENT —what the writer or artist wants the audience to believe, feel, or do. Identify the text's THESIS, and decide how convincingly it supports that thesis. Then write a sentence or two summarizing the argument and your reactions to it.

Think about the larger context. To analyze a text's role in its larger context, you may need to do additional research on where and when it was originally published, what else was happening or being discussed at the time, and whether the text responded to other ideas or arguments. Then write a sentence or two describing the larger context and how it affects your understanding of the text.

Consider what you know about the writer or artist. A person's credentials, other work, reputation, stance, and beliefs are all useful windows into understanding a text. Write a sentence or two summarizing what you know about the writer and how that information affects your understanding.

Come up with a thesis. Once you've studied the text thoroughly, you need to identify your analytical goal: Do you want to show that the text has a certain meaning? Uses certain techniques to achieve its purposes? Tries to influence its audience in particular ways? Relates to some larger context in some significant manner? Something else? Come up with a tentative **THESIS** to guide you—but be aware that your thesis may change as you work.

Ways of organizing a textual analysis. Consider how to organize the information you've gathered to best support your thesis. Your analysis might be structured in at least two ways. You might discuss patterns or themes that run through the text. Alternatively, you might analyze each text or section of text separately.

[Thematically]

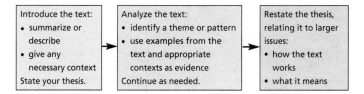

| Introduce the text:
• summarize or describe
• give any necessary context
State your thesis. | Analyze the text:
• identify a theme or pattern
• use examples from the text and appropriate contexts as evidence
Continue as needed. | Restate the thesis, relating it to larger issues:
• how the text works
• what it means |

[Part by part, or text by text]

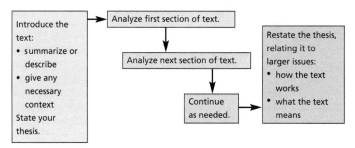

| Introduce the text:
• summarize or describe
• give any necessary context
State your thesis. | Analyze first section of text.
Analyze next section of text.
Continue as needed. | Restate the thesis, relating it to larger issues:
• how the text works
• what the text means |

>> **SEE W-1** for help analyzing your writing context. See **W-2** for guidelines on drafting, revising, editing, and proofreading a textual analysis. To read an example textual analysis, go to **wwnorton.com/write/little-seagull-handbook**.

W-7 Reports

Many kinds of writing report information. Newspapers report on local and world events; textbooks give information about biology, history, writing; websites provide information about products (jcrew.com), people (johnnydepp.com), institutions (smithsonian.org). You've likely done a lot of writing that reports information, from a third-grade report on the water cycle to an essay for a history class reporting on migrants during the Great Depression. Very often this kind of writing calls for research: you need to know your subject in order to report on it. This chapter describes the key elements found in most reports and offers tips for writing one.

W-7a Key Elements of a Report

A tightly focused topic. The goal of this kind of writing is to inform readers about something without digressing—and without, in general, bringing in the writer's own opinions. If you're writing a report on the causes of air turbulence, for example, you probably don't need to describe the delays on your last flight.

Accurate, well-researched information. Reports usually require some research. The kind of research depends on the topic. Library research may be necessary for some topics—for a report on migrant laborers during the Great Depression, for example. Very current topics may require Internet research. Other topics may require FIELD RESEARCH —interviews, observations, and so on. For a report on local farming, for example, you might interview some area farmers.

Various writing strategies. You'll usually use a number of organizing STRATEGIES —to describe something, explain a process, and so on. For example, a report on the benefits of exercise might require that you classify types of exercise, analyze the effects of each type, and compare the benefits of each.

Clear definitions. Reports need to provide clear **DEFINITIONS** of any key terms that their audience may not know. For a report on the 2008 financial crisis for a general audience, for example, you might need to define terms such as *mortgage-backed security* and *predatory lending*.

Appropriate design. Some information is best presented in paragraphs, but some may be easier to present (and to read) in lists, tables, diagrams, and other visuals. Numerical data, for instance, can be easier to understand in a table than in a paragraph. A photograph can help readers see a subject, such as an image of someone talking on a cell phone while driving in a report on multitasking.

W-7b Tips for Writing a Report

Choosing a topic. What interests you? What do you wish you knew more about? The possible topics for informational reports are limitless, but the topics that you're most likely to write well on are those that engage you. They may be academic in nature or reflect your personal interests or both.

If your topic is assigned, be sure to understand what you're required to do. Some assignments are specific: "Explain the physics of roller coasters." If, however, your assignment is broad—"Explain some aspect of the U.S. government"—try focusing on a more limited aspect of that topic, preferably one that interests you: federalism, majority rule, political parties, states' rights. Even if an assignment seems to offer little flexibility, you will need to decide how to research the topic and how to develop your report to appeal to your audience. And sometimes even narrow topics can be shaped to fit your own interests.

Generating ideas and text. Start by exploring whatever you know or want to know about your topic, perhaps by **FREEWRITING**, **LOOPING**, or **CLUSTERING**, all activities that will help you come up with ideas. Then you'll need to narrow your focus.

Narrow your topic. You may know which aspect of the topic you want to focus on, but often you'll need to do some research first—and that research may change your thinking and your focus. Start with sources that can give you a general sense of the subject, such as an encyclopedia article, a Wikipedia entry, or an interview with an expert. Your goal at this point is to find topics to report on and then to focus on one that you will be able to cover.

Come up with a tentative thesis. Once you narrow your topic, write out a statement saying what you plan to report on or explain. A good THESIS is potentially interesting (to you and your readers) and limits your topic enough to be manageable. For a report on the benefits of exercise, for instance, your thesis might be "While weight lifting can build strength and endurance, regular cardiovascular exercise offers greater overall health benefits."

Do any necessary research. Focus your efforts by OUTLINING what you expect to discuss. Identify any aspects you'll need to research. Think about what kinds of information will be most informative for your audience, and be sure to consult multiple sources and perspectives. Revisit and finalize your thesis in light of your research findings.

Ways of organizing a report

[Reports on topics that are unfamiliar to readers]

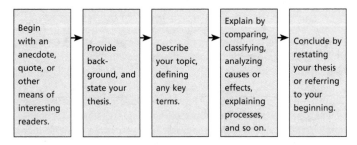

| Begin with an anecdote, quote, or other means of interesting readers. | → | Provide background, and state your thesis. | → | Describe your topic, defining any key terms. | → | Explain by comparing, classifying, analyzing causes or effects, explaining processes, and so on. | → | Conclude by restating your thesis or referring to your beginning. |

[Reports on an event]

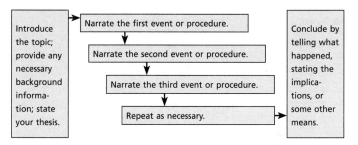

[Reports that compare and contrast]

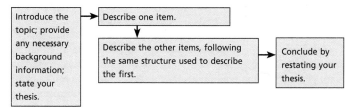

» **SEE W-1** for help analyzing your writing context. See **W-2** for guidelines on drafting, revising, editing, and proofreading your report. To read an example report, go to **wwnorton.com/write/ little-seagull-handbook**.

W-8   Personal Narratives

Narratives are stories, and we read and tell them for many different purposes. Parents read their children bedtime stories as an evening ritual. Preachers base their Sunday sermons on Bible stories to teach lessons about moral behavior. Grandparents tell how things used to be, sometimes the same stories year after year. College applicants write about significant moments in their lives. Writing students are often called on to compose narratives to explore their personal experiences. This chapter describes the key elements of personal narratives and provides tips for writing one.

W-8a Key Elements of a Personal Narrative

A well-told story. Most narratives set up some sort of situation that needs to be resolved. That need for resolution makes readers want to keep reading. You might write about a challenge you've overcome, for example, such as learning a new language or encountering some kind of discrimination.

Vivid detail. Details can bring a narrative to life by giving readers vivid mental images of the sights, sounds, smells, tastes, and textures of the world in which your story takes place. The details you use when DESCRIBING something can help readers picture places, people, and events; DIALOGUE can help them hear what is being said. To give readers a picture of your childhood home in the country, you might describe the gnarled apple trees in your backyard and the sound of crickets chirping on a spring night. Similarly, dialogue that lets readers hear your father's sharp reprimand after you hit a ball through the back window can help them understand how you felt at the time.

Some indication of the narrative's significance. Narratives usually have a point; you need to make clear why the incident matters to you, or how the narrative supports a larger argument. You may reveal

46- 49 + 230-235

its significance in various ways, but try not to state it too directly, as if it were a kind of moral of the story. A story about the lasting impression of a conversation with your grandfather about the novel he started but never finished will likely be less effective if you were to end by saying, "He taught me to value creative writing."

W-8b Tips for Writing a Personal Narrative

Choosing a topic. In general, it's a good idea to focus on a single event that took place during a relatively brief period of time:

- an event that was interesting, humorous, or embarrassing
- something you found (or find) especially difficult or challenging
- the origins of a current attitude or belief
- a memory from childhood that you recall vividly

Make a list of possible topics, and then choose one that you think will be interesting to you and to others—and that you're willing to share with others.

Generating ideas and text. Start by writing out what you remember about the setting and those involved, perhaps BRAINSTORMING, LOOPING, or QUESTIONING to help you generate ideas.

Describe the setting. List the places where your story unfolds. For each place, write informally for a few minutes, DESCRIBING what you remember seeing, hearing, smelling, tasting, and feeling.

Think about the key people. Narratives include people whose actions play an important role in the story. To develop your understanding of the people in your narrative, you might begin by describing them—their movements, their posture, their bearing, their facial expressions. Then try writing several lines of DIALOGUE between two people in your narrative, including distinctive words or phrases they used. If you can't remember an actual conversation, make up one that could have happened.

Write about "what happened." At the heart of every good narrative is the answer to the question "What happened?" The action may be as dramatic as winning a championship or as subtle as a conversation between two friends; both contain action, movement, or change that the narrative dramatizes for readers. Try narrating the action using active and specific verbs (*pondered*, *shouted*, *laughed*) to capture what happened.

Consider the significance. You need to make clear why the event you are writing about matters. How did it change or otherwise affect you? What aspects of your life now can you trace to that event? How might your life have been different if this event had not happened?

Ways of organizing a personal narrative. Don't assume that the only way to tell your story is just as it happened. That's one way—starting at the beginning of the action and continuing to the end. You might also start in the middle—or even at the end.

[Chronologically, from beginning to end]

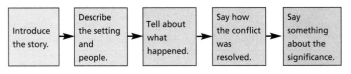

[Beginning in the middle]

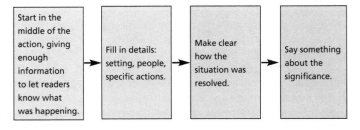

[Beginning at the end]

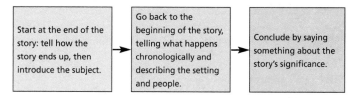

Start at the end of the story: tell how the story ends up, then introduce the subject.

→

Go back to the beginning of the story, telling what happens chronologically and describing the setting and people.

→

Conclude by saying something about the story's significance.

>> **SEE** W-1 for help analyzing your writing context. See W-2 for guidelines on drafting, revising, editing, and proofreading your narrative. To read an example narrative, go to **wwnorton.com/ write/little-seagull-handbook**.

2-30 -238

W-9 Literary Analyses

Literary analyses are essays in which we examine literary texts closely to understand their messages, interpret their meanings, and appreciate their writers' techniques. You might look for a pattern in the images of blood in Shakespeare's *Macbeth,* or point out the differences between Stephen King's *The Shining* and Stanley Kubrick's screenplay based on that novel. In both cases, you go below the surface to deepen your understanding of how the texts work and what they mean. This chapter describes the key elements found in most literary analyses and provides tips for writing one.

W-9a Key Elements of a Literary Analysis

An arguable thesis. In a literary analysis, you are arguing that your ANALYSIS of a work is valid. Your thesis, then, should be arguable. You might argue, for example, that the dialogue between two female characters in a short story reflects current stereotypes about gender roles. But a mere summary—"In this story, two women discuss their struggles to succeed"—would not be arguable and therefore is not a good thesis. (See W-5a for help developing an arguable thesis.)

Careful attention to the language of the text. Specific words, images, metaphors—these are the foundation of a text's meaning, and are where analysis begins. You may also bring in contextual information or refer to similar texts, but the words, phrases, and sentences that make up the text you are analyzing are your primary source. That's what literature teachers mean by "close reading": reading with the assumption that every word of a text is meaningful.

Attention to patterns or themes. Literary analyses are usually built on evidence of meaningful patterns or themes within a text or among several texts. For example, you might analyze how the images of snow, ice, and wind and the repetition of the word "nothing" contribute to a sense of loneliness and desolation in a poem about a winter scene.

A clear interpretation. When you write a literary analysis, you show one way the text may be understood, using evidence from the text and, sometimes, relevant contextual evidence to support your particular INTERPRETATION.

MLA style. Literary analyses usually follow **MLA** style.

W-9b Tips for Writing a Literary Analysis

Generating ideas and text. Start by considering whether your assignment specifies a particular kind of analysis or critical approach. Look for words that say what to do: *analyze, compare, interpret,* and so on. Then you'll want to take a close look at the literary work.

Choose a method for analyzing the text. If your assignment doesn't specify a particular method, three common approaches are to focus on the text itself; on your own experience reading it; and on other cultural, historical, or literary contexts:

- *The text itself.* Trace the development and expression of themes, characters, and language through the work. How do they help to create particular meaning, tone, or effects?

- *Your own response as a reader.* Explore the way the text affects you as you read through it. Read closely, noticing how the elements of the text shape your responses, both intellectual and social. How has the author evoked your response?

- *Context.* Analyze the text as part of some larger context—as part of a certain time or place in history or of a certain culture; or as one of many other texts like it, a representative of a genre.

Read the work more than once. When you first experience a piece of literature, you usually focus on the story, the plot, the overall meaning. By experiencing the work repeatedly, you can see how its effects are achieved, what the pieces are and how they fit together, where different patterns emerge, and how the author crafted the work.

Compose a strong thesis. The **THESIS** of a literary analysis should be specific, limited, and open to potential disagreement. In addition, it should be **ANALYTICAL**, not **EVALUATIVE**. Your goal is not to pass judgment but to suggest one way of seeing the text.

Do a close reading. Find specific, brief passages that support your interpretation; then analyze those passages in terms of their language, their context, and your reaction to them as a reader. Do a close reading, questioning as you go:

- What does each word (phrase, passage) mean exactly? Why does the writer choose *this* language, *these* words?
- What images or metaphors are used? What is their effect?
- What patterns of language, imagery, or plot do you see? If something is repeated, what significance does the pattern have?
- What words, phrases, or passages connect to a larger context?
- How do these various elements of language, image, and pattern support your thesis?

Support your argument with evidence. The parts of the text you examine in your close reading become the evidence you use to support your interpretation. Treat your analysis like any other **ARGUMENT**: discuss how the text creates an effect or expresses a theme, and then show **EVIDENCE** from the text—significant plot or structural elements; important characters; patterns of language, imagery, or action—to back up your argument.

Pay attention to matters of style. Literary analyses have certain conventions for using pronouns and verbs. In informal papers, it's okay to use the first person: "I believe Frost's narrator provides little basis for claiming that one road is 'less traveled.'" In more formal essays, make assertions directly: "Frost's narrator provides no basis for claiming that one road is 'less traveled.'" Discuss textual features in the present tense even if quotations from the text are in another tense. Describe the historical context of the setting in the past tense.

One way of organizing a literary analysis

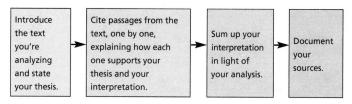

Introduce the text you're analyzing and state your thesis. → Cite passages from the text, one by one, explaining how each one supports your thesis and your interpretation. → Sum up your interpretation in light of your analysis. → Document your sources.

≫ SEE W-1 for help analyzing your writing context. See **W-12** for more help reading with a critical eye. For guidelines on drafting, revising, editing, and proofreading, see **W-2**. To read an example literary analysis, go to **wwnorton.com/write/little-seagull-handbook**.

W-10 Annotated Bibliographies

Annotated bibliographies describe, give publication information for, and sometimes evaluate each work on a list of sources. You may be assigned to create annotated bibliographies to weigh the potential usefulness of sources and to document your search efforts. This chapter describes the key elements of an annotated bibliography and provides tips for writing two kinds of annotations: *descriptive* and *evaluative*.

Descriptive annotations simply SUMMARIZE the contents of each work, without comment or evaluation. They may be very short, just long enough to capture the flavor of the work, like this excerpt from a bibliography of books and articles on teen films, documented MLA style and published in the *Journal of Popular Film and Television*.

> Doherty, Thomas. *Teenagers and Teenpics: The Juvenilization of American Movies in the 1950s.* Boston: Unwin Hyman, 1988. Print. A historical discussion of the identification of teenagers as a targeted film market.
>
> Foster, Harold M. "Film in the Classroom: Coping with Teen Pics." *English Journal* 76.3 (1987): 86–88. Print. An evaluation of the potential of using teen films such as *Sixteen Candles* and *The Karate Kid* to instruct adolescents on the difference between film as communication and film as exploitation.
> —Michael Benton, Mark Dolan, and Rebecca Zisch, "Teen Film$"

Evaluative annotations offer opinions on a source as well as describe it. They are often helpful in assessing how useful a source will be for your own writing. The following evaluative annotation is from an APA-style bibliography written by a student.

> Gore, A. (2006). *An inconvenient truth: The planetary emergency of global warming and what we can do about it.* New York: Rodale.

This publication, which is based on Gore's slide show on global warming, stresses the urgency of the global warming crisis. It centers on how the atmosphere is very thin and how greenhouse gases such as carbon dioxide are making it thicker. The thicker atmosphere traps more infrared radiation, causing warming of Earth. Gore argues that carbon dioxide, which is created by burning fossil fuels, cutting down forests, and producing cement, accounts for 80 percent of greenhouse gas emissions. He includes several examples of problems caused by global warming. Penguins and polar bears are at risk because the glaciers they call home are quickly melting. Coral reefs are being bleached and destroyed when their inhabitants overheat and leave. Global warming is now affecting people's lives as well. For example, many highways in Alaska are only frozen enough to be driven on fewer than eighty days of the year. In China and elsewhere, record-setting floods and droughts are taking place. Hurricanes are on the rise.

This source's goal is to inform its audience about the global warming crisis and to inspire change. It is useful because it relies on scientific data that can be referred to easily and it provides a solid foundation for me to build on. For example, it explains how carbon dioxide is produced and how it is currently affecting plants and animals. This evidence could potentially help my research on how humans are biologically affected by global warming. It will also help me structure my essay, using its general information to lead into the specifics of my topic. For example, I could introduce the issue by explaining the thinness of the atmosphere and the effect of greenhouse gases, then focus on carbon dioxide and its effects on organisms.   —Jessica Ann Olson, "Global Warming"

W-10a Key Elements of an Annotated Bibliography

A statement of scope. You may need a brief introductory statement to explain what you're covering. This might be one paragraph or several—but it should establish a context for the bibliography and announce your purpose for compiling it.

Complete bibliographic information. Provide all the information about the source following one documentation system (**MLA**,

APA, *Chicago*, CSE, or another one) so that your readers or other researchers will be able to find each source easily.

A concise description of the work. A good annotation describes each item as carefully and objectively as possible, giving accurate, specific information and showing that you understand the source—and how it relates to your topic.

Relevant commentary. If you write an evaluative bibliography, your comments should be relevant to your purpose and audience. To achieve relevance, consider what questions a potential reader might have about the sources. Your evaluation might also focus on the text's suitability as a source for your writing.

Consistent presentation. All annotations should be consistent in content, sentence structure, and format. If you're evaluating, evaluate each source, not just some sources. If one annotation is written in complete sentences, they should all be. Also be sure to use one documentation style—and to treat all book titles consistently, all italicized and following a consistent capitalization style.

W-10b Tips for Annotating a Bibliography

Generating ideas and text. You'll need to do some research to locate potential sources for your bibliography. As you consider which to include, keep your AUDIENCE and PURPOSE in mind.

Decide what sources to include. Though you may be tempted to include every source you find, a better strategy is to include only those sources that you or your readers may find useful in researching your topic. Consider these qualities:

- *Appropriateness.* Is this source relevant to your topic? Is it a PRIMARY or SECONDARY source? Is it general or specialized?

- *Credibility.* Are the author and the publisher or sponsor reputable? Do their ideas agree with those in other sources you've read?

- *Balance.* Does the source present enough evidence? Does it show any particular bias? Does it present COUNTERARGUMENTS?
- *Timeliness.* Does the source reflect current thinking or research?

Decide whether the bibliography should be descriptive or evaluative. If you're writing a descriptive bibliography, your reading goal will be to understand and capture each writer's message clearly. If you're writing an evaluative bibliography, your annotations must also include your own comments on the source.

Read carefully. To write an annotation, you must understand the source's argument, but for some assignments, you may have neither the time nor the need to read the whole text. To quickly determine whether a source is likely to serve your needs, first check the publisher or sponsor; then read the preface, abstract, or introduction; skim the table of contents or the headings; and read the parts that relate specifically to your topic.

Research the writer, if necessary. You may need to find information about the writer's credentials; try looking him or her up on a search engine or in *Contemporary Authors.* In any case, information about the writer should take up no more than one sentence in your annotation.

Summarize the work. Sumarize it as objectively as possible: even if you are writing an evaluative annotation, you can evaluate the central point of a work better by stating it clearly first. Your SUMMARY should be concise, but try to be specific and detailed enough to give readers a clear understanding not only of the scope and content of the source, but also of the author's perspective on the topic. *If you're writing a descriptive annotation, you're done.*

If you're writing an evaluative bibliography, EVALUATE your sources in terms of their usefulness for your project, their STANCE, and their overall credibility. If you can generalize about the worth of the entire work, fine. You may find, however, that some parts are useful while others are not, and your evaluation should reflect that mix.

Ways of organizing an annotated bibliography. Depending on their purpose, annotated bibliographies may or may not include an introduction. Consult the documentation system you're using for details about alphabetizing works appropriately.

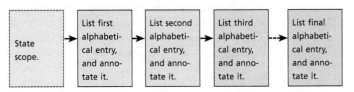

Sometimes an annotated bibliography needs to be organized into several subject areas (or genres, periods, or some other category), and the entries are listed alphabetically within each category.

[Multi-category bibliography]

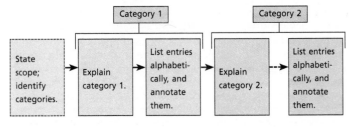

>> **SEE W-1** for help analyzing your writing context. See **W-2** for guidelines on drafting, revising, editing, and proofreading your bibliography. For help finding and evaluating sources, see **R-1** and **R-2**. To read an example annotated bibliography, go to **wwnorton.com/write/little-seagull-handbook**.

W-11   Abstracts

Abstracts are brief summaries written to give readers the gist of a report or presentation. You may be required to include an abstract in a REPORT or as a preview of a presentation you plan to give at an academic or professional conference. This chapter provides tips for writing three common kinds: *informative, descriptive,* and *proposal.*

Informative abstracts state in one paragraph the essence of a whole paper about a study or a research project. That one paragraph must mention all the main points or parts of the paper: a description of the study or project, its methods, the results, and the conclusions. Here is an example of the abstract accompanying a seven-page essay that appeared in 2002 in *The Journal of Clinical Psychology:*

> The relationship between boredom proneness and health-symptom reporting was examined. Undergraduate students (N = 200) completed the Boredom Proneness Scale and the Hopkins Symptom Checklist. A multiple analysis of covariance indicated that individuals with high boredom-proneness total scores reported significantly higher ratings on all five subscales of the Hopkins Symptom Checklist (Obsessive-Compulsive, Somatization, Anxiety, Interpersonal Sensitivity, and Depression). The results suggest that boredom proneness may be an important element to consider when assessing symptom reporting. Implications for determining the effects of boredom proneness on psychological- and physical-health symptoms, as well as the application in clinical settings, are discussed.   —Jennifer Sommers and Stephen J. Vodanovich, "Boredom Proneness"

Descriptive abstracts are usually much briefer than informative abstracts; they provide a quick overview that invites the reader to read the whole paper. They usually do not summarize the entire paper, give or discuss results, or set out the conclusion or its implications. A descriptive abstract of the boredom-proneness essay might simply include the first sentence from the informative abstract plus a final sentence of its own:

> The relationship between boredom proneness and health-symptom reporting was examined. The findings and their application in clinical settings are discussed.

Proposal abstracts contain the same basic information as informative abstracts. You prepare them to persuade someone to let you write on a topic, pursue a project, conduct an experiment, or present a paper at a scholarly conference; often the abstract is written before the paper itself. Titles and other aspects of the proposal deliberately reflect the theme of the proposed work, and you may use the future tense to describe work not yet completed. Here is a possible proposal for doing research on boredom and health problems:

> Undergraduate students will complete the Boredom Proneness Scale and the Hopkins Symptom Checklist. A multiple analysis of covariance will be performed to determine the relationship between boredom-proneness total scores and ratings on the five subscales of the Hopkins Symptom Checklist (Obsessive-Compulsive, Somatization, Anxiety, Interpersonal Sensitivity, and Depression).

W-11a Key Elements of an Abstract

A summary of basic information. An informative abstract includes enough information to substitute for the report itself; a descriptive abstract offers only enough information to let the audience decide whether to read further; and a proposal abstract gives an overview of the planned work.

Objective description. Abstracts present information on the contents of a report or a proposed study; they do not present arguments about or personal perspectives on those contents.

Brevity. Although the length of abstracts may vary, journals and organizations often restrict them to 120–200 words—meaning you must carefully select and edit your words.

W-11b Tips for Writing an Abstract

Generating ideas and text. Unless you are writing a proposal abstract, write the paper first. You can then use the finished work as the guide for the abstract, which should follow the same basic structure.

Copy and paste key statements. If you've already written the work, highlight your THESIS, objective, or purpose; basic information on your methods; your results; and your conclusion. Copy and paste those sentences into a new document to create a rough draft.

Pare down the information to key ideas. SUMMARIZE the report, editing out any nonessential words and details. Introduce the overall scope of your study, and include any other information that seems crucial to understanding your paper. In general, you probably won't want to use "I"; an abstract should cover ideas, not say what you think or will do.

Conform to any requirements. In general, an informative abstract should be at most 10 percent as long as the original and no longer than the maximum length allowed. Descriptive abstracts should be shorter still, and proposal abstracts should conform to the requirements of the organization calling for the proposal.

Ways of organizing an abstract

[An informative abstract]

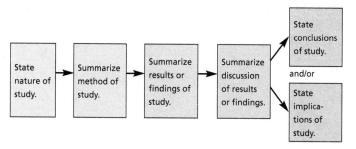

[A descriptive abstract]

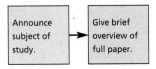

[A proposal abstract]

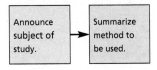

>> **SEE** W-1 for help analyzing your writing context. See W-2 for guidelines on drafting, revising, editing, and proofreading your abstract.

Reading Strategies

We read newspapers and websites to learn about the events of the day. We read cookbooks to find out how to make brownies and textbooks to learn about history, biology, and other academic topics. We read short stories for pleasure—and, in literature classes, to analyze plot, theme, and the like. And as writers, we read our own drafts to make sure they say what we mean. In other words, we read for many different purposes. This chapter offers strategies for reading texts—and the arguments they make—with a critical eye.

W-12a Reading with a Critical Eye

Different texts require different strategies. Some can be read quickly, if you're reading to get a general overview. But most of the time you'll need to read carefully, skimming to get the basic ideas, then reading again to pay close attention to the details. Following are some strategies for reading with a critical eye.

Preview the text. Start by skimming to get the basic ideas; read the title and subtitle, any headings, the first and last paragraphs, the first sentences of all the other paragraphs. Study any visuals.

Consider the writing context. What is the PURPOSE of the text—to inform? persuade? entertain? Who is the intended AUDIENCE? If you're not a member of that group, are there terms or concepts you'll need to look up? What is the GENRE—a report? an analysis? something else? What do you know about the writer, and what is his or her STANCE—Critical? Objective? Something else? Is the text print or electronic—and how does the MEDIUM affect what it says?

Think about your initial response. Read the text to get a sense of it; then jot down brief notes about your initial reaction and think about why you reacted as you did. What about the text accounts for this reaction?

Annotate. Highlight key words and phrases, connect ideas with lines or symbols, and write comments or questions in the margins. What you annotate depends on your purpose. If you're analyzing an argument, you might underline any thesis statement and the reasons and evidence that support it. If you are looking for patterns, try highlighting each one in a different color.

Analyze how the text works. Outline the text paragraph by paragraph. If you're interested in analyzing its ideas, identify what each paragraph *says*. Are there any patterns in the topics the writer addresses? How has the writer arranged ideas, and how does that arrangement develop the topic? If, on the other hand, you're concerned with how the ideas are presented, pay attention to what each paragraph *does*: Does it introduce a topic? Provide background? Describe something? Entice you to read further?

Summarize. Restate a text's main ideas in your own words, leaving out most examples and other details. This approach can help you both to see the relationships among the text's ideas and to understand what it's saying.

Identify patterns. Look for notable patterns in the text: recurring words and their synonyms, repeated phrases and metaphors, and types of sentences. Does the author rely on any particular writing strategies? Is the evidence offered more opinion than fact? Nothing but statistics? Is there a predominant pattern to how sources are presented? As quotations? Paraphrases? Summaries? In visual texts, are there any patterns of color, shape, and line? What isn't there that you would expect to find? Is there anything that doesn't really fit in?

Consider the larger context. All texts are part of an ongoing conversation with other texts, and that larger context can help you better understand what you're reading. What's motivating the text? What other arguments is the writer responding to? Whom does the writer cite? Do those cited have a particular academic specialty, or share similar beliefs? Why does the topic matter?

W-12b Analyzing an Argument

All texts make some kind of argument, claiming something and then offering reasons and evidence as support for the claim. As a critical reader, you need to look closely at the argument a text makes.

- *What is the claim?* What is the main point the writer is trying to make? Is there a clearly stated **THESIS**, or is it merely implied?

- *What support does the writer offer for the claim?* What **REASONS** are given to support the claim, and what **EVIDENCE** backs up those reasons? Are the reasons plausible and sufficient?

- *How evenhandedly does the writer present the issues?* Are the arguments appropriately qualified? Is there any mention of **COUNTER-ARGUMENTS** —and if so, how does the writer deal with them?

- *What authorities or other sources of information are cited?* How credible and current are they?

- *How does the writer address you as the reader?* Does the writer assume that you know something about what's being discussed? Does his or her language include you, or not? (Hint: if you see the word *we*, do you feel included?)

Be sure to check for **FALLACIES**, arguments that rely on faulty reasoning. Such arguments can seem plausible, and they can be persuasive —so be sure to check the legitimacy of such reasoning when you run across it.

Research

Research is formalized curiosity.
It is poking and prying with a purpose.

— Zora Neale Hurston

R-1   Doing Research

We do research all the time, for many different reasons. We search the Web for information about a new computer, ask friends about the best place to get coffee, try on several pairs of jeans before deciding which ones to buy. This chapter will help you to get started with the kind of research you'll need to do for academic work.

R-1a Considering the Context for Your Research

When you begin a research project, you need to consider the overall context for your project.

- What is your PURPOSE for the project? Is the project is part of an assignment, does it specify a specific GENRE of writing—To argue for a position? Report on a topic? Analyze something? Something else?

- Who is your AUDIENCE and what do they know about your topic? Will you need to provide background information? What kinds of evidence will your audience find persuasive? What attitudes do they hold, and how can you best appeal to them?

- What kinds of sources will you need to find to learn about your TOPIC? Think about your own STANCE on your topic—are you objective? Skeptical? Confused? Indifferent?

- Do you get to choose your MEDIUM? If so, which medium will best reach your audience, and how will that medium affect the kind of information you search for?

- How much time do you have to complete the project? Is there a due date? How much time will your project take, and how can you best schedule your time in order to complete it?

R-1b Choosing a Topic, Narrowing Its Focus

If you need to choose a topic for your research project, consider your interests. What do you want to learn more about? If your topic is assigned, read the assignment carefully to make sure you understand what it asks you to do. If the assignment offers only broad guidelines, identify the requirements and range of possibilities, and define your topic within those constraints.

As you consider topics, look to narrow your focus on a topic to make it specific enough to cover in a research paper. For example, "ethanol and the environment" is probably too broad a topic; a better one might be "the potential environmental effects of increasing the use of gasoline mixed with ethanol." Narrowing your topic will make it easier to find and manage specific information that you can address in your project.

Doing some preliminary research can help you explore your topic and define the focus for further research. You might start by consulting encyclopedias and other reference works to get an overview of the scholarship on your topic and find potential paths to follow. Discipline-specific encyclopedias can be more helpful than general reference works; they usually cover topics in more depth and may provide scholarly references that can be a starting point for your research. Be sure to keep a **WORKING BIBLIOGRAPHY** that lists any sources you consult so that you can easily find and cite them. Your bibliography should include all the information you'll need in order to document each source; you'll find more on documentation in the chapters on **MLA** style, **APA** style, *Chicago* style, and **CSE** style.

R-1c Posing a Research Question, Drafting a Tentative Thesis

Posing a research question. Once you have narrowed your topic, you need to come up with a research question—a specific question that you will then work to answer through your research. Generate a list of questions beginning with *What? When? Where? Who? How? Why? Would? Could?* and *Should?* For example, here are some questions about the tentative topic "the potential environmental effects of increasing the use of ethanol":

How much energy does producing ethanol require?

Why do some environmental groups oppose the use of ethanol?

Should ethanol use be increased?

Select one question and use it to help guide your research.

Drafting a tentative thesis. When your research has led you to a possible answer to your question, try to formulate your answer as a tentative **THESIS**. Here are three tentative thesis statements, each one based on a previous research question about ethanol.

Producing ethanol uses more fossil fuels than burning it saves.

Some environmental groups are opposed to ethanol because it's not as "green" as liquid propane gas.

The federal government should require the use of ethanol as a gasoline additive.

A tentative thesis will help guide your research, but be ready to revise it as you continue to learn about your subject and consider many points of view. If you hold too tightly to a tentative thesis, you risk focusing only on evidence that supports your own views—but research should be a process of inquiry in which you approach a topic with an open mind, ready to learn.

R-1d Finding Appropriate Sources

You'll need to choose from many sources for your research—from reference works, books, periodicals, and the Web to surveys, interviews, and other kinds of field research that you yourself conduct. Which kinds of sources you turn to will depend on your topic. If you're researching a literary topic, you might consult biographical reference works, scholarly books and articles, literary works, and works of criticism. If you're researching a current issue, you would likely consult newspapers and other periodicals, websites, and books on your topic.

Check your assignment to see if you are required to use primary or secondary sources—or both. Primary sources are original works, such as historical documents, literary works, eyewitness accounts, diaries, letters, and lab studies, as well as any original field research you do. Secondary sources include scholarly books and articles, reviews, biographies, and other works that interpret or discuss primary sources. For example, novels and poems are primary sources; articles interpreting them are secondary sources.

Whether a work is considered primary or secondary often depends on your topic and purpose. If you're analyzing a poem, a critic's article analyzing the poem is a secondary source—but if you're investigating the critic's work, the article would be a primary source.

Library websites. When you conduct academic research, it is often better to start with your library's website rather than with a commercial search engine such as *Google*. Library websites provide access to a range of well-organized resources, including scholarly databases through which you can access authoritative articles that have been screened by librarians or subject-matter specialists.

R-1e Searching Electronically

When you search for subjects on the Web or in library catalogs, indexes, or databases, you need to come up with KEYWORDS that will focus on the information you need. Specific commands vary among search engines and databases, but most search engines offer "Advanced Search" options that allow you to narrow your search by typing keywords into text boxes with the following labels:

- All of these words
- The exact phrase
- Any of these words
- None of these words

In addition, you may filter the results to include only full-text articles (articles that are available in full online); only certain domains (such as *.edu*, for educational sites; *.gov*, for government sites; or *.org*, for nonprofit sites); and, in library databases, only scholarly, peer-reviewed sites. Type quotation marks around words to search for an exact phrase: "Louisiana Purchase" or "Spike Jonze."

Some databases may require you to limit searches through the use of various symbols or Boolean operators (AND, OR, NOT). See the "Advanced Search" instructions for help with such symbols, which may be called "field tags."

If a search turns up too many sources, be more specific (*homeopathy* instead of *medicine*). If your original keywords don't generate good results, try synonyms (*home remedy* instead of *folk medicine*). Keep in mind that searching requires flexibility, both in the words you use and the methods you try.

R-1f Reference Works

Every library has a reference section, where you will find encyclopedias, dictionaries, atlases, almanacs, bibliographies, and other reference works that can provide an overview as you begin your search. For some topics, you might find specialized reference works such as the *Film Encyclopedia* or *Dictionary of Philosophy*, which provide in-depth information on a single field or topic and can often lead you to more specific sources. Many reference works are also online, but some may be available only in the library. You may be tempted to look up your topic in *Wikipedia*, but keep in mind that anyone can edit wiki entries, so you cannot be certain about the accuracy of information you find there.

You should also look for bibliographies, which list published works on particular topics along with the information you'll need to find each work. You can also find bibliographies in many scholarly articles and books. Check with a reference librarian for help finding bibliographies on your research topic.

R-1g Books / Searching the Library Catalog

To find books, you can search the library catalog by author, title, subject, or keyword. A keyword search will yield books the library has on the topic and may also provide related subject headings that could lead to other useful materials in the library. Library catalogs also supply a call number, which identifies the book's location on the shelves.

R-1h Periodicals / Searching Indexes and Databases

To find journal, magazine, and newspaper articles, you need to search periodical indexes and databases. Indexes list articles by topics; databases usually provide full texts or abstracts. While some databases and indexes are freely available online, most must be accessed through a library. For pre-1980 articles, you may need to check print indexes such as *The Reader's Guide to Periodical Literature*.

A reference librarian can help you determine which databases will be most helpful to you, but here are some useful ones:

GENERAL INDEXES AND DATABASES

Academic Search Complete contains articles from more than 7,900 journals and indexes over 11,900 journals.

EBSCOhost provides databases of abstracts and complete articles from periodicals and government documents.

InfoTrac offers over 20 million full-text articles from a variety of sources, including the *New York Times*.

JSTOR archives many scholarly journals, but not current issues.

LexisNexis Academic Universe contains articles from a large number of sources—newspapers; business, legal, and medical sources; and references such as the *World Almanac*.

ProQuest provides full-text articles from thousands of periodicals and newspapers from 1986 to the present.

SINGLE-SUBJECT INDEXES AND DATABASES

BIOSIS Previews provides abstracts and indexes for over 5,500 sources on biological sciences, the environment, and agriculture.

ERIC is the database of the U.S. Department of Education.

Humanities International Index contains bibliographies for over 2,200 humanities journals.

MLA International Bibliography indexes scholarly articles on modern languages, literature, folklore, and linguistics.

PsychINFO indexes scholarly literature in psychology.

To search a database, start with a keyword search. If a keyword does not lead to enough sources, try a synonym; if it leads to too many sources, try narrowing your search using the strategies in R-1e.

R-1i The Web

The Web contains countless sites sponsored by governments, educational institutions, organizations, businesses, and individuals. Because the Web is so vast and dynamic, however, finding information can be a challenge. There are several ways to search the Web:

- *Keyword searches.* *Google, Bing, Ask.com, Yahoo!, AltaVista,* and *Lycos* all scan the Web looking for the keywords you specify.

- *Metasearches.* *Copernic Agent, SurfWax,* and *Dogpile* let you use several search engines simultaneously.

- *Academic searches.* For peer-reviewed academic writing in many disciplines, try *Google Scholar*; or use *Scirus* for scientific, technical, and medical documents.

Although many websites provide authoritative information, keep in mind that Web content varies greatly in its stability and reliability: what you see on a site today may be different (or gone) tomorrow, so save or make copies of pages you use and evaluate carefully what you find there (see R-2). Following is a list of just a few of the many resources available on the Web.

- *Indexes, databases, and directories.* Information put together by specialists and grouped by topics can be especially helpful. You may want to consult *Librarians' Internet Index* (an annotated subject directory of more than 20,000 websites selected by librarians); *Infomine* (a huge collection of databases, mailing lists, catalogs, articles, directories, and more); or the *World Wide Web Virtual Library* (a catalog of websites on numerous subjects, compiled by experts).

- *News sites.* Many newspapers, magazines, and radio and TV stations have websites that provide both up-to-the-minute information and also archives of older news articles. Through *Google News* and *NewsLink,* for example, you can access current news worldwide, whereas *Google News Archive Search* has files extending to the 1700s.

- *Government sites.* Many government agencies and departments maintain websites where you can find government reports, statistics, legislative information, and other resources. *USA.gov* offers information, services, and other resources from the U.S. government.

- *Digital archives.* These sites collect and organize materials from the past, including drawings, maps, recordings, speeches, and historic documents, often focusing on a particular subject or country. The National Archives and Records Administration and the Library of Congress both archive U.S. materials, for example.

- *Discussion lists and forums.* Online mailing lists, newsgroups, discussion groups, and forums let members post and receive messages from other members. To join a discussion with people who are knowledgeable about your topic, try searching for your topic—for example, for "Thomas Jefferson discussion forum." Or consult a site such as *Google Groups,* where you can find online discussions on your topic.

R-1j Field Research

Sometimes you'll need to go beyond the information you find in published sources and gather your own data by doing field research. Three kinds of field research you might consider are interviews, observations, and surveys.

Interviewing experts. Some kinds of writing—a **PROFILE** of a living person, for instance—almost require that you conduct an interview, whether it's face-to-face, over the telephone, or via email.

1. *Before the interview,* email or phone to ask for an appointment and state your purpose for the interview. If you wish to record the interview, ask for permission. Write out questions in advance—and bear in mind that open-ended questions are likely to elicit a more extended response than those that can be answered with a simple yes or no.

2. *At the interview,* record the full name of the person and the date, time, and place. Take notes, even if you are recording the interview, and don't take more time than you agreed to beforehand.

3. *After the interview,* flesh out your notes with details right away, and send a thank-you note or email.

Observation. Some writing projects are based on information you get by observing something.

1. *Before observing,* think about your research purpose. How does this observation relate to your research goals, and what do you expect to find? If necessary, set up an appointment and ask your subjects' permission to observe them.

2. *While observing,* divide each page of your notepaper down the middle and write only on the left side. Describe who is there, what they are doing, what they look like, what they say, and any other relevant details. Jot down details about the setting.

3. *After observing,* use the right side of your pages to jot down additional details. Then analyze your notes, looking for patterns. What did you learn?

Surveys. One way of gathering information from a large number of people is with a questionnaire.

1. *Start by thinking* about your research question and what can you learn with a survey.

2. *Decide who you'll send it to* and how you'll reach them: Face-to-face? On the phone? On a website such as *SurveyMonkey*? Via email?

3. **Write questions** that ask for specific answers and can be answered easily. Multiple-choice questions will be easier to tally than open-ended questions.

4. **If you're mailing the survey**, write an introduction that explains its purpose. Include a stamped and addressed envelope, and be sure to give a due date. Remember to say thank you.

5. **Test your questions** on several people, making sure that the questions and any instructions are clear.

R-2   Evaluating Sources

Searching the *Health Source* database for information on the incidence of meningitis among college students, you find seventeen articles. A *Google* search on the same topic produces over ten thousand hits. How do you decide which sources to read? This chapter presents advice on evaluating sources and reading them critically.

R-2a Considering the Reliability and Usefulness of Sources

As you consider potential sources, keep your PURPOSE in mind. If you're trying to persuade readers to believe something, be sure to find sources representing various stances; if you're reporting on a topic, you may need sources that are more factual or informative. Reconsider your AUDIENCE. What kinds of sources will they find persuasive? If you're writing for readers in a particular field, what counts as EVIDENCE in that field? The following questions can help you select reliable and useful sources:

- **Is it relevant?** How does the source relate to your purpose? What will it add to your work? Look at the title and at any introductory material to see what it covers.

- **What are the author's credentials?** Has the author written other works on this subject? Is he or she known for a particular position on it? If the author's credentials are not stated, you might do a Web search to see what else you can learn about him or her.

- **What is the STANCE?** Does the source cover various points of view or advocate only one perspective? Does its title suggest a certain slant? If you're evaluating a website, check to see whether it includes links to sites expressing other perspectives. You'll want to consult sources with various viewpoints.

- **Who is the publisher?** If it's a book, what kind of company published it; if an article, what kind of periodical did it appear in? Books published by university presses and articles in scholarly journals are reviewed by experts before they are published. But books and articles written for general audiences—and many websites—do not undergo rigorous review or fact-checking.

- **If it's a website, who is the sponsor?** Is the site maintained by an organization, interest group, government agency, or individual? If the site doesn't give this information on its home page, look for clues in the URL domain: *.edu* is used mostly by colleges and universities, *.gov* by government agencies, *.org* by nonprofit organizations, .mil by the military, and *.com* by commercial organizations. What is the site's purpose: To argue a position? To present information? To sell a product?

- **What is the level of the material?** Texts written for a general audience might be easier to understand but may not be authoritative enough for academic work. Scholarly texts will be more authoritative but may be hard to comprehend.

- **How current is the source?** Check to see when books and articles were published and when websites were last updated. (If a site lists no date, see if links to other sites still work; if not, the site is probably too dated to use.) A recent publication date or updating, however, does not necessarily mean the source is better—some topics require current information whereas others call for older sources.

- *Is the source cited in other works?* If so, you can probably assume that some other writers regard it as trustworthy. If it's a book and your school's library doesn't have it, can you get it through inter-library loan?

- *Does it include other useful information?* Is there a bibliography that might lead you to other sources? How current or authoritative are the sources it cites?

R-2b Reading with a Critical Eye

Approach your sources with an open mind but consider their arguments with a critical eye. Pay attention to what they say, to the reasons and evidence they offer to support what they say, and to whether they address viewpoints other than their own. Assume that each author is responding to some other argument—and that you in turn will be joining the conversation.

- *What ARGUMENTS does the author make?* Does he or she present several different positions or argue for a particular position? What arguments is he or she responding to?

- *How persuasive do you find the argument?* What REASONS and EVIDENCE does the author provide? Are there citations or links—and if so, are they credible? Are any of the author's assumptions questionable? How thoroughly does he or she consider alternative arguments?

- *What is the author's STANCE?* Does he or she seem objective, or does the language reveal a particular bias? Is the author associated with a special interest that might signal a certain perspective? Does he or she consider opposing views?

- *Does the publisher bring a certain stance to the work?* Book publishers, periodicals, or websites that are clearly liberal or conservative or advance a particular agenda will likely express views reflecting their stance.

- *Do you recognize ideas you've run across in other sources?* Does the source leave out any information that other sources include?

- *Does this source support or challenge your own position—or does it do both?* Does it support a different argument altogether? Represent a position you need to address? Don't reject a source just because it challenges your views.

- *What can you tell about the intended* AUDIENCE *and* PURPOSE*?* Are you a member of the audience addressed—and if not, does that affect the way you interpret what you read? Is the main purpose to inform readers about a topic or to argue a certain point?

R-3   Synthesizing Ideas

Whatever topic you are researching, you need to be constantly synthesizing the information you find—to sift through your sources in order to identify patterns, themes, and main points—and then to use that data to help you generate your own argument. This chapter focuses on going beyond what your sources say to using what they say to inspire and support what *you* want to say.

R-3a Reading for Patterns and Connections

Your task as a writer is to find as much information as you can on your topic, and then to study the data you find to determine and support what you yourself will write. Read with an open mind, taking careful notes to help you see patterns, themes, and connections among your sources. Take notes on your own thoughts as well, and pay attention to your first reactions. You'll likely have many ideas to work with, but your first thoughts can often lead somewhere interesting. Here are some questions that can help you discover key patterns and connections:

- What sources make the strongest arguments? What makes them so strong?

- Which arguments do you agree with? Disagree with?

- Are there any arguments, themes, or data that you see in more than one source?

- Are there any disagreements among sources? Any that you need to address in what you write?

- How have your sources affected your thinking on your topic? Have you discovered new questions you need to investigate?

- Have you found the information you need that will achieve your **PURPOSE**, appeal to your **AUDIENCE**, and suit your **MEDIUM**?

The ideas and insights that emerge from this questioning can become the basis for your own ideas, and for what *you* have to say about the topic.

R-3b Synthesizing Information to Support Your Own Ideas

If you're doing research for a **REPORT**, your ideas will be communicated primarily through the choices you make about what information to include from your sources and how you organize that information. If you're writing a research-based **ARGUMENT**, on the other hand, your synthesis must support that argument. No matter what kind of writing you're doing, however, the challenge is to synthesize ideas and information from your research to develop and support *your own* ideas.

Entering the conversation. As you read and think about your topic, you will come to an understanding of the concepts, interpretations, and controversies relating to your topic—and you'll become aware that there's a larger conversation going on. When you begin to find connections among your sources, you will begin to see your own place in that conversation, to discover your own ideas, your own stance on your topic. This is the exciting part of a research project, for when you write out your own ideas on the topic, you will find yourself entering that conversation. Remember that your STANCE as an author needs to be clear: simply stringing together the words and ideas of others isn't enough. You need to show readers how your source materials relate to one another and to your THESIS.

R-4 Integrating Sources, Avoiding Plagiarism

When you work with the ideas and words of others, you need to clearly distinguish those ideas and words from your own and give credit to their authors. This chapter will help you with the specifics of integrating source materials in your writing and acknowledging your sources appropriately.

R-4a Incorporating the Words and Ideas of Others into Your Text

When you want to incorporate source materials into your own writing, you'll need to decide how to do so—whether to quote, paraphrase, or summarize. You might follow this rule of thumb: QUOTE texts when the wording is worth repeating, when you want to cite the exact words of a known authority on your topic, when his or her opinions challenge or disagree with those of others, or when the source is one you want to emphasize. PARAPHRASE sources that are not worth quoting but contain details you need to include. SUMMARIZE longer passages whose main points are important but whose details are not.

In addition, you'll need to introduce any words or ideas that are not your own with a SIGNAL PHRASE in order to clearly distinguish what your sources say from what you have to say—and to document any words or ideas that are not your own.

R-4b Quoting

Quoting is a way of weaving someone's exact words into your text. When you quote, you reproduce the source exactly, though you can omit unnecessary details (adding ellipses to show that you've done so) or modify the quotation to make it fit smoothly into your text (enclosing any changes in brackets).

Incorporate short quotations into your text, enclosed in quotation marks. What counts as a short quotation varies, however; consult the chapters on **MLA**, **APA**, *Chicago*, or **CSE** for guidelines in each of those styles. The following examples are shown MLA style.

> Gerald Graff argues that colleges leave many students with "the misconception that the life of the mind is a secret society for which only an elite few qualify" (1).

To quote three lines or less of poetry MLA style, run them in with your text, enclosed in quotation marks. Separate lines with slashes, leaving one space on each side of the slash. Include the line numbers in parentheses at the end of the quotation.

> Emma Lazarus almost speaks for the Statue of Liberty with the words inscribed on its pedestal: "Give me your tired, your poor, / Your huddled masses yearning to breathe free, / The wretched refuse of your teeming shore" (lines 10–12).

Set off long quotations block style. Longer quotations should not be run in with quotation marks but instead are set off from your text and indented from the left margin. Block quotations are usually introduced by a full sentence. Again, what counts as long varies across disciplines; consult the chapters on MLA, APA, *Chicago*, or CSE for specific guidelines on when to format a quotation as a block and how much to indent. Whatever style you're following, do not add quotation marks; the indent signals that you are quoting someone's exact words. Remember to add a citation to the source, using the format required by the style you're following. Here is an example shown MLA style.

> Organizations such as Oxfam rely on visual representations of the poor. What better way to get our attention, asks Diana George:
>
>> In a culture saturated by the image, how else do we convince Americans that—despite the prosperity they see all around them—there is real need out there? The solution for most nonprofits has been to show the despair. To do that they must represent poverty as something that can be seen and easily recognized: fallen down shacks and trashed out public housing, broken windows, dilapidated porches, barefoot kids with stringy hair, emaciated old women and men staring out at the camera with empty eyes. (210)

If you quote four or more lines of poetry MLA style, they need to be set off block style the same way:

> Emily Dickinson, like many poets, asserts that we cannot know truth directly but must apprehend it through indirect means:
>
>> Tell all the Truth but tell it slant—
>> Success in Circuit lies
>> Too bright for our infirm Delight
>> The Truth's superb surprise (lines 1–4)

Indicate any omissions with ellipses, inserting three ellipsis marks with space around each one to indicate deleted words. Be careful not to distort your source's meaning.

> In her essay, Antonia Peacocke argues that *Family Guy* provides an astute satire of American society, though she concedes that it does sometimes "seem to cross . . . the line of indecency" (266).

If you omit a sentence or more in the middle of a quotation, put a period before the three ellipsis dots.

> According to Kathleen Welch, "Television is more acoustic than visual. . . . One can turn one's gaze away from the television, but one cannot turn one's ears from it without leaving the area where the monitor leaks its aural signals into every corner" (102).

Indicate any additions or changes with brackets. Sometimes you'll need to change or add words to make a quotation fit grammatically within your sentence, or to add a comment. Here the writer changes the word *our* to *their* so the quotation fits grammatically into her own text.

> Writing about the dwindling attention of some composition scholars to the actual teaching of writing, Susan Miller notes that "few discussions of writing pedagogy take it for granted that one of [their] goals is to teach how to write" (480).

In this example, brackets are used to add an explanatory word:

> As Barbosa notes, Chico Buarque's lyrics include "many a metaphor of *saudades* [yearning] so characteristic of *fado* music" (207).

Keep in mind that too many ellipses and brackets can make a text choppy and hard to read, however, so it's best to keep such editing to a minimum.

>> **SEE P-4** for guidance in using other punctuation inside or outside quotation marks.

R-4c Paraphrasing

When you paraphrase, you restate information from a source in your own words, using your own sentence structures. Paraphrase when the source material is important but the original wording is not. Because it includes all the main points of the source, a paraphrase is usually about the same length as the original.

Here is an excerpt from a source, followed by three paraphrases. The first two demonstrate some of the challenges of paraphrasing:

ORIGINAL SOURCE

In 1938, in a series of now-classic experiments, exposure to synthetic dyes derived from coal and belonging to a class of chemicals called aromatic amines was shown to cause bladder cancer in dogs. These results helped explain why bladder cancers had become so prevalent among dyestuffs workers. With the invention of mauve in 1854, synthetic dyes began replacing natural plant-based dyes

in the coloring of cloth and leather. By the beginning of the twentieth century, bladder cancer rates among this group of workers had skyrocketed, and the dog experiments helped unravel this mystery.
—Sandra Steingraber, "Pesticides, Animals, and Humans," p. 976.

UNACCEPTABLE PARAPHRASE: WORDING TOO CLOSE

<u>Now-classic experiments</u> in 1938 showed that when dogs were exposed to aromatic amines, chemicals used in <u>synthetic dyes derived from coal</u>, they developed bladder cancer. Similar cancers were <u>prevalent among dyestuffs workers,</u> and these experiments helped to <u>explain why</u>. Mauve, a synthetic dye, was invented in 1854, after which <u>cloth and leather</u> manufacturers replaced most of the natural plant-based dyes with synthetic dyes. <u>By the early twentieth century, this group of workers had skyrocketing</u> rates of bladder cancer, a <u>mystery the dog experiments helped to unravel</u> (Steingraber 976).

This paraphrase borrows too much of the language of the original or changes it only slightly, as the underlined words and phrases show.

UNACCEPTABLE PARAPHRASE: SENTENCE STRUCTURE TOO CLOSE

In 1938, several pathbreaking experiments showed that being exposed to synthetic dyes that are made from coal and belong to a type of chemicals called aromatic amines caused dogs to get bladder cancer. These results helped researchers identify why cancers of the bladder had become so common among textile workers who worked with dyes. With the development of mauve in 1854, synthetic dyes began to be used instead of dyes based on plants in the dyeing of leather and cloth. By the end of the nineteenth century, rates of bladder cancer among these workers had increased dramatically, and the experiments using dogs helped clear up this oddity (Steingraber 976).

This paraphrase uses different language but follows the sentence structure of Steingraber's text too closely.

ACCEPTABLE PARAPHRASE

Biologist Sandra Steingraber explains that pathbreaking experiments in 1938 demonstrated that dogs exposed to aromatic amines

> (chemicals used in coal-derived synthetic dyes) developed cancers of the bladder that were similar to cancers common among dyers in the textile industry. After mauve, the first synthetic dye, was invented in 1854, leather and cloth manufacturers replaced most natural dyes made from plants with synthetic dyes, and by the early 1900s textile workers had very high rates of bladder cancer. The experiments with dogs proved the connection (976).

Use your own words and sentence structure. If you use a few words from the original, put them in quotation marks.

R-4d Summarizing

A summary states the main ideas found in a source concisely and in your own words. Unlike a paraphrase, a summary does *not* present all the details, so it is generally as brief as possible. Summaries may boil down an entire book or essay into a single sentence, or they may take a paragraph or more to present the main ideas. Here, for example, is a summary of the original excerpt from Steingraber:

> Steingraber explains that experiments with dogs demonstrated that aromatic amines, chemicals used in synthetic dyes, can cause bladder cancer (976).

As with a paraphrase, if you include any language from the original, put it in quotation marks.

R-4e Incorporating Source Materials into Your Text

You need to introduce quotations, paraphrases, and summaries with a signal phrase, usually letting readers know who the author is and, if need be, something about his or her credentials. Consider this sentence:

> Professor and textbook author Elaine Tyler May argues that many high school history books are far too bland to interest young readers (531).

The signal phrase ("Professor and textbook author Elaine Tyler May argues") tells readers who is making the assertion and why she has the authority to speak on the topic.

Signal verbs. The verb you use in a signal phrase can be neutral—*says* or *thinks*—or it can suggest something about the **STANCE**—the source's or your own. The example above referring to the textbook author uses the verb *argues*, suggesting that what she says is disputable (or that the writer believes it is).

SOME COMMON SIGNAL VERBS

acknowledge	claim	disagree	observe
admit	comment	dispute	point out
advise	conclude	emphasize	reason
agree	concur	grant	reject
argue	confirm	illustrate	report
assert	contend	imply	respond
believe	declare	insist	suggest
charge	deny	note	think

Though "he says" or "she thinks" will sometimes be the most appropriate phrasing, you can usually make your writing more precise and lively by choosing verbs that better signal the stance of the ideas you're introducing—and by varying the placement of your signal phrases. For example:

> As the critic X argues, "_____."
> In their book, _____, X and Y suggest that _____.
> Writing in the journal _____, X observes, "_____."
> "_____," X contends.
> On the other hand, X has continued to insist that _____.

Verb tenses. Each documentation style has its own conventions regarding the verbs that are used in signal phrases.

MLA requires present tense verbs (*writes, notes, contends*) in signal phrases that introduce source material. If, however, you mention the date when the source was written, the verb should be in the past tense.

> As Benjamin Franklin <u>notes</u> in *Poor Richard's Almanack*, "He that cannot obey, cannot command" (739).

> Back in 1736, Benjamin Franklin <u>wrote</u> that "He that cannot obey, cannot command" (739).

APA uses the past tense or PRESENT PERFECT to introduce quotations or to present research results.

> Dowdall, Crawford, and Wechsler (1998) <u>observed</u> that women attending women's colleges are less likely to engage in binge drinking than are women who attend coeducational colleges (p. 713).

> Dowdall, Crawford, and Wechsler (1998) <u>have observed</u> that . . . .

To discuss the implications of an experiment or conclusions that are generally agreed on, however, APA requires the use of the present tense: *the findings of the study <u>suggest</u>, most researchers <u>concur</u>.*

Chicago uses the present tense (*As Eric Foner <u>notes</u>*) or PRESENT PERFECT (*As Eric Foner <u>has noted</u>*) to introduce most quotations. Use the past tense, however, when you are focusing on the fact that the point was made in the past: *Just before signing the Declaration of Independence, John Adams <u>wrote</u> his wife Abigail.*

CSE uses the past tense or PRESENT PERFECT to refer to research from the past (*Gillen's 2005 paper <u>argued</u>, his early studies <u>have demonstrated</u>*) or to discuss methods (*our subjects <u>received</u>*) or findings: *his earlier studies (1999, 2003) <u>showed</u>.* Use the present tense, however, when citing research reports: *Gillen (2010) <u>provides</u> the most detailed evidence.*

Statistics. You may introduce a statistic or a specific fact with a signal phrase—but you don't need to. Most of the time, it will be clear that you are citing only the statistic or fact. The following examples introduce statistics with and without a signal phrase in MLA style.

47% of people arrested for arson were juveniles (2).

Almost half the 47% of people arrested for arson in 2008 were juveniles (Puzzanchera 2).

R-4f Acknowledging Sources

When you insert in your text information that you've obtained from others, your reader needs to know where your source's words or ideas begin and end. Usually you should introduce a source by naming the author in a SIGNAL PHRASE and follow it with a brief citation. Conventions for acknowledging sources vary across disciplines, however; see the chapters on MLA, APA, *Chicago*, and CSE for specific advice. Whatever style you use, you need only a brief citation here, since your readers will find full publication information in your WORKS CITED, REFERENCES, or BIBLIOGRAPHY.

Sources that need acknowledgment

- Direct quotations, paraphrases, and summaries
- Controversial statements
- Information that may not be common knowledge
- The opinions and ideas of others
- Any information that you didn't generate yourself—charts, graphs, interviews, statistics, visuals, anything you did not create
- Help from others

Sources that don't need acknowledgment. Widely available information and common knowledge do not require acknowledgment—but what constitutes common knowledge isn't always clear. When in doubt, provide a citation or ask your instructor for advice. You generally do not need to cite the following sources:

- Facts that most readers are likely to know or that are found in reference sources (such as the date when President Lincoln was assassinated)

- Information that you see mentioned in several sources
- Well-known quotations
- Material you created or gathered yourself, such as photos you took or data from your own field research (make sure, however, that readers know the work is yours)

A good rule of thumb: *when in doubt, cite your source.* You won't be criticized for citing too much—but you may invite charges of plagiarism by citing too little.

R-4g Avoiding Plagiarism

When you use the words or ideas of others, you need to acknowledge them; if you don't credit your sources, you are guilty of plagiarism. Plagiarism is often unintentional—as when a writer paraphrases someone else's ideas in language that is close to the original. It is essential, therefore, to know what constitutes plagiarism: (1) using another writer's words or ideas without in-text citation and documentation, (2) using another writer's exact words without quotation marks, and (3) paraphrasing or summarizing someone else's ideas using language or sentence structures that are too close to theirs. The following practices will help you avoid plagiarizing:

- *Take careful notes*, clearly labeling quotations and using your own phrasing and sentence structure in paraphrases and summaries.

- *Know what sources you must document*, and give credit to them both in the text and in a works-cited list (MLA), a references list (APA or CSE), or a bibliography (*Chicago*).

- *Be especially careful with online material*—copying source material directly into a document you are writing is all too easy. Like other sources, information from the Web must be acknowledged.

- *Check all paraphrases and summaries* to be sure they are in *your* words and sentence structures—and that you put quotation marks around any of the source's original phrasing.

- *Check to see that all quotations are documented;* it is not enough just to include quotation marks or indent a block quotation.

Whether it's deliberate or accidental, plagiarism has consequences. Students who plagiarize fail courses or might even be expelled from school. If you're having trouble completing an assignment, seek assistance from your instructor or your school's writing center.

R-4h Understanding Documentation Styles

When we write up the results of a research project, we cite the sources we use and acknowledge those sources through DOCUMENTATION. Documenting our sources not only helps establish our credibility as researchers and writers, but it also enables our readers to find our sources themselves (if they wish to).

The Little Seagull Handbook provides guidelines on four documentation styles, each of which is commonly used in specific disciplines:

- MLA (Modern Language Association): mainly used in English, foreign languages, and other humanities
- APA (American Psychological Association): mainly used in psychology and other social sciences
- *Chicago* (University of Chicago Press): mainly used in history, philosophy, and other humanities
- CSE (Council of Science Editors): mainly used in physical and biological sciences and mathematics

Each system has two parts: (1) an in-text citation for each quotation, paraphrase, or summary and (2) a detailed list of sources at the end of the text. Although the specific guidelines for the styles differ, they all require that you provide basic information about the authors, titles, and publication information for your sources. To help you see the crucial parts of each citation in this book, the examples throughout the following chapters are color-coded: tan for author and editor, yellow for title, and gray for publication information: place of publication, name of publisher, date of publication, page number(s), medium of publication, and so on.

MLA Style

Modern Language Association style calls for (1) brief in-text documentation and (2) complete documentation in a list of works cited at the end of your text. The models in this chapter draw on the *MLA Handbook for Writers of Research Papers*, 7th edition (2009). Additional information is available at www.mla.org.

A DIRECTORY TO MLA STYLE

List of Works Cited   103

Throughout this chapter, you'll find models and examples that are color-coded to help you see how writers include source information in their texts and lists of works cited: tan for author or editor, yellow for title, gray for publication information: place of publication, publisher, date of publication, page number(s), and so on.

MLA-a In-Text Documentation

Brief documentation in your text makes clear to your reader what you took from a source and where in the source you found the information.

In your text, you have three options for citing a source: QUOTING, PARAPHRASING, and SUMMARIZING. As you cite each source, you will need to decide whether or not to name the author in a signal phrase—"as Toni Morrison writes"—or in parentheses—"(Morrison 24)."

The first examples in this chapter show basic in-text citations of a work by one author. Variations on those examples follow. The examples illustrate the MLA style of using quotation marks around titles of short works and italicizing titles of long works.

1. AUTHOR NAMED IN A SIGNAL PHRASE

If you mention the author in a signal phrase, put only the page number(s) in parentheses. Do not write *page* or *p.*

> McCullough describes John Adams's hands as those of someone
> used to manual labor (18).

2. AUTHOR NAMED IN PARENTHESES

If you do not mention the author in a signal phrase, put his or her last name in parentheses along with the page number(s). Do not use punctuation between the name and the page number(s).

> Adams is said to have had "the hands of a man accustomed to
> pruning his own trees, cutting his own hay, and splitting his
> own firewood" (McCullough 18).

Whether you use a signal phrase and parentheses or parentheses only, try to put the parenthetical citation at the end of the sentence or as close as possible to the material you've cited without awkwardly interrupting the sentence. Notice that in the example above, the parenthetical reference comes after the closing quotation marks but before the period at the end of the sentence.

3. TWO OR MORE WORKS BY THE SAME AUTHOR

If you cite multiple works by one author, include the title of the work you are citing either in the signal phrase or in parentheses. Give the full title if it's brief; otherwise, give a short version.

> Kaplan insists that understanding power in the Near East
> requires "Western leaders who know when to intervene, and do
> so without illusions" (*Eastward* 330).

Include a comma between author and title if you include both in
the parentheses.

> Understanding power in the Near East requires "Western leaders
> who know when to intervene, and do so without illusions"
> (Kaplan, *Eastward* 330).

4. AUTHORS WITH THE SAME LAST NAME

Give the author's first name in any signal phrase or the author's first
initial in the parenthetical reference.

> *Imaginative* applies not only to modern literature (E. Wilson)
> but also to writing of all periods, whereas *magical* is often used
> in writing about Arthurian romances (A. Wilson).

5. TWO OR MORE AUTHORS

For a work by two or three authors, name all the authors, either in
a signal phrase or in the parentheses.

> Carlson and Ventura's stated goal is to introduce Julio Cortázar,
> Marjorie Agosín, and other Latin American writers to an
> audience of English-speaking adolescents (v).

For a work with four or more authors, either mention all their names
or include just the name of the first author followed by *et al.*, Latin
for "and others."

> One popular survey of American literature breaks the contents
> into sixteen thematic groupings (Anderson et al. A19–24).

6. ORGANIZATION OR GOVERNMENT AS AUTHOR

Cite the organization either in a signal phrase or in parentheses. It's
acceptable to shorten long names.

> The U.S. government can be direct when it wants to be. For
> example, it sternly warns, "If you are overpaid, we will recover
> any payments not due you" (Social Security Administration 12).

7. AUTHOR UNKNOWN

If you don't know the author, use the work's title or a shortened version of the title in the parentheses.

> A powerful editorial in last week's paper asserts that healthy
> liver donor Mike Hurewitz died because of "frightening" faulty
> postoperative care ("Every Patient's Nightmare").

8. LITERARY WORKS

When referring to literary works that are available in many different editions, cite the page numbers from the edition you are using, followed by information that will let readers of any edition locate the text you are citing.

NOVELS. Give the page and chapter number.

> In *Pride and Prejudice,* Mrs. Bennet shows no warmth toward
> Jane and Elizabeth when they return from Netherfield (105;
> ch. 12).

VERSE PLAYS. Give the act, scene, and line numbers; separate them with periods.

> Macbeth continues the vision theme when he addresses the
> Ghost with "Thou hast no speculation in those eyes / Which
> thou dost glare with" (3.3.96–97).

POEMS. Give the part and the line numbers (separated by periods). If a poem has only line numbers, use the word *line(s)* in the first reference.

> Whitman sets up not only opposing adjectives but also opposing
> nouns in "Song of Myself" when he says, "I am of old and

young, of the foolish as much as the wise, / . . . a child as well
as a man" (16.330–32).

One description of the mere in *Beowulf* is "not a pleasant
place!" (line 1372). Later, the label is "the awful place" (1378).

9. WORK IN AN ANTHOLOGY

Name the author(s) of the work, not the editor of the anthology—
either in a signal phrase or in parentheses.

"It is the teapots that truly shock," according to Cynthia Ozick
in her essay on teapots as metaphor (70).

In *In Short: A Collection of Creative Nonfiction,* readers will find
both an essay on Scottish tea (Hiestand) and a piece on teapots
as metaphors (Ozick).

10. ENCYCLOPEDIA OR DICTIONARY

Cite an entry in an encyclopedia or dictionary using the author's
name, if available. For an entry in a reference work without an author,
give the entry's title in parentheses. If entries are arranged alphabetically, no page number is needed.

Katz notes that before *Spartacus,* Kubrick went without work
for two years ("Stanley Kubrick").

11. LEGAL AND HISTORICAL DOCUMENTS

For legal cases and acts of law, name the case or act in a signal phrase
or in parentheses. Italicize the name of a legal case.

In 2005, the Supreme Court confirmed in *MGM Studios, Inc. v.
Grokster, Ltd.* that peer-to-peer file sharing is illegal copyright
infringement.

Do not italicize the titles of laws, acts, or well-known historical documents such as the Declaration of Independence. Give the title and any
relevant articles and sections in parentheses. It's okay to use common
abbreviations such as *art.* or *sec.* and to abbreviate well-known titles.

> The United States Constitution grants the president the right to
> make recess appointments (US Const., art. 2, sec. 2).

12. SACRED TEXT

When citing sacred texts such as the Bible or the Qur'an, give the
title of the edition used, and in parentheses give the book, chapter,
and verse (or their equivalent), separated by periods. MLA style recommends that you abbreviate the names of the books of the Bible
in parenthetical references.

> The wording from *The New English Bible* follows: "In the
> beginning of creation, when God made heaven and earth, the
> earth was without form and void, with darkness over the face
> of the abyss, and a mighty wind that swept over the surface of
> the waters" (Gen. 1.1–2).

13. MULTIVOLUME WORK

If you cite more than one volume of a multivolume work, each time
you cite one of the volumes, give the volume *and* the page numbers
in parentheses, separated by a colon.

> Sandburg concludes with the following sentence about those
> paying last respects to Lincoln: "All day long and through the
> night the unbroken line moved, the home town having its
> farewell" (4: 413).

If your works-cited list includes only a single volume of a multivolume work, give just the page number in parentheses.

14. TWO OR MORE WORKS CITED TOGETHER

If you're citing two or more works closely together, you will sometimes need to provide a parenthetical citation for each one.

> Tanner (7) and Smith (viii) have looked at works from a cultural
> perspective.

If you include both in the same parentheses, separate the references with a semicolon.

> Critics have looked at both *Pride and Prejudice* and *Frankenstein* from a cultural perspective (Tanner 7; Smith viii).

15. SOURCE QUOTED IN ANOTHER SOURCE

When you are quoting text that you found quoted in another source, use the abbreviation *qtd. in* in the parenthetical reference.

> Charlotte Brontë wrote to G. H. Lewes: "Why do you like Miss Austen so very much? I am puzzled on that point" (qtd. in Tanner 7).

16. WORK WITHOUT PAGE NUMBERS

For works without page numbers, including many online sources, identify the source using the author or other information either in a SIGNAL PHRASE or in parentheses.

> Studies reported in *Scientific American* and elsewhere show that music training helps children to be better at multitasking later in life ("Hearing the Music").

If the source has paragraph or section numbers, use them with the abbreviation *par.* or *sec.*: ("Hearing the Music," par. 2). If an online work is available as a PDF, cite its page numbers in parentheses.

17. AN ENTIRE WORK OR ONE-PAGE ARTICLE

If you cite an entire work rather than a part of it, or if you cite a single-page article, identify the author in a signal phrase or in parentheses. There's no need to include page numbers.

> At least one observer considers Turkey and Central Asia explosive (Kaplan).

MLA-b Notes

Sometimes you may need to give information that doesn't fit into the text itself—to thank people who helped you, provide additional details, refer readers to other sources, or to add comments about sources. Such information can be given in a *footnote* (at the bottom of the page) or an *endnote* (on a separate page with the heading *Notes* just before your works-cited list). Put a superscript number at the appropriate point in your text, signaling to readers to look for the note with the corresponding number. If you have multiple notes, number them consecutively throughout your paper.

TEXT

This essay will argue that small liberal arts colleges should not recruit athletes and, more specifically, that giving student athletes preferential treatment undermines the larger educational goals.[1]

NOTE

[1]I want to thank all those who have contributed to my thinking on this topic, especially my classmates and my teachers Marian Johnson and Diane O'Connor.

MLA-c List of Works Cited

A works-cited list provides full bibliographic information for every source cited in your text. See page 132 for guidelines on preparing this list; for a sample works-cited list, see page 135.

Books

For most books, you'll need to provide information about the author; the title and any subtitle; and the place of publication, publisher, and date. At the end of the citation provide the medium—Print.

IMPORTANT DETAILS FOR CITING BOOKS

- **AUTHORS:** Include the author's middle name or initials, if any.

- **TITLES:** Capitalize all principal words in titles and subtitles. Do not capitalize *a, an, the, to,* or any prepositions or coordinating conjunctions unless they are the first or last word of a title or subtitle.

- **PUBLICATION PLACE:** If there's more than one city, use the first.

- **PUBLISHER:** Use a short form of the publisher's name (Norton for W. W. Norton & Company, Yale UP for Yale University Press).

- **DATES:** If more than one year is given, use the most recent one.

1. ONE AUTHOR

Author's Last Name, First Name. *Title.* Publication City: Publisher, Year of publication. Medium.

Anderson, Curtis. *The Long Tail: Why the Future of Business Is Selling Less of More.* New York: Hyperion, 2006. Print.

2. TWO OR MORE WORKS BY THE SAME AUTHOR(S)

Give the author's name in the first entry, and then use three hyphens in the author slot for each of the subsequent works, listing them alphabetically by the first important word of each title.

Author's Last Name, First Name. *Title That Comes First Alphabetically.* Publication City: Publisher, Year of publication. Medium.

---. *Title That Comes Next Alphabetically.* Publication City: Publisher, Year of publication. Medium.

Kaplan, Robert D. *The Coming Anarchy: Shattering the Dreams of the Post Cold War.* New York: Random, 2000. Print.

---. *Eastward to Tartary: Travels in the Balkans, the Middle East, and the Caucasus.* New York: Random, 2000. Print.

Documentation Map (MLA)

BOOK

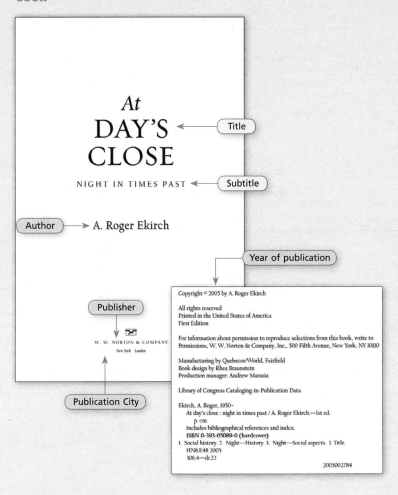

At
DAY'S
CLOSE
⟵ Title

NIGHT IN TIMES PAST ⟵ Subtitle

Author ⟶ A. Roger Ekirch

Year of publication

Publisher

W. W. NORTON & COMPANY
New York London

Publication City

Copyright © 2005 by A. Roger Ekirch

All rights reserved
Printed in the United States of America
First Edition

For information about permission to reproduce selections from this book, write to
Permissions, W. W. Norton & Company, Inc., 500 Fifth Avenue, New York, NY 10110

Manufacturing by Quebecor/World, Fairfield
Book design by Rhea Braunstein
Production manager: Andrew Marasia

Library of Congress Cataloging-in-Publication Data

Ekirch, A. Roger, 1950–
    At day's close : night in times past / A. Roger Ekirch.—1st ed.
        p. cm.
    Includes bibliographical references and index.
    ISBN 0-393-05089-0 (hardcover)
1. Social history. 2. Night—History. 3. Night—Social aspects. I. Title.
HN8.E48 2005
306.4—dc22

                                                          2005002784

Ekirch, A. Roger. *At Day's Close: Night in Times Past.* New York:
    Norton, 2005. Print.

3. TWO OR THREE AUTHORS

First Author's Last Name, First Name, Second Author's First and Last
Names, and Third Author's First and Last Names. *Title.*
Publication City: Publisher, Year of publication. Medium.

Malless, Stanley, and Jeffrey McQuain. *Coined by God: Words and
Phrases That First Appear in the English Translations of the
Bible.* New York: Norton, 2003. Print.

Sebranek, Patrick, Verne Meyer, and Dave Kemper. *Writers INC: A
Guide to Writing, Thinking, and Learning.* Burlington: Write
Source, 1990. Print.

4. FOUR OR MORE AUTHORS

You may give each author's name or the name of the first author
only, followed by *et al.*, Latin for "and others."

First Author's Last Name, First Name, Second Author's First and Last
Names, Third Author's First and Last Names, and Final Author's
First and Last Names. *Title.* Publication City: Publisher, Year of
publication. Medium.

Anderson, Robert, John Malcolm Brinnin, John Leggett, Gary Q.
Arpin, and Susan Allen Toth. *Elements of Literature: Literature
of the United States.* Austin: Holt, 1993. Print.

Anderson, Robert, et al. *Elements of Literature: Literature of the
United States.* Austin: Holt, 1993. Print.

5. ORGANIZATION OR GOVERNMENT AS AUTHOR

Organization Name. *Title.* Publication City: Publisher, Year of
publication. Medium.

Diagram Group. *The Macmillan Visual Desk Reference.* New York:
Macmillan, 1993. Print.

For a government publication, give the name of the government first,
followed by the names of any department and agency.

United States. Dept. of Health and Human Services. Natl. Inst. of
    Mental Health. *Autism Spectrum Disorders.* Washington: GPO,
    2004. Print.

6. ANTHOLOGY

Editor's Last Name, First Name, ed. *Title*. Publication City: Publisher,
    Year of publication. Medium.
Hall, Donald, ed. *The Oxford Book of Children's Verse in America*.
    New York: Oxford UP, 1985. Print.

If there is more than one editor, list the first editor last-name-first
and the others first-name-first.

Kitchen, Judith, and Mary Paumier Jones, eds. *In Short: A Collection
    of Brief Creative Nonfiction*. New York: Norton, 1996. Print.

7. WORK(S) IN AN ANTHOLOGY

Author's Last Name, First Name. "Title of Work." *Title of Anthology*.
    Ed. Editor's First and Last Names. Publication City: Publisher,
    Year of publication. Pages. Medium.
Achebe, Chinua. "Uncle Ben's Choice." *The Seagull Reader:
    Literature*. Ed. Joseph Kelly. New York: Norton, 2005. 23–27.
    Print.

To document two or more selections from one anthology, list each
selection by author and title, followed by the anthology editor(s)'
names and the pages of the selection. Then include an entry for the
anthology itself (see no. 6).

Author's Last Name, First Name. "Title of Work." Anthology Editor's
    Last Name Pages.
Hiestand, Emily. "Afternoon Tea." Kitchen and Jones 65–67.
Ozick, Cynthia. "The Shock of Teapots." Kitchen and Jones 68–71.

8. AUTHOR AND EDITOR

Start with the author if you've cited the text itself.

> Author's Last Name, First Name. *Title*. Ed. Editor's First and Last
>   Names. Publication City: Publisher, Year of publication.
>   Medium.

> Austen, Jane. *Emma*. Ed. Stephen M. Parrish. New York: Norton,
>   2000. Print.

Start with the editor to cite his or her contribution rather than the author's.

> Editor's Last Name, First Name, ed. *Title*. By Author's First and Last
>   Names. Publication City: Publisher, Year of publication.
>   Medium.

> Parrish, Stephen M., ed. *Emma*. By Jane Austen. New York: Norton,
>   2000. Print.

9. NO AUTHOR OR EDITOR

> *Title*. Publication City: Publisher, Year of publication. Medium.
> *2008 New York City Restaurants*. New York: Zagat, 2008. Print.

10. TRANSLATION

Start with the author to emphasize the work itself.

> Author's Last Name, First Name. *Title*. Trans. Translator's First and
>   Last Names. Publication City: Publisher, Year of publication.
>   Medium.

> Dostoevsky, Fyodor. *Crime and Punishment*. Trans. Richard Pevear
>   and Larissa Volokhonsky. New York: Vintage, 1993. Print.

Start with the translator to emphasize the translation.

> Pevear, Richard, and Larissa Volokhonsky, trans. *Crime and
>   Punishment*. By Fyodor Dostoevsky. New York: Vintage, 1993.
>   Print.

11. GRAPHIC NARRATIVE

Start with the person whose work is most relevant to your research, and include labels to indicate each collaborator's role.

> Pekar, Harvey, writer. *American Splendor.* Illus. R. Crumb. New York: Four Walls, 1996. Print.
>
> Crumb, R., illus. *American Splendor.* By Harvey Pekar. New York: Four Walls, 1996. Print.

If the work was written and illustrated by the same person, format the entry like that of any other book.

12. FOREWORD, INTRODUCTION, PREFACE, OR AFTERWORD

> Part Author's Last Name, First Name. Name of Part. *Title of Book.* By Author's First and Last Names. Publication City: Publisher, Year of publication. Pages. Medium.
>
> Tanner, Tony. Introduction. *Pride and Prejudice.* By Jane Austen. London: Penguin, 1972. 7–46. Print.

13. MULTIVOLUME WORK

If you cite all the volumes of a multivolume work, give the number of volumes after the title.

> Author's Last Name, First Name. *Title of Complete Work.* Number of vols. Publication City: Publisher, Year of publication. Medium.
>
> Sandburg, Carl. *Abraham Lincoln: The War Years.* 4 vols. New York: Harcourt, 1939. Print.

If you cite only one volume, give the volume number after the title.

> Sandburg, Carl. *Abraham Lincoln: The War Years.* Vol. 2. New York: Harcourt, 1939. Print.

14. ARTICLE IN A REFERENCE BOOK

Provide the author's name if the article is signed. If the reference work is well known, give only the edition and year of publication.

> Author's Last Name, First Name. "Title of Article." *Title of Reference
>   Book.* Edition number. Year of publication. Medium.
> "Kiwi." *Merriam-Webster's Collegiate Dictionary.* 11th ed. 2003.
>   Print.

If the reference work is less familiar or more specialized, give full publication information. If it has only one volume or is in its first edition, omit that information.

> Author's Last Name, First Name. "Title of Article." *Title of Reference
>   Book.* Ed. Editor's First and Last Name. Edition number.
>   Number of vols. Publication City: Publisher, Year of
>   publication. Medium.
> Campbell, James. "The Harlem Renaissance." *The Oxford Companion
>   to Twentieth-Century Poetry.* Ed. Ian Hamilton. Oxford: Oxford
>   UP, 1994. Print.

15. BOOK IN A SERIES

> Editor's Last Name, First Name, ed. *Title of Book.* By Author's First
>   and Last Names. Publication City: Publisher, Year of
>   publication. Medium. Series Title abbreviated.
> Wall, Cynthia, ed. *The Pilgrim's Progress.* By John Bunyan. New York:
>   Norton, 2007. Print. Norton Critical Ed.

16. SACRED TEXT

If you have cited a specific edition of a religious text, you need to include it in your works-cited list.

> *The New English Bible with the Apocrypha.* New York: Oxford UP,
>   1971. Print.
> *The Torah: A Modern Commentary.* Ed. W. Gunther Plaut. New York:
>   Union of Amer. Hebrew Congregations, 1981. Print.

17. BOOK WITH TITLE WITHIN THE TITLE

When the title of a book contains the title of another long work, do not italicize that title.

> Walker, Roy. *Time Is Free: A Study of* Macbeth. London: Dakers, 1949. Print.

When the book title contains the title of a short work, put the short work in quotation marks, and italicize the entire title.

> Thompson, Lawrance Roger. *"Fire and Ice": The Art and Thought of Robert Frost.* New York: Holt, 1942. Print.

18. EDITION OTHER THAN THE FIRST

> Author's Last Name, First Name. *Title*. Name or number of ed. Publication City: Publisher, Year of publication. Medium.
> Hirsch, E. D., Jr., ed. *What Your Second Grader Needs to Know: Fundamentals of a Good Second-Grade Education.* Rev. ed. New York: Doubleday, 1998. Print.

19. REPUBLISHED WORK

Give the original publication date after the title, followed by the publication information of the republished edition.

> Author's Last Name, First Name. *Title.* Year of original edition. Publication City: Current Publisher, Year of republication. Medium.
> Bierce, Ambrose. *Civil War Stories.* 1909. New York: Dover, 1994. Print.

20. PUBLISHER AND IMPRINT

Some sources may provide both a publisher's name and an imprint on the title page; if so, include both, with a hyphen between the imprint and the publisher.

> Author's Last Name, First Name. *Title*. Publication City: Imprint-
>   Publisher, Year of publication. Medium.

Rowling, J. K. *Harry Potter and the Goblet of Fire*. New York:
    Levine–Scholastic, 2000. Print.

Periodicals

For most articles, you'll need to provide information about the author, the article title and any subtitle, the periodical title, any volume or issue number, the date, inclusive page numbers, and the medium—Print.

IMPORTANT DETAILS FOR CITING PERIODICALS

- **AUTHORS:** If there is more than one author, list the first author last-name-first and the others first-name-first.

- **TITLES:** Capitalize titles and subtitles as you would for a book. For periodical titles, omit any initial *A, An,* or *The.*

- **DATES:** Abbreviate the names of months except for May, June, or July: Jan., Feb., Mar., Apr., Aug., Sept., Oct., Nov., Dec. Journals paginated by volume or issue need only the year (in parentheses).

- **PAGES:** If an article does not fall on consecutive pages, give the first page with a plus sign (55+).

21. ARTICLE IN A JOURNAL

> Author's Last Name, First Name. "Title of Article." *Title of Journal*
>   Volume.Issue (Year): Pages. Medium.

Cooney, Brian C. "Considering *Robinson Crusoe*'s 'Liberty of
    Conscience' in an Age of Terror." *College English* 69.3 (2007):
    197–215. Print.

22. ARTICLE IN A JOURNAL NUMBERED BY ISSUE

> Author's Last Name, First Name. "Title of Article." *Title of Journal*
>   Issue (Year): Pages. Medium.

Documentation Map (MLA)

ARTICLE IN A JOURNAL

Pious Princes and Red-Hot Lovers: The Politics of ◄─ Title of Article
Shakespeare's **Romeo and Juliet**

Author ──► Jerry Weinberger
Michigan State University

Shakespeare's *Romeo and Juliet* is obviously a tragedy of impetuous young love. But it is also a play about politics, especially politics as conditioned by Christian morality and religion. The play's action is determined by the conflict between secular and priestly authority, and by the complex interaction among mercy, love, and punishment as practiced by Escalus, Prince of Verona, and Friar Laurence, the Franciscan. In the course of this action, the Veronese regime is transformed, and the common good determined, in ways more compatible with the friar's interests than with those of the Prince. *Romeo and Juliet* is one of Shakespeare's pictures of the unique problems that determined modern, as opposed to ancient, political life.

Critical opinion now agrees that Shakespeare presents a sophisticated teaching about politics, ancient as well as modern. While it was long thought that Shakespeare knew little about ancient politics, we now have a different view, for instance, of the Roman plays: *Coriolanus* depicts the Republic's subtle constitutional balance; *Julius Caesar* depicts the end of Republican liberty; *Antony and Cleopatra* describes the political, moral, and psychological conditions of the Empire (Cantor 1976). As regards modern politics, critics have long acknowledged that Shakespeare was a keen interpreter of the quintessential modern, Machiavelli. "It can hardly be doubted," said E. M. W. Tillyard in 1944, that Shakespeare knew well the doctrines of Machiavelli (Tillyard 1991, 28–30). More recent critics—from both ends of the ideological spectrum—agree. One conservative sees *Measure for Measure* as "a Machiavellian scheme to bring good government to a bad city" (Jaffa 1981, 189), while a leading cultural materialist tells us that "Shakespeare's Henry plays . . . can be seen to confirm the Machiavellian hypothesis of the origin of princely power in force and fraud even as they draw their audiences irresistibly toward the celebration of that power" (Greenblatt 1985, 20). Whereas Hume (1873, 357–58) once faulted Shakespeare for his indifference to English civil liberty (in the English history plays), we now know that

Volume   Issue

I thank Paul A. Cantor, Werner J. Dannhauser, Arthur Melzer, and Richard Zinman for their helpful criticism of this article's earlier drafts.

THE JOURNAL OF POLITICS, Vol. 65, No. 2, May 2003, Pp. 350–375 ◄── Pages
© 2003 Blackwell Publishing, 350 Main St., Malden, MA 02148, USA, and PO Box 1354, 9600 Garsington Road, Oxford OX4 2DQ, UK.

Title of Journal   Year

Weinberger, Jerry. "Pious Princes and Red-Hot Lovers: The Politics of Shakespeare's *Romeo and Juliet.*" *Journal of Politics* 65.2 (2003): 350–75. Print.

Documentation Map (MLA)

ARTICLE IN A MAGAZINE

Title of Article

Author

Page

Month and year

Title of Magazine

Fox, Michael W. "The Wolf in Your Dog." *Bark* Mar.–Apr. 2008: 85–87. Print.

Flynn, Kevin. "The Railway in Canadian Poetry." *Canadian Literature*
174 (2002): 70–95. Print.

23. ARTICLE IN A MAGAZINE

Author's Last Name, First Name. "Title of Article." *Title of Magazine*
Day Month Year: Pages. Medium.

Walsh, Bryan. "Not a Watt to Be Wasted." *Time* 17 Mar. 2008: 46–47.
Print.

For a monthly magazine, include only the month and year.

Fellman, Bruce. "Leading the Libraries." *Yale Alumni Magazine* Feb.
2002: 26–31. Print.

24. ARTICLE IN A DAILY NEWSPAPER

Author's Last Name, First Name. "Title of Article." *Name of
Newspaper* Day Month Year: Pages. Medium.

Springer, Shira. "Celtics Reserves Are Whizzes vs. Wizards." *Boston
Globe* 14 Mar. 2005: D4+. Print.

If you are citing a particular edition of a newspaper, list the edition
(late ed., natl. ed., etc.) after the date. And if a section is not identified
by a letter, put the name of the section after the edition information.

Burns, John F., and Miguel Helft. "Under Pressure, YouTube
Withdraws Muslim Cleric's Videos." *New York Times* 4 Nov.
2010, late ed., sec. 1: 13. Print.

25. UNSIGNED ARTICLE

"Title of Article." *Name of Publication* Day Month Year: Pages.
Medium.

"Being Invisible Closer to Reality." *Atlanta Journal-Constitution* 11
Aug. 2008: A3. Print.

26. EDITORIAL

> "Title." Editorial. *Name of Publication* Day Month Year: Page.
> Medium.

> "Gas, Cigarettes Are Safe to Tax." Editorial. *Lakeville Journal* 17 Feb.
> 2005: A10. Print.

27. LETTER TO THE EDITOR

> Author's Last Name, First Name. "Title (if any)." Letter. *Name of
> Publication* Day Month Year: Page. Medium.

> Festa, Roger. "Social Security: Another Phony Crisis." Letter. *Lakeville
> Journal* 17 Feb. 2005: A10. Print.

28. REVIEW

> Reviewer's Last Name, First Name. "Title (if any) of Review." Rev. of
> *Title of Work,* by Author's First and Last Names. *Title of
> Periodical* Day Month Year: Pages. Medium.

> Frank, Jeffrey. "Body Count." Rev. of *The Exception,* by Christian
> Jungersen. *New Yorker* 30 July 2007: 86–87. Print.

Online Sources

Not every online source gives you all the data that MLA would like
to see in a works-cited entry. Ideally, you will be able to list the
author's name, the title, information about print publication, information about electronic publication (title of site, editor, date of first
electronic publication and /or most recent revision, name of the publisher or sponsoring institution), the publication medium, date of
access, and, if necessary, a URL.

IMPORTANT DETAILS FOR CITING ONLINE SOURCES

- **AUTHORS OR EDITORS** and **TITLES:** Format authors and titles as you
  would for a print book or periodical.

- **PUBLISHER:** If the name of the publisher or sponsoring institution
  is unavailable, use *N.p.*

- **DATES:** Abbreviate the months as you would for a print periodical. Although MLA asks for the date when materials were first posted or most recently updated, you won't always be able to find that information; if it's unavailable, use *n.d.* Be sure to include the date on which you accessed the source.

- **PAGES:** If the citation calls for page numbers but the source is unpaginated, use *n. pag.* in place of page numbers.

- **MEDIUM:** Indicate the medium—Web, email, CD-ROM, and so on.

- **URL:** MLA assumes that readers can locate most sources on the Web by searching for the author, title, or other identifying information, so they don't require a URL for most online sources. When users can't locate the source without a URL, give the address of the website in angle brackets. When a URL won't fit on one line, break it only after a slash (and do not add a hyphen). If a URL is very long, consider giving the URL of the site's home or search page instead.

29. ENTIRE WEBSITE

For websites with an editor, compiler, director, narrator, or translator, follow the name with the appropriate abbreviation (*ed., comp.*).

> Author's Last Name, First Name. *Title of Site*. Publisher or Sponsoring Institution, Date posted or last updated. Medium. Day Month Year of access.

Zalta, Edward N., ed. *Stanford Encyclopedia of Philosophy.* Metaphysics Research Lab, Center for the Study of Language and Information, Stanford U, 2007. Web. 14 Nov. 2010.

PERSONAL WEBSITE

> Author's Last Name, First Name. Home page. Sponsor, Date posted or last updated. Medium. Day Month Year of access.

Nunberg, Geoffrey. Home page. School of Information, U of California, Berkeley, 2009. Web. 13 Apr. 2009.

Documentation Map (MLA)

WORK FROM A WEBSITE

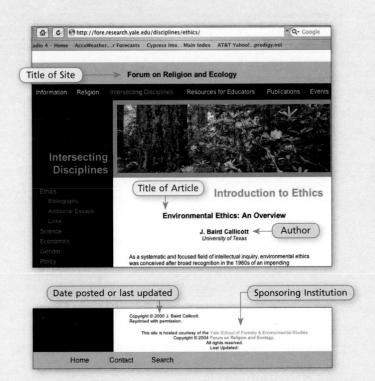

Title of Site → **Forum on Religion and Ecology**

Information   Religion   Intersecting Disciplines   Resources for Educators   Publications   Events

Intersecting Disciplines

Ethics
  Bibliography
  Additional Essays
  Links
Science
Economics
Gender
Policy

Title of Article → **Introduction to Ethics**

Environmental Ethics: An Overview

J. Baird Callicott ← Author
University of Texas

As a systematic and focused field of intellectual inquiry, environmental ethics was conceived after broad recognition in the 1960s of an impending

Date posted or last updated   Sponsoring Institution

Copyright © 2000 J. Baird Callicott.
Reprinted with permission.

This site is hosted courtesy of the Yale School of Forestry & Environmental Studies
Copyright © 2004 Forum on Religion and Ecology.
All rights reserved.
Last Updated:

Home   Contact   Search

Callicott, J. Baird. "Environmental Ethics: An Overview." *Forum on Religion and Ecology*. Yale School of Forestry & Environmental Studies, 2000. Web. 17 Sept. 2008.

30. WORK FROM A WEBSITE

> Author's Last Name, First Name. "Title of Work." *Title of Site*. Ed.
> Editor's First and Last Names. Sponsor, Date posted or last
> updated. Medium. Day Month Year of access.

Buff, Rachel Ida. "Becoming American." *Immigration History
Research Center*. U of Minnesota, 24 Mar. 2008. Web. 4 Apr.
2008.

31. ONLINE BOOK OR PART OF A BOOK

Cite a book you access online as you would a print book, adding the
name of the site or database, the medium, and the date of access.

Anderson, Sherwood. *Winesburg, Ohio*. New York: B. W. Huebsch,
1919. *Bartleby.com*. Web. 7 Apr. 2008.

If you are citing a part of a book, put the part in quotation marks
before the book title. If the online book is paginated, give the pages;
if not, use N. *pag*.

Anderson, Sherwood. "The Strength of God." *Winesburg, Ohio*.
New York: B. W. Huebsch, 1919. N. pag. *Bartleby.com*. Web.
7 Apr. 2008.

To cite a book you've downloaded onto a Kindle, Nook, or other digital device, follow the setup for a print book, but indicate the ebook
format at the end of your citation.

Larson, Erik. *The Devil in the White City: Murder, Mayhem, and
Madness at the Fair That Changed America*. New York:
Vintage, 2004. Kindle.

32. ARTICLE IN AN ONLINE SCHOLARLY JOURNAL

If a journal does not number pages or if it numbers each article
separately, use *n. pag.* in place of page numbers.

> Author's Last Name, First Name. "Title of Article." *Title of Journal*
> Volume.Issue (Year): Pages. Medium. Day Month Year of access.

Gleckman, Jason. "Shakespeare as Poet or Playwright? The Player's
　　　Speech in *Hamlet.*" *Early Modern Literary Studies* 11.3 (2006):
　　　n. pag. Web. 24 June 2008.

33. ARTICLE IN AN ONLINE NEWSPAPER

Author's Last Name, First Name. "Title of Article." *Title of
　　　Newspaper.* Publisher, Day Month Year. Medium. Day Month
　　　Year of access.

Banerjee, Neela. "Proposed Religion-Based Program for Federal
　　　Inmates Is Canceled." *New York Times.* New York Times, 28
　　　Oct. 2006. Web. 24 June 2008.

34. ARTICLE IN AN ONLINE MAGAZINE

Author's Last Name, First Name. "Title of Article." *Title of Magazine.*
　　　Publisher, Date of publication. Medium. Day Month Year of
　　　access.

Lithwick, Dahlia. "Privacy Rights Inc." *Slate.* Washington Post–
　　　Newsweek Interactive, 14 Oct. 2010. Web. 25 Oct. 2010.

35. BLOG ENTRY

Author's Last Name, First Name. "Title of Entry." *Title of Blog.* Sponsor,
　　　Day Month Year posted. Medium. Day Month Year of access.

Gladwell, Malcolm. "Enron and Newspapers." *Gladwell.com.* N.p.,
　　　4 Jan. 2007. Web. 26 Aug. 2008.

If the entry has no title, use "Blog entry" without quotation marks.
Cite a whole blog as you would an entire website (see no. 29). If the
publisher or sponsor is unavailable, use *N.p.*

36. ARTICLE ACCESSED THROUGH A DATABASE

For articles accessed through a library's subscription services, such
as InfoTrac and EBSCOhost, cite the publication information for the
source, followed by the name of the database.

Author's Last Name, First Name. "Title of Article." *Title of Periodical
Date or Volume.Issue (Year): Pages. Database Name.* Medium.
Day Month Year of access.

Stalter, Sunny. "Subway Ride and Subway System in Hart Crane's 'The
Tunnel.'" *Journal of Modern Literature* 33.2 (2010): 70–91.
Academic Search Complete. Web. 28 May 2010.

37. ONLINE EDITORIAL

"Title of Editorial." Editorial. *Title of Site.* Publisher, Day Month Year
of publication. Medium. Day Month Year of access.

"Keep Drinking Age at 21." Editorial. *ChicagoTribune.com.* Chicago
Tribune, 25 Aug. 2008. Web. 28 Aug. 2008.

38. ONLINE FILM REVIEW

Reviewer's Last Name, First Name. "Title of Review." Rev. of *Title of
Work,* dir. First and Last Names. *Title of Site.* Publisher, Day
Month Year posted. Medium. Day Month Year of access.

Edelstein, David. "Best Served Cold." Rev. of *The Social Network,* dir.
David Fincher. *New York Magazine.* New York Media, 1 Oct.
2010. Web. 3 Nov. 2010.

39. EMAIL

Writer's Last Name, First Name. "Subject Line." Message to the
author. Day Month Year of message. Medium.

Smith, William. "Teaching Grammar—Some Thoughts." Message to
the author. 19 Nov. 2007. Email.

40. POSTING TO AN ONLINE FORUM

Writer's Last Name, First Name. "Title of Posting." *Name of Forum.*
Sponsor, Day Month Year of posting. Medium. Day Month
Year of access.

Mintz, Stephen H. "Manumission During the Revolution." *H-Net List
on Slavery.* Michigan State U, 14 Sept. 2006. Web. 18 Apr. 2009.

Documentation Map (MLA)

ARTICLE ACCESSED THROUGH A DATABASE

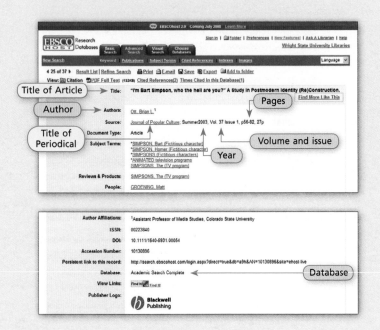

Ott, Brian L. "'I'm Bart Simpson, Who the Hell Are You?' A
   Study in Postmodern Identity (Re)Construction." *Journal of
   Popular Culture* 37.1 (2003): 56–82. *Academic Search
   Complete.* Web. 24 Mar. 2008.

41. ARTICLE IN AN ONLINE REFERENCE WORK

"Title of Article." *Title of Reference Work.* Sponsor, Date of work.
Medium. Day Month Year of access.

"Dubai." *MSN Encarta.* Microsoft Corporation, 2008. Web. 20 June
2008.

42. WIKI ENTRY

"Title of Entry." *Title of Wiki.* Sponsor, Day Month Year updated.
Medium. Day Month Year of access.

"Pi." *Wikipedia.* Wikimedia Foundation, 28 Aug. 2008. Web. 2 Sept.
2008.

43. PODCAST

Performer or Host's Last Name, First Name. "Title of Podcast."
Host Host's First and Last Name. *Title of Program.* Sponsor, Day
Month Year posted. Medium. Day Month Year of access.

Blumberg, Alex, and Adam Davidson. "The Giant Pool of Money."
Host Ira Glass. *This American Life.* Chicago Public Radio, 9 May
2008. Web. 18 Sept. 2008.

Other Kinds of Sources (including online versions)

Many of the sources in this section can be found online, and you'll
find examples here for how to cite them. If there is no Web model
here, start with the guidelines most appropriate for the source you
need to cite, omit the original medium, and end your citation with
the title of the website, italicized; the medium (Web); and the day,
month, and year of access.

44. ADVERTISEMENT

Product or Company. Advertisement. *Title of Periodical* Date or
Volume.Issue (Year): Page. Medium.

Empire BlueCross BlueShield. Advertisement. *Fortune* 8 Dec. 2003:
208. Print.

ADVERTISEMENT ON THE WEB

Rolex. Advertisement. *Time.* Time, n.d. Web. 1 Apr. 2009.

45. ART

Artist's Last Name, First Name. *Title of Art.* Medium. Year. Institution,
    City.

Van Gogh, Vincent. *The Potato Eaters.* Oil on canvas. 1885. Van
    Gogh Museum, Amsterdam.

ART ON THE WEB

Warhol, Andy. *Self-Portrait.* 1979. J. Paul Getty Museum, Los
    Angeles. *The Getty.* Web. 29 Mar. 2007.

Cite photographs you find online by giving the photographer, title,
and date of the image, if available. If the date is unavailable, use *n.d.*
For photographs you take yourself, see no. 64.

Donnell, Ryan. *At a Pre-Civil War Railroad Construction Site Outside
    of Philadelphia.* 2010. Smithsonian Institution. *Smithsonian.
    com.* Web. 3 Nov. 2010.

46. CARTOON

Artist's Last Name, First Name. "Title of Cartoon (if titled)." Cartoon.
    Title of Periodical Date or Volume.Issue (Year): Page. Medium.

Chast, Roz. "The Three Wise Men of Thanksgiving." Cartoon. *New
    Yorker* 1 Dec. 2003: 174. Print.

CARTOON ON THE WEB

Horsey, David. Cartoon. *Seattle Post-Intelligencer.* Seattle Post-
    Intelligencer, 20 Apr. 2008. Web. 21 Apr. 2008.

47. DISSERTATION

Treat a published dissertation as you would a book, but after its
title, add the abbreviation *Diss.*, the institution, and the date of the
dissertation.

Author's Last Name, First Name. *Title*. Diss. Institution, Year.
    Publication City: Publisher, Year. Medium.
Goggin, Peter N. *A New Literacy Map of Research and Scholarship in
    Computers and Writing*. Diss. Indiana U of Pennsylvania, 2000.
    Ann Arbor: UMI, 2001. Print.

For unpublished dissertations, put the title in quotation marks and
end with the degree-granting institution and the year.

Kim, Loel. "Students Respond to Teacher Comments: A Comparison
    of Online Written and Voice Modalities." Diss. Carnegie
    Mellon U, 1998. Print.

48. CD-ROM OR DVD-ROM

Title. Any pertinent information about the edition, release, or
    version. Publication City: Publisher, Year of publication.
    Medium.
Othello. Princeton: Films for the Humanities and Sciences, 1998.
    CD-ROM.

If you are citing only part of the CD-ROM or DVD-ROM, name the part
as you would a part of a book.

"Snow Leopard." *Encarta Encyclopedia 2007*. Seattle: Microsoft,
    2007. CD-ROM.

49. FILM, DVD, OR VIDEO CLIP

Title. Dir. Director's First and Last Names. Perf. Lead Actors' First and
    Last Names. Distributor, Year of release. Medium.
Casablanca. Dir. Michael Curtiz. Perf. Humphrey Bogart, Ingrid
    Bergman, and Claude Rains. Warner, 1942. Film.

To cite a particular person's work, start with that name.

Cody, Diablo, scr. *Juno*. Dir. Jason Reitman. Perf. Ellen Page, Michael
    Cera, Jennifer Garner, and Jason Bateman. Fox Searchlight,
    2007. DVD.

Cite a video clip on YouTube or a similar site as you would a short work from a website.

> Director's Last Name, First Name, dir. "Title of Video." *Title of Site.*
>> Sponsor, Day Month Year of release. Medium. Day Month Year
>> of access.
> PivotMasterDX, dir. "Bounce!" *YouTube.* YouTube, 14 June 2008.
>> Web. 21 June 2008.

50. BROADCAST INTERVIEW

> Subject's Last Name, First Name. Interview. *Title of Program.*
>> Network. Station, City, Day Month Year. Medium.
> Gates, Henry Louis, Jr. Interview. *Fresh Air.* NPR. WNYC, New York,
>> 9 Apr. 2002. Radio.

51. PUBLISHED INTERVIEW

> Subject's Last Name, First Name. Interview, or "Title of Interview."
>> *Title of Periodical* Date or Volume.Issue (Year): Pages. Medium.
> Stone, Oliver. Interview. *Esquire* Nov. 2004: 170. Print.

52. PERSONAL INTERVIEW

> Subject's Last Name, First Name. Personal interview. Day Month Year.
> Roddick, Andy. Personal interview. 17 Aug. 2008.

53. UNPUBLISHED LETTER

For medium, use MS for a hand-written letter and TS for a typed one.

> Author's Last Name, First Name. Letter to the author. Day Month
>> Year. Medium.
> Quindlen, Anna. Letter to the author. 11 Apr. 2002. MS.

54. PUBLISHED LETTER

> Letter Writer's Last Name, First Name. Letter to First and Last Names.
>> Day Month Year of letter. *Title of Book.* Ed. Editor's First and

Last Names. City: Publisher, Year of publication. Pages.
Medium.

White, E. B. Letter to Carol Angell. 28 May 1970. *Letters of E. B.*
White. Ed. Dorothy Lobarno Guth. New York: Harper, 1976.
600. Print.

55. MAP OR CHART

Title of Map. Map. City: Publisher, Year of publication. Medium.

Toscana. Map. Milan: Touring Club Italiano, 1987. Print.

MAP ON THE WEB

"Portland, Oregon." Map. *Google Maps.* Google, 25 Apr. 2009. Web.
25 Apr. 2009.

56. MUSICAL SCORE

Composer's Last Name, First Name. *Title of Composition.* Year of
composition. Publication City: Publisher, Year of publication.
Medium. Series Information (if any).

Beethoven, Ludwig van. *String Quartet No. 13 in B Flat, Op. 130.*
1825. New York: Dover, 1970. Print.

57. SOUND RECORDING

Artist's Last Name, First Name. *Title of Long Work.* Other pertinent
details about the artists. Manufacturer, Year of release.
Medium.

Beethoven, Ludwig van. *Missa Solemnis.* Perf. Westminster Choir and
New York Philharmonic. Cond. Leonard Bernstein. Sony, 1992.
CD.

Whether you list the composer, conductor, or performer first depends
on where you want to place the emphasis. If you are citing a specific
song, put it in quotation marks before the name of the recording.

Brown, Greg. "Canned Goods." *The Live One.* Red House, 1995. MP3
file.

For a spoken-word recording, you may begin with the writer, speaker, or producer, depending on your emphasis.

> Dale, Jim, narr. *Harry Potter and the Deathly Hallows.* By J. K. Rowling. Random House Audio, 2007. CD.

58. ORAL PRESENTATION

> Speaker's Last Name, First Name. "Title of Lecture." Sponsoring Institution. Site, City. Day Month Year. Medium.
>
> Cassin, Michael. "Nature in the Raw—The Art of Landscape Painting." Berkshire Institute for Lifetime Learning. Clark Art Institute, Williamstown. 24 Mar. 2005. Lecture.

59. PAPER FROM PROCEEDINGS OF A CONFERENCE

> Author's Last Name, First Name. "Title of Paper." *Title of Conference Proceedings.* Date, City. Ed. Editor's First and Last Names. Publication City: Publisher, Year. Pages. Medium.
>
> Zolotow, Charlotte. "Passion in Publishing." *A Sea of Upturned Faces: Proceedings of the Third Pacific Rim Conference on Children's Literature.* 1986, Los Angeles. Ed. Winifred Ragsdale. Metuchen: Scarecrow P, 1989. 236–49. Print.

60. PERFORMANCE

> Title. By Author's First and Last Names. Other appropriate details about the performance. Site, City. Day Month Year. Medium.
>
> *Take Me Out.* By Richard Greenberg. Dir. Scott Plate. Perf. Caleb Sekeres. Dobama Theatre, Cleveland. 17 Aug. 2007. Performance.

61. TELEVISION OR RADIO PROGRAM

> "Title of Episode." *Title of Program.* Other appropriate information about the writer, director, actors, etc. Network. Station, City, Day Month Year of broadcast. Medium.

"Tabula Rasa." *Criminal Minds.* Writ. Dan Dworkin. Dir. Steve Boyum. NBC. WCNC, Charlotte, 14 May 2008. Television.

TELEVISION OR RADIO ON THE WEB

"Bush's War." *Frontline.* Writ. and dir. Michael Kirk. PBS, 24 Mar. 2008. *PBS.org.* Web. 10 Apr. 2009.

62. PAMPHLET, BROCHURE, OR PRESS RELEASE

Author's Last Name, First Name. *Title of Publication.* Publication City: Publisher, Year. Medium.

Bowers, Catherine. *Can We Find a Home Here? Answering Questions of Interfaith Couples.* Boston: UUA Publications, n.d. Print.

To cite a press release, include the day and month before the year.

63. LEGAL SOURCE

The name of a court case is not italicized in a works-cited entry.

Names of the First Plaintiff v. First Defendant. Volume Name Page numbers of law report. Name of Court. Year of decision. Source information for medium consulted.

District of Columbia v. Heller. 540 US 290. Supreme Court of the US. 2008. *Supreme Court Collection.* Legal Information Inst., Cornell U Law School, n.d. Web. 18 Mar. 2009.

For acts of law, include both the Public Law number and the Statutes at Large volume and page numbers.

Name of Law. Public law number. Statutes at Large Volume Stat. Pages. Day Month Year enacted. Medium.

Military Commissions Act. Pub. L. 109-366. 120 Stat. 2083–2521. 17 Oct. 2006. Print.

64. MP3, JPEG, PDF, OR OTHER DIGITAL FILE

For downloaded songs, photographs, PDFs, and other documents stored on your computer or another digital device, follow the guidelines for the type of work you are citing (art, journal article, and so on) and give the file type as the medium.

> Talking Heads. "Burning Down the House." *Speaking in Tongues.* Sire, 1983. Digital file.
>
> Taylor, Aaron. "Twilight of the Idols: Performance, Melodramatic Villainy, and *Sunset Boulevard.*" *Journal of Film and Video* 59 (2007): 13–31. PDF file.

Citing Sources Not Covered by MLA

To cite a source for which MLA does not provide guidelines, look for models similar to the source you are citing. Give any information readers will need in order to find your source themselves—author; title, subtitle; publisher and/or sponsor; medium; dates; and any other pertinent information. You might want to try out your citation yourself, to be sure it will lead others to your source.

MLA-d Formatting a Paper

Name, course, title. MLA does not require a separate title page. In the upper left-hand corner of your first page, include your name, your professor's name, the name of the course, and the date. Center the title of your paper on the next line after the date; capitalize it as you would a book title.

Page numbers. In the upper right-hand corner of each page, one-half inch below the top of the page, include your last name and the page number. Number pages consecutively throughout your paper.

Spacing, margins, and indents. Double-space the entire paper, including your works-cited list. Set one-inch margins at the top, bottom, and sides of your text; do not justify your text. The first line of each paragraph should be indented one-half inch from the left margin.

Long quotations. When quoting more than three lines of poetry, more than four lines of prose, or dialogue between two or more characters from a drama, set off the quotation from the rest of your text, indenting it one inch (or ten spaces) from the left margin. Do not use quotation marks, and put any parenthetical documentation *after* the final punctuation.

> In *Eastward to Tartary,* Kaplan captures ancient and contemporary Antioch for us:
>
>> At the height of its glory in the Roman-Byzantine age, when it had an amphitheater, public baths, aqueducts, and sewage pipes, half a million people lived in Antioch. Today the population is only 125,000. With sour relations between Turkey and Syria, and unstable politics throughout the Middle East, Antioch is now a backwater—seedy and tumbledown, with relatively few tourists. I found it altogether charming. (123)

> In the first stanza of Arnold's "Dover Beach," the exclamations make clear that the speaker is addressing a companion who is also present in the scene:
>
>> Come to the window, sweet is the night air!
>> Only, from the long line of spray
>> Where the sea meets the moon-blanched land,
>> Listen! You hear the grating roar
>> Of pebbles which the waves draw back, and fling. (6–10)

Illustrations. Insert illustrations in your paper close to the text that discusses them. For tables, provide a number (*Table* 1) and a title on separate lines above the table. Below the table, include a caption and provide information about the source. For figures (graphs, charts, photos, and so on), provide a figure number (*Fig.* 1), caption, and source information below the figure. If you give only brief information about the source (such as a parenthetical citation), or if the source is cited elsewhere in your text, include the source in your list of works cited. Be sure to discuss any illustrations, and make it clear how they relate to the rest of your text.

List of Works Cited. Start your list on a new page, following any notes. Center the title and double-space the entire list. Each entry should begin at the left margin, and subsequent lines should be indented one-half inch (or five spaces). Alphabetize the list by authors' last names (or by editors' or translators' names, if appropriate). Alphabetize works that have no identifiable author or editor by title, disregarding *A, An,* and *The.* If you cite more than one work by a single author, list them all alphabetically by title, and use three hyphens in place of the author's name after the first entry (see no. 2 on p. 104).

MLA-e Sample Pages

The following sample pages are from "Against the Odds: Harry S. Truman and the Election of 1948," a report written by Dylan Borchers for a first-year writing course. They are formatted according to the guidelines of the *MLA Handbook for Writers of Research Papers,* 7th edition (2009). To read the complete report, go to **wwnorton.com/write/little-seagull-handbook**.

Sample Page of Research Paper, MLA Style

Borchers   1   Last name
and page
number.

1"

Dylan Borchers

Professor Bullock

English 102, Section 4

31 March 2009

Against the Odds: Title centered.

Harry S. Truman and the Election of 1948   Double-spaced
throughout.

"Thomas E. Dewey's Election as President Is a Foregone

Conclusion," read a headline in the *New York Times* during the

presidential election race between incumbent Democrat Harry S.

Truman and his Republican challenger, Thomas E. Dewey. Earlier,

Life magazine had put Dewey on its cover with the caption "The

Next President of the United States" (qtd. in "1948 Truman-Dewey

Election"). In a *Newsweek* survey of fifty prominent political writers,

each one predicted Truman's defeat, and *Time* correspondents   1"

declared that Dewey would carry 39 of the 48 states (Donaldson

210). Nearly every major media outlet across the United States

endorsed Dewey and lambasted Truman. As historian Robert H.

Ferrell observes, even Truman's wife, Bess, thought he would be   Author named
in signal
beaten (270).   phrase, page
numbers in
parentheses.

The results of an election are not so easily predicted, as the

famous photograph in fig. 1 shows. Not only did Truman win the

election, but he won by a significant margin, with 303 electoral

votes and 24,179,259 popular votes, compared to Dewey's 189

electoral votes and 21,991,291 popular votes (Donaldson 204–07).

In fact, many historians and political analysts argue that Truman

would have won by an even greater margin had third-party

Progressive candidate Henry A. Wallace not split the Democratic

1"

Sample Page of Research Paper, MLA Style

Borchers   2

Illustration close to the text to which it relates. Figure number, caption, and parenthetical source citation included.

Fig. 1. President Harry S. Truman holds up an Election Day edition of the *Chicago Daily Tribune,* which mistakenly announced "Dewey Defeats Truman." St. Louis. 4 Nov. 1948 (Rollins).

vote in New York State and Dixiecrat Strom Thurmond not won four states in the South (McCullough 711). Although Truman's defeat was heavily predicted, those predictions themselves, Dewey's passiveness as a campaigner, and Truman's zeal turned the tide for a Truman victory.

Paragraphs indent ½ inch or 5 spaces.

In the months preceding the election, public opinion polls predicted that Dewey would win by a large margin. Pollster Elmo Roper stopped polling in September, believing there was no reason to continue, given a seemingly inevitable Dewey landslide. Although the margin narrowed as the election drew near, the other

No signal phrase; author and page numbers in parentheses.

pollsters predicted a Dewey win by at least 5 percent (Donaldson 209). Many historians believe that these predictions aided the president in the long run. First, surveys showing Dewey in the lead

Sample Works Cited List, MLA Style

Borchers   8

Heading centered. ....• Works Cited

Alphabetized by authors' last names.

Donaldson, Gary A. *Truman Defeats Dewey.* Lexington: UP of •⋯⋯
Kentucky, 1999. Print.

Ferrell, Robert H. *Harry S. Truman: A Life.* Columbia: U of Missouri P,
1994. Print.

Double-spaced.

Hamby, Alonzo L., ed. "Harry S. Truman (1945-1953)."
AmericanPresident.org. Miller Center of Public Affairs, U of
Virginia, 11 Dec. 2003. Web. 17 Mar. 2009.

Each entry begins at the left margin; subsequent lines indented.

---. *Man of the People: A Life of Harry S. Truman.* New York: Oxford UP, •
1995. Print.

Holbrook, Thomas M. "Did the Whistle-Stop Campaign Matter?" *PS:
Political Science and Politics* 35.1 (2002): 59-66. Print.

Multiple works by a single author listed alphabetically by title.

Karabell, Zachary. *The Last Campaign: How Harry Truman Won the
1948 Election.* New York: Knopf, 2000. Print.

McCullough, David. *Truman.* New York: Simon, 1992. Print.

McDonald, Daniel G., Carroll J. Glynn, Sei-Hill Kim, and Ronald E.
Ostman. "The Spiral of Silence in the 1948 Presidential
Election." *Communication Research* 28.2 (2001): 139-55. Print.

"1948: The Great Truman Surprise." *Media and Politics Online Projects:
Media Coverage of Presidential Campaigns.* Dept. of Political
Science and International Affairs, Kennesaw State U, 29 Oct.
2003. Web. 20 Mar. 2009.

"1948 Truman-Dewey Election." *Electronic Government Project:
Eagleton Digital Archive of American Politics.* Eagleton Inst. of
Politics, Rutgers, State U of New Jersey, 2004. Web. 19 Mar.
2009.

APA Style

American Psychological Association (APA) style calls for (1) brief documentation in parentheses near each in-text citation and (2) complete documentation in a list of references at the end of your text. The models in this chapter draw on the *Publication Manual of the American Psychological Association*, 6th edition (2010). Additional information is available at www.apastyle.org.

A DIRECTORY TO APA STYLE

Reference List   144

Throughout this chapter, you'll find models and examples that are color-coded to help you see how writers include source information in their texts and reference lists: tan for author or editor, yellow for title, gray for publication information: place of publication, publisher, date of publication, page number(s), and so on.

APA-a In-Text Documentation

Brief documentation in your text makes clear to your reader precisely what you took from a source and, in the case of a quotation, precisely where (usually, on which page) in the source you found the text you are quoting.

PARAPHRASES and SUMMARIES are more common than QUOTATIONS in APA-style projects. See R-4 for more on all three kinds of citation. As you cite each source, you will need to decide whether to name the author in a signal phrase—"as McCullough (2001) wrote"—or in parentheses—"(McCullough, 2001)." Note that APA requires you to use the past tense or present perfect tense for verbs in SIGNAL PHRASES: "Moss (2003) argued," "Moss (2003) has argued."

1. AUTHOR NAMED IN A SIGNAL PHRASE

If you are quoting, you must give the page number(s). You are not required to give the page number(s) with a paraphrase or a summary, but APA encourages you to do so, especially if you are citing a long or complex work; most of the models in this chapter do include page numbers.

AUTHOR QUOTED

Put the date in parentheses right after the author's name; put the page in parentheses as close to the quotation as possible.

> McCullough (2001) described John Adams as having "the hands of a man accustomed to pruning his own trees, cutting his own hay, and splitting his own firewood" (p. 18).

Notice that in this example, the parenthetical reference with the page number comes *after* the closing quotation marks but *before* the period at the end of the sentence.

AUTHOR PARAPHRASED

Put the date in parentheses right after the author's name; follow the date with the page.

> John Adams's hands were those of a laborer, according to McCullough (2001, p. 18).

2. AUTHOR NAMED IN PARENTHESES

If you do not mention an author in a signal phrase, put his or her name, a comma, and the year of publication in parentheses as close as possible to the quotation, paraphrase, or summary.

AUTHOR QUOTED

Give the author, date, and page in one parenthesis, or split the information between two parentheses.

> One biographer (McCullough, 2001) has said John Adams had "the hands of a man accustomed to pruning his own trees, cutting his own hay, and splitting his own firewood" (p. 18).

AUTHOR PARAPHRASED OR SUMMARIZED

Give the author, date, and page in one parenthesis toward the beginning or the end of the paraphrase.

> John Adams's hands were those of a laborer (McCullough, 2001, p. 18).

3. AUTHORS WITH THE SAME LAST NAME

If your reference list includes more than one person with the same last name, include initials in all documentation to distinguish the authors from one another.

> Eclecticism is common in contemporary criticism (J. M. Smith, 1992, p. vii).

4. TWO AUTHORS

Always mention both authors. Use *and* in a signal phrase, but use an ampersand (&) in parentheses.

> Carlson and Ventura (1990, p. v) wanted to introduce Julio Cortázar, Marjorie Agosín, and other Latin American writers to an audience of English-speaking adolescents.

> According to the Peter Principle, "In a hierarchy, every employee tends to rise to his level of incompetence" (Peter & Hull, 1969, p. 26).

5. THREE OR MORE AUTHORS

In the first reference to a work by three to five persons, name all contributors. In subsequent references, name the first author followed by *et al.*, Latin for "and others." Whenever you refer to a work by six or more contributors, name only the first author, followed by *et al.* Use *and* in a signal phrase, but use an ampersand (&) in parentheses.

> Faigley, George, Palchik, and Selfe (2004, p. xii) have argued
> that where there used to be a concept called *literacy,* today's
> multitude of new kinds of texts has given us *literacies.*

> Peilen et al. (1990, p. 75) supported their claims about corporate
> corruption with startling anecdotal evidence.

6. ORGANIZATION OR GOVERNMENT AS AUTHOR

If an organization name is recognizable by its abbreviation, give the full name and the abbreviation the first time you cite the source. In subsequent citations, use only the abbreviation. If the organization does not have a familiar abbreviation, always use its full name.

FIRST CITATION

(American Psychological Association [APA], 2008)

SUBSEQUENT CITATIONS

(APA, 2008)

7. AUTHOR UNKNOWN

Use the complete title if it is short; if it is long, use the first few words of the title under which the work appears in the reference list.

> *Webster's New Biographical Dictionary* (1988) identifies William
> James as "American psychologist and philosopher" (p. 520).

> A powerful editorial asserted that healthy liver donor Mike
> Hurewitz died because of "frightening" faulty postoperative
> care ("Every Patient's Nightmare," 2007).

8. TWO OR MORE WORKS CITED TOGETHER

If you cite multiple works in the same parenthesis, place them in the order that they appear in your reference list, separated by semicolons.

> Many researchers have argued that what counts as "literacy" is not necessarily learned at school (Heath, 1983; Moss, 2003).

9. TWO OR MORE WORKS BY ONE AUTHOR IN THE SAME YEAR

If your list of references includes more than one work by the same author published in the same year, order them alphabetically by title, adding lowercase letters ("a," "b," and so on) to the year.

> Kaplan (2000a) described orderly shantytowns in Turkey that did not resemble the other slums he visited.

10. SOURCE QUOTED IN ANOTHER SOURCE

When you cite a source that was quoted in another source, let the reader know that you used a secondary source by adding the words *as cited in*.

> During the meeting with the psychologist, the patient stated repeatedly that he "didn't want to be too paranoid" (as cited in Oberfield & Yasik, 2004, p. 294).

11. WORK WITHOUT PAGE NUMBERS

Instead of page numbers, some electronic works have paragraph numbers, which you should include (preceded by the abbreviation *para.*) if you are referring to a specific part of such a source. In sources with neither page nor paragraph numbers, refer readers to a particular part of the source if possible, perhaps indicating a heading and the paragraph under the heading.

> Russell's dismissals from Trinity College at Cambridge and from City College in New York City have been seen as examples of the controversy that marked his life (Irvine, 2006, para. 2).

12. AN ENTIRE WORK

You do not need to give a page number if you are directing readers' attention to an entire work.

> Kaplan (2000) considered Turkey and Central Asia explosive.

When you are citing an entire website, give the URL in the text. You do not need to include the website in your reference list. To cite part of a website, see no. 20 on page 153.

> Beyond providing diagnostic information, the website for the
> Alzheimer's Association includes a variety of resources for family
> and community support of patients suffering from Alzheimer's
> (http://www.alz.org).

13. PERSONAL COMMUNICATION

Cite email, telephone conversations, interviews, personal letters, messages from nonarchived electronic discussion sources, and other personal texts as *personal communication,* along with the person's initial(s), last name, and the date. You do not need to include such personal communications in your reference list.

> L. Strauss (personal communication, December 6, 2006) told
> about visiting Yogi Berra when they both lived in Montclair,
> New Jersey.

APA-b Notes

You may need to use content notes to give an explanation or information that doesn't fit into your text. To signal a content note, place a superscript numeral at the appropriate point in your text. Put the notes on a separate page with the heading *Notes,* after your text but before the reference list. If you have multiple notes, number them consecutively throughout your text. Here is an example from *In Search of Solutions: A New Direction in Psychotherapy* (2003).

TEXT WITH SUPERSCRIPT

An important part of working with teams and one-way mirrors is taking the consultation break, as at Milan, BFTC, and MRI.[1]

CONTENT NOTE

[1]It is crucial to note here that, while working within a team is fun, stimulating, and revitalizing, it is not necessary for successful outcomes. Solution-oriented therapy works equally well when working solo.

APA-c Reference List

A reference list provides full bibliographic information for every source cited in your text with the exception of entire websites and personal communications. See page 164 for guidelines on preparing such a list; for a sample reference list, see page 169.

Books

For most books, you'll need to provide the author, the publication date, the title and any subtitle, and the place of publication and publisher.

IMPORTANT DETAILS FOR CITING BOOKS

- **AUTHORS:** Use the author's last name but replace the first and middle names with initials (D. Kinder for Donald Kinder).
- **DATES:** If more than one year is given, use the most recent one.
- **TITLES:** Capitalize only the first word and proper nouns and proper adjectives in titles and subtitles.
- **PUBLICATION PLACE:** Give city followed by state (abbreviated) or country, if outside the United States (for example, Boston, MA; London, England; Toronto, Ontario, Canada). If more than one city is given, use the first. Do not include the state or country if the publisher is a university whose name includes that information.

- **PUBLISHER**: Use a shortened form of the publisher's name (Little, Brown for Little, Brown and Company), but retain *Association, Books,* and *Press* (American Psychological Association, Princeton University Press).

1. ONE AUTHOR

> Author's Last Name, Initials. (Year of publication). *Title*. Publication City, State or Country: Publisher.

> Lewis, M. (2003). *Moneyball: The art of winning an unfair game.* New York, NY: Norton.

2. TWO OR MORE WORKS BY THE SAME AUTHOR

If the works were published in different years, list them chronologically.

> Lewis, B. (1995). *The Middle East: A brief history of the last 2,000 years.* New York, NY: Scribner.

> Lewis, B. (2003). *The crisis of Islam: Holy war and unholy terror.* New York, NY: Modern Library.

If the works were published in the same year, list them alphabetically by title, adding "a," "b," and so on to the year.

> Kaplan, R. D. (2000a). *The coming anarchy: Shattering the dreams of the post cold war.* New York, NY: Random House.

> Kaplan, R. D. (2000b). *Eastward to Tartary: Travels in the Balkans, the Middle East, and the Caucasus.* New York, NY: Random House.

3. TWO OR MORE AUTHORS

For two to seven authors, use this format.

> First Author's Last Name, Initials, Next Author's Last Name, Initials, & Final Author's Last Name, Initials. (Year of publication). *Title*. Publication City, State or Country: Publisher.

> Levitt, S. D., & Dubner, S. J. (2005). *Freakonomics: A rogue economist explores the hidden side of everything.* New York, NY: Morrow.

Documentation Map (APA)

BOOK

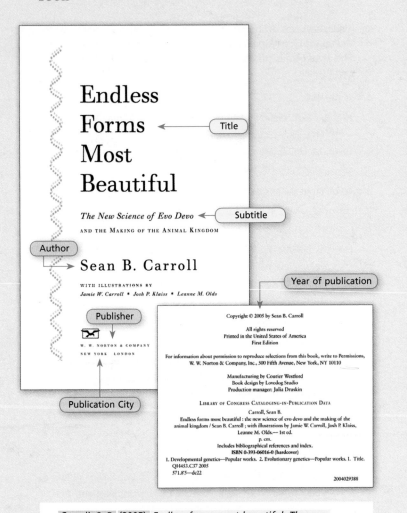

Carroll, S. B. (2005). *Endless forms most beautiful: The new science of evo devo and the making of the animal kingdom.* New York, NY: Norton.

For a work by eight or more authors, name just the first six authors, followed by three ellipses, and end with the final author (see no. 21 for an example from a magazine article).

4. ORGANIZATION OR GOVERNMENT AS AUTHOR

Sometimes a corporation or government organization is both author and publisher. If so, use the word *Author* as the publisher.

Organization Name or Government Agency. (Year of publication). *Title*. Publication City, State or Country: Publisher.

Catholic News Service. (2002). *Stylebook on religion 2000: A reference guide and usage manual*. Washington, DC: Author.

5. AUTHOR AND EDITOR

Author's Last Name, Initials. (Year of edited edition). *Title*. (Editor's Initials Last Name, Ed.). Publication City, State or Country: Publisher. (Original work[s] published year[s])

Dick, P. F. (2008). *Five novels of the 1960s and 70s*. (J. Lethem, Ed.). New York, NY: Library of America. (Original works published 1964–1977)

6. EDITED COLLECTION

First Editor's Last Name, Initials, Next Editor's Last Name, Initials, & Final Editor's Last Name, Initials. (Eds.). (Year of edited edition). *Title*. Publication City, State or Country: Publisher.

Raviv, A., Oppenheimer, L., & Bar-Tal, D. (Eds.). (1999). *How children understand war and peace: A call for international peace education*. San Francisco, CA: Jossey-Bass.

7. WORK IN AN EDITED COLLECTION

Author's Last Name, Initials. (Year of publication). Title of article or chapter. In Initials Last Name (Ed.), *Title* (pp. pages). Publication City, State or Country: Publisher.

Harris, I. M. (1999). Types of peace education. In A. Raviv, L. Oppenheimer, & D. Bar-Tal (Eds.), *How children understand war and peace: A call for international peace education* (pp. 46–70). San Francisco, CA: Jossey-Bass.

8. UNKNOWN AUTHOR

Title. (Year of publication). Publication City, State or Country: Publisher.

Webster's new biographical dictionary. (1988). Springfield, MA: Merriam-Webster.

If the title page of a work lists the author as *Anonymous*, treat the reference-list entry as if the author's name were Anonymous, and alphabetize it accordingly.

9. EDITION OTHER THAN THE FIRST

Author's Last Name, Initials. (Year). *Title* (name or number ed.). Publication City, State or Country: Publisher.

Burch, D. (2008). *Emergency navigation: Find your position and shape your course at sea even if your instruments fail* (2nd ed.). Camden, ME: International Marine/McGraw-Hill.

10. TRANSLATION

Author's Last Name, Initials. (Year of publication). *Title* (Translator's Initials Last Name, Trans.). Publication City, State or Country: Publisher. (Original work published Year)

Hugo, V. (2008). *Les misérables* (J. Rose, Trans.). New York, NY: Modern Library. (Original work published 1862)

11. MULTIVOLUME WORK

Author's Last Name, Initials. (Year). *Title* (Vols. numbers). Publication City, State or Country: Publisher.

Nastali, D. P., & Boardman, P. C. (2004). *The Arthurian annals: The tradition in English from 1250 to 2000* (Vols. 1–2). New York, NY: Oxford University Press USA.

ONE VOLUME OF A MULTIVOLUME WORK

Author's Last Name, Initials. (Year). *Title of whole work* (Vol. number). Publication City, State or Country: Publisher.

Spiegelman, A. (1986). *Maus* (Vol. 1). New York, NY: Random House.

12. ARTICLE IN A REFERENCE BOOK

UNSIGNED

Title of entry. (Year). In *Title of reference book* (Name or number ed., Vol. number, pp. pages). Publication City, State or Country: Publisher.

Macrophage. (2003). In *Merriam-Webster's collegiate dictionary* (10th ed., p. 698). Springfield, MA: Merriam-Webster.

SIGNED

Author's Last Name, Initials. (Year). Title of entry. In *Title of reference book* (Vol. number, pp. pages). Publication City, State or Country: Publisher.

Wasserman, D. E. (2006). Human exposure to vibration. In *International encyclopedia of ergonomics and human factors* (Vol. 2, pp. 1800–1801). Boca Raton, FL: CRC.

Periodicals

For most articles, you'll need to provide information about the author; the date; the article title and any subtitle; the periodical title; and any volume or issue number and inclusive page numbers. (APA also recommends including a DOI if one is available; for more on DOIs, see page 153. For an example of a journal article that shows a DOI, see no. 21.)

IMPORTANT DETAILS FOR CITING PERIODICALS

- **AUTHORS**: List authors as you would for a book.
- **DATES**: For journals, give year only. For magazines and newspapers, give year followed by a comma and then month or month and day.

- **TITLES:** Capitalize article titles as you would for a book. Capitalize the first and last words and all principal words of periodical titles. Do not capitalize *a, an, the,* or any prepositions or coordinating conjunctions unless they begin the title of the periodical.

- **VOLUME AND ISSUE:** For journals and magazines, give volume or volume and issue, depending on the journal's pagination method. For newspapers, do not give volume or issue.

- **PAGES:** Use *p.* or *pp.* for a newspaper article but not for a journal or magazine article. If an article does not fall on consecutive pages, give all the page numbers (for example, 45, 75–77 for a journal or magazine; pp. C1, C3, C5–C7 for a newspaper).

13. ARTICLE IN A JOURNAL PAGINATED BY VOLUME

Author's Last Name, Initials. (Year). Title of article. *Title of Journal, volume,* pages.

Gremer, J. R., Sala, A., & Crone, E. E. (2010). Disappearing plants: Why they hide and how they return. *Ecology, 91,* 3407–3413.

14. ARTICLE IN A JOURNAL PAGINATED BY ISSUE

Author's Last Name, Initials. (Year). Title of article. *Title of Journal, volume*(issue), pages.

Weaver, C., McNally, C., & Moerman, S. (2001). To grammar or not to grammar: That is *not* the question! *Voices from the Middle, 8*(3), 17–33.

15. ARTICLE IN A MAGAZINE

If a magazine is published weekly, include the day and the month. If there are a volume number and an issue number, include them after the magazine title.

Author's Last Name, Initials. (Year, Month Day). Title of article. *Title of Magazine, volume*(issue), page(s).

Gregory, S. (2008, June 30). Crash course: Why golf carts are more hazardous than they look. *Time, 171*(26), 53.

If a magazine is published monthly, include the month(s) only.

Documentation Map (APA)

ARTICLE IN A MAGAZINE

Title of article

Author

Volume and issue

Title of Magazine

Month, day, and year

Page

Cullen, L. T. (2008, March 24). Freshen up your drink: Reusing water bottles is good ecologically, but is it bad for your health? How to drink smart. *Time, 171*(12), 65.

16. ARTICLE IN A NEWSPAPER

If page numbers are consecutive, separate them with a dash. If not, separate them with a comma.

> Author's Last Name, Initials. (Year, Month Day). Title of article. *Title of Newspaper,* p(p). page(s).
>
> Schneider, G. (2005, March 13). Fashion sense on wheels. *The Washington Post,* pp. F1, F6.

17. ARTICLE BY AN UNKNOWN AUTHOR

> Title of article. (Year, Month Day). *Title of Periodical, volume*(issue), pages *or* p(p). page(s).
>
> Hot property: From carriage house to family compound. (2004, December). *Berkshire Living, 1*(1), 99.

18. BOOK REVIEW

> Reviewer's Last Name, Initials. (Date of publication). Title of review [Review of the book *Title of Work,* by Author's Initials Last Name]. *Title of Periodical, volume*(issue), page(s).
>
> Brandt, A. (2003, October). Animal planet [Review of the book *Intelligence of apes and other rational beings,* by D. R. Rumb & D. A. Washburn]. *National Geographic Adventure, 5*(10), 47.

If the review does not have a title, include the bracketed information about the work being reviewed, immediately after the date of publication.

19. LETTER TO THE EDITOR

> Author's Last Name, Initials. (Date of publication). Title of letter [Letter to the editor]. *Title of Periodical, volume*(issue), page(s). *or* p(p). page(s).
>
> Hitchcock, G. (2008, August 3). Save our species [Letter to the editor]. *San Francisco Chronicle,* p. P-3.

Online Sources

Not every online source gives you all the data that APA would like to see in a reference entry. Ideally, you will be able to list an author's or editor's name; date of first electronic publication or most recent revision; title of document; information about print publication if any; and retrieval information: DOI (Digital Object Identifier, a string of letters and numbers that identifies an online document) or URL. In some cases, additional information about electronic publication may be required (title of site, retrieval date, name of sponsoring institution).

IMPORTANT DETAILS FOR CITING ONLINE SOURCES

- **AUTHORS**: List authors as you would for a print book or periodical.

- **TITLES**: For websites and electronic documents, articles, or books, capitalize title and subtitles as you would for a book; capitalize periodical titles as you would for a print periodical.

- **DATES**: After the author, give the year of the document's original publication on the Web or of its most recent revision. If neither of those years is clear, use *n.d.* to mean "no date." For undated content or content that may change (for example, a wiki entry), include the month, day, and year that you retrieved the document. You don't need to include the retrieval date for content that's unlikely to change.

- **DOI OR URL**: Include the DOI instead of the URL in the reference whenever one is available. If no DOI is available, provide the URL of the home page or menu page. If you do not identify the sponsoring institution, you do not need a colon before the URL or DOI. When a URL won't fit on the line, break the URL before most punctuation, but do not break *http://*.

20. WORK FROM A NONPERIODICAL WEBSITE

Author's Last Name, Initials. (Date of publication). Title of work. *Title of site*. DOI or Retrieved Month Day, Year (if necessary), from URL

Cruikshank, D. (2009, June 15). Unlocking the secrets and powers of the brain. *National Science Foundation*. Retrieved from http://www.nsf.gov/discoveries/disc_summ.jsp?cntn_id=114979&org=NSF

To cite an entire website, include the URL in parentheses in an in-text citation. Do not list the website in your list of references.

21. ARTICLE IN AN ONLINE PERIODICAL

When available, include the volume number and issue number as you would for a print source. If no DOI has been assigned, provide the URL of the home page or menu page of the journal or magazine, even for articles that you access through a database.

ARTICLE IN AN ONLINE JOURNAL

Author's Last Name, Initials. (Year). Title of article. *Title of Journal, volume*(issue), pages. DOI or Retrieved from URL

Corbett, C. (2007). Vehicle-related crime and the gender gap. *Psychology, Crime & Law, 13,* 245–263. doi:10.1080/10683160600822022

ARTICLE IN AN ONLINE MAGAZINE

Author's Last Name, Initials. (Year, Month Day). Title of article. *Title of Magazine, volume*(issue). DOI or Retrieved from URL

Barreda, V. D., Palazzesi, L., Tellería, M. C., Katinas, L., Crisci, J. N., Bromer, K., . . . Bechis, F. (2010, September 24). Eocene Patagonia fossils of the daisy family. *Science, 329*(5999). doi:10.1126/science.1193108

ARTICLE IN AN ONLINE NEWSPAPER

If the article can be found by searching the site, give the URL of the home page or menu page.

Author's Last Name, Initials. (Year, Month Day). Title of article. *Title of Newspaper.* Retrieved from URL

Collins, G. (2008, June 21). Vice is nice. *The New York Times.* Retrieved from http://www.nytimes.com

Documentation Map (APA)

WORK FROM A WEBSITE

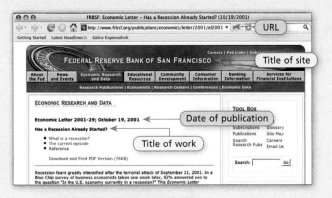

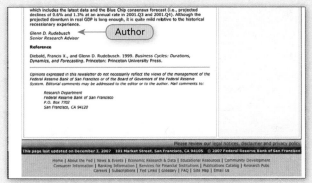

Rudebusch, G. D. (2001, October 19). Has a recession already
      started? *Federal Reserve Bank of San Francisco*. Retrieved
      April 3, 2008, from http://www.frbsf.org/publications
      /economics/letter/2001/el2001-29.html

Documentation Map (APA)

ARTICLE IN A JOURNAL WITH DOI

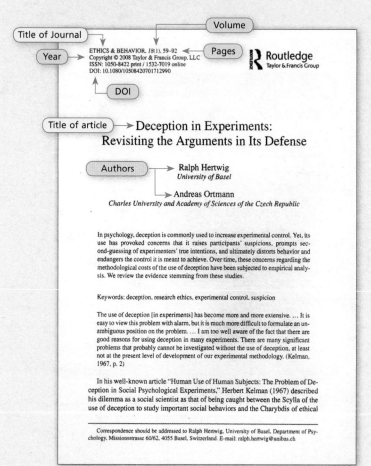

Title of Journal · Volume · Year · Pages · DOI

ETHICS & BEHAVIOR, *18*(1), 59–92
Copyright © 2008 Taylor & Francis Group, LLC
ISSN: 1050-8422 print / 1532-7019 online
DOI: 10.1080/10508420701712990

Routledge
Taylor & Francis Group

Title of article →

Deception in Experiments:
Revisiting the Arguments in Its Defense

Authors →

Ralph Hertwig
University of Basel

Andreas Ortmann
Charles University and Academy of Sciences of the Czech Republic

In psychology, deception is commonly used to increase experimental control. Yet, its use has provoked concerns that it raises participants' suspicions, prompts second-guessing of experimenters' true intentions, and ultimately distorts behavior and endangers the control it is meant to achieve. Over time, these concerns regarding the methodological costs of the use of deception have been subjected to empirical analysis. We review the evidence stemming from these studies.

Keywords: deception, research ethics, experimental control, suspicion

The use of deception [in experiments] has become more and more extensive. ... It is easy to view this problem with alarm, but it is much more difficult to formulate an unambiguous position on the problem. ... I am too well aware of the fact that there are good reasons for using deception in many experiments. There are many significant problems that probably cannot be investigated without the use of deception, at least not at the present level of development of our experimental methodology. (Kelman, 1967, p. 2)

In his well-known article "Human Use of Human Subjects: The Problem of Deception in Social Psychological Experiments," Herbert Kelman (1967) described his dilemma as a social scientist as that of being caught between the Scylla of the use of deception to study important social behaviors and the Charybdis of ethical

Correspondence should be addressed to Ralph Hertwig, University of Basel, Department of Psychology, Missionsstrasse 60/62, 4055 Basel, Switzerland. E-mail: ralph.hertwig@unibas.ch

Hertwig, R. & Ortmann, A. (2008). Deception in experiments: Revisiting the arguments in its defense. *Ethics & Behavior, 18,* 59–92. doi:10.1080/10508420701712990

Documentation Map (APA)

ARTICLE ACCESSED THROUGH A DATABASE WITH DOI

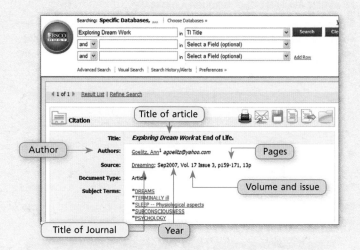

Goelitz, A. (2007). Exploring dream work at end of life.
Dreaming, 17(3), 159–171. doi:10.1037/1053-079717.3.159

22. ARTICLE AVAILABLE ONLY THROUGH A DATABASE

Some sources, such as an out-of-print journal or rare book, can be accessed only through a database. When no DOI is provided, give either the name of the database or its URL.

> Author's Last Name, Initials. (Year). Title of article. *Title of Journal, volume*(issue), pages. DOI or Retrieved from Name of database or URL
>
> Simpson, M. (1972). Authoritarianism and education: A comparative approach. *Sociometry, 35*(2), 223–234. Retrieved from http:// www.jstor.org/stable/2786619

23. ARTICLE OR CHAPTER IN A WEB DOCUMENT OR ONLINE REFERENCE WORK

For a chapter in a Web document or an article in an online reference work, give the URL of the chapter or entry if no DOI is provided.

> Author's Last Name, Initials. (Year). Title of entry. In Initials Last Name (Ed.), *Title of reference work*. DOI or Retrieved from URL
>
> Korfmacher, C. (2006). Personal identity. In J. Fieser & B. Dowden (Eds.), *Internet encyclopedia of philosophy*. Retrieved from http://www.iep.utm.edu/person-i/

24. ELECTRONIC BOOK

> Author's Last Name, Initials. (Year). *Title of book*. DOI or Retrieved from URL
>
> TenDam, H. (n.d.). *Politics, civilization & humanity*. Retrieved from http://onlineoriginals.com/showitem.asp?itemID=46&page=2

For an ebook based on a print version, include a description of the digital format in brackets after the book title.

> Blain, M. (2009). *The sociology of terror: Studies in power, subjection, and victimage ritual* [Adobe Digital Editions version]. Retrieved from http://www.powells.com/sub /AdobeDigitalEditionsPolitics.html?sec_big_link=1

25. WIKI ENTRY

Give the entry title and the date of posting, or *n.d.* if there is no date.
Then include the retrieval date, the name of the wiki, and the URL
for the entry.

> Title of entry. (Year, Month Day). Retrieved Month Day, Year, from
>> Title of wiki: URL
>
> Discourse. (n.d.). Retrieved November 8, 2010, from Psychology Wiki:
>> http://psychology.wikia.com/wiki/Discourse

26. ONLINE DISCUSSION SOURCE

If the name of the list to which to the message was posted is not
part of the URL, include it after *Retrieved from*. The URL you provide
should be for the archived version of the message or post.

> Author's Last Name, Initials. (Year, Month Day). Subject line of
>> message [Descriptive label]. Retrieved from URL
>
> Baker, J. (2005, February 15). Re: Huffing and puffing [Electronic
>> mailing list message]. Retrieved from American Dialect Society
>> electronic mailing list: http://listserv.linguistlist.org/cgi-bin
>> /wa?A2=ind0502C&L=ADS-L&P=R44

Do not include email or other nonarchived discussions in your list
of references. Simply cite the sender's name in your text. See no. 13
on page 143 for guidelines on identifying such sources in your text.

27. BLOG ENTRY

> Author's Last Name, Initials. (Year, Month Day). Title of post [Blog
>> post]. Retrieved from URL
>
> Collins, C. (2009, August 19). Butterfly benefits from warmer springs?
>> [Blog post]. Retrieved from http://www.intute.ac.uk
>> /blog/2009/08/19/butterfly-benefits-from-warmer-springs/

28. ONLINE VIDEO

> Last Name, Initials (Writer), & Last Name, Initials (Producer). (Year,
> Month Day posted). *Title* [Descriptive label]. Retrieved from URL

Coulter, J. (Songwriter & Performer), & Booth, M. S. (Producer).
(2006, September 23). *Code monkey* [Video file]. Retrieved
from http://www.youtube.com/watch?v=v4Wy7gRGgeA

29. PODCAST

> Writer's Last Name, Initials. (Writer), & Producer's Last Name, Initials.
> (Producer). (Year, Month Day). Title of podcast. *Title of site or
> program* [Audio podcast]. Retrieved from URL

Britt, M. A. (Writer & Producer). (2009, June 7). Episode 97: Stanley
Milgram study finally replicated. *The Psych Files Podcast*
[Audio podcast]. Retrieved from http://www.thepsychfiles.com/

Other Kinds of Sources

30. FILM, VIDEO, OR DVD

> Last Name, Initials (Producer), & Last Name, Initials (Director). (Year).
> *Title* [Motion picture]. Country: Studio.

Wallis, H. B. (Producer), & Curtiz, M. (Director). (1942). *Casablanca*
[Motion picture]. United States: Warner.

31. MUSIC RECORDING

> Composer's Last Name, Initials. (Year of copyright). Title of song. On
> *Title of album* [Medium]. City, State or Country: Label.

Veloso, C. (1997). Na baixado sapateiro. On *Livros* [CD]. Los Angeles,
CA: Nonesuch.

32. PROCEEDINGS OF A CONFERENCE

> Author's Last Name, Initials. (Year of publication). Title of paper. In
> *Proceedings Title* (pp. pages). Publication City, State or
> Country: Publisher.

Heath, S. B. (1997). Talking work: Language among teens. In
Symposium about Language and Society–Austin (pp. 27–45).
Austin: Department of Linguistics at the University of Texas.

33. TELEVISION PROGRAM

Last Name, Initials (Writer), & Last Name, Initials (Director). (Year).
Title of episode [Descriptive label]. In Initials Last Name
(Producer), *Series title.* City, State or Country: Network.
Mundy, C. (Writer), & Bernaro, E. A. (Director). (2007). In birth and
death [Television series episode]. In E. A. Bernaro (Executive
Producer), *Criminal minds.* New York, NY: NBC.

34. SOFTWARE OR COMPUTER PROGRAM

Title and version number [Computer software]. (Year). Publication
City, State or Country: Publisher.
The Sims 2: Holiday edition [Computer software]. (2005). Redwood
City, CA: Electronic Arts.

35. GOVERNMENT DOCUMENT

Government Agency. (Year of publication). *Title.* Publication City,
State or Country: Publisher.
U.S. Department of Health and Human Services, Centers for Disease
Control and Prevention. (2009). *Fourth national report on
human exposure to environmental chemicals.* Washington, DC:
Government Printing Office.

ONLINE GOVERNMENT DOCUMENT

Government Agency. (Year of publication). *Title* (Publication No. [if
any]). Retrieved from URL
U.S. Department of Health and Human Services, National Institutes
of Health, National Institute of Mental Health. (2006). *Bipolar
disorder* (NIH Publication No. 06-3679). Retrieved from http://

www.nimh.nih.gov/health/publications/bipolar-disorder/
nimh-bipolar-adults.pdf

36. DISSERTATION

Include the database name and accession number for dissertations that you retrieve from a database.

> Author's Last Name, Initials. (Year). *Title of dissertation* (Doctoral dissertation). Retrieved from Name of database. (accession number)
>
> Knapik, M. (2008). *Adolescent online trouble-talk: Help-seeking in cyberspace* (Doctoral dissertation). Retrieved from ProQuest Dissertation and Theses database. (AAT NR38024)

For a dissertation that you access on the Web, include the name of the institution after *Doctoral dissertation*. For example: (Doctoral dissertation, University of North Carolina). End your citation with *Retrieved from* and the URL.

37. TECHNICAL OR RESEARCH REPORT

> Author's Last Name, Initials. (Year). *Title of report* (Report number). Publication City, State or Country: Publisher.
>
> Elsayed, T., Namata, G., Getoor, L., & Oard., D. W. (2008). *Personal name resolution in email: A heuristic approach* (Report No. LAMP-TR-150). College Park: University of Maryland.

Citing Sources Not Covered by APA

To cite a source for which APA does not provide guidelines, look at models similar to the source you are citing. Give any information readers will need in order to find it themselves—author; date of publication; title; publisher; information about electronic retrieval (DOI or URL); and any other pertinent information. You might want to try your citation yourself, to be sure it will lead others to your source.

APA-d Formatting a Paper

Title page. APA does not provide guidelines specifically for the title page of a paper written for a college course; check with your instructor about his or her preferences. Be sure to provide the full title; your name; the course and section number; your instructor's name; and the date. Center each element on a separate line.

Page numbers. Beginning with the title page, insert a shortened title in capital letters in the upper left-hand corner of each page; place the page number in the upper right-hand corner. Number pages consecutively throughout your paper.

Spacing, margins, and indents. Double-space the entire paper, including any notes and your list of references. Leave one-inch margins at the top, bottom, and sides of your text; do not justify the text. The first line of each paragraph should be indented one-half inch (or five-to-seven spaces) from the left margin. APA recommends using two spaces after end-of-sentence punctuation.

Headings. Though they are not required in APA style, headings can help readers follow your text. The first level of heading should be bold, centered, and capitalized as you would any other title; the second level of heading should be bold and flush with the left margin; the third level should be bold and indented, with only the first letter and proper nouns capitalized and with a period at the end of the heading.

First Level Heading

Second Level Heading

Third level heading.

Abstract. An abstract is a concise summary of your paper that introduces readers to your topic and main points. Most scholarly journals require an abstract; check with your instructor about his or her preference. Put your abstract on the second page, with the word *Abstract* centered at the top. Unless your instructor specifies a length, limit your abstract to 120 words or fewer.

Long quotations. Indent quotations of more than forty words one-half inch (or five-to-seven spaces) from the left margin. Do not use quotation marks, and place the page number(s) in parentheses *after* the end punctuation.

> Kaplan (2000) captured ancient and contemporary Antioch for us:
>> At the height of its glory in the Roman-Byzantine age,
>> when it had an amphitheater, public baths, aqueducts,
>> and sewage pipes, half a million people lived in Antioch.
>> Today the population is only 125,000. With sour
>> relations between Turkey and Syria, and unstable
>> politics throughout the Middle East, Antioch is now a
>> backwater—seedy and tumbledown, with relatively
>> few tourists. (p. 123)
>
> Antioch's decline serves as a reminder that the fortunes of cities
> can change drastically over time.

List of references. Start your list on a new page after any notes. Center the title and double-space the entire list. Each entry should begin at the left margin, and subsequent lines should be indented one-half inch (or five-to-seven spaces). Alphabetize the list by authors' last names (or by editors' names, if appropriate). Alphabetize works that have no author or editor by title, disregarding *A, An,* and *The.* Be sure every source listed is cited in the text; do not include sources that you consulted but did not cite.

Illustrations. For each table, provide a number (*Table* 1) and a descriptive title on separate lines above the table; below the table, include a note with information about the source. For figures—charts, diagrams, graphs, photos, and so on—include a figure number (*Figure* 1) and information about the source in a note below the figure. Number tables and figures separately, and be sure to discuss any illustrations so that readers know how they relate to the rest of your text.

Table 1

Hours of Instruction Delivered per Week

	American classrooms	Japanese classrooms	Chinese classrooms
First Grade			
Language Arts	10.5	8.7	10.4
Mathematics	2.7	5.8	4.0
Fifth Grade			
Language Arts	7.9	8.0	11.1
Mathematics	3.4	7.8	11.7

Note. Adapted from "Peeking Out from Under the Blinders: Some Factors We Shouldn't Forget in Studying Writing," by J. R. Hayes, 1991, National Center for the Study of Writing and Literacy (Occasional Paper No. 25). Retrieved from National Writing Project website: http://www.nwp.org/

APA-e Sample Pages

The following sample pages are from "It's in Our Genes: The Biological Basis of Human Mating Behavior," a paper submitted by Carolyn Stonehill for a first-year writing course. They are formatted according to the guidelines of the *Publication Manual of the American Psychological Association*, 6th edition (2010). To read the complete paper, go to **wwnorton.com/write/little-seagull-handbook**.

Sample Title Page, APA Style

Shortened title.

Running head: IT'S IN OUR GENES

Page number.

1

Title, name, and school name.

It's in Our Genes:

The Biological Basis of Human Mating Behavior

Carolyn Stonehill

Wright State University

Sample Abstract, APA Style

Abstract

While cultural values and messages certainly play a part in the process of mate selection, the genetic and psychological predispositions developed by our ancestors play the biggest role in determining to whom we are attracted. Women are attracted to strong, capable men with access to resources to help rear children. Men find women attractive based on visual signs of youth, health, and, by implication, fertility. While perceptions of attractiveness are influenced by cultural norms and reinforced by advertisements and popular media, the persistence of mating behaviors that have no relationship to societal realities suggests that they are part of our biological heritage.

Heading centered.

Limited to 120 words or fewer.

Two spaces after end punctuation.

Sample Page of Research Paper, APA Style

Title centered.

It's in Our Genes:

The Biological Basis of Human Mating Behavior

Double-spaced throughout.

Consider the following scenario: It's a sunny afternoon on campus, and Jenny is walking to her next class. Out of the corner of her eye, she catches sight of her lab partner, Joey, parking his car. She stops to admire how tall, muscular, and stylishly dressed he is, and she does not take her eyes off him as he walks away from his shiny new BMW. As he flashes her a pearly white smile, Jenny melts, then quickly adjusts her skirt and smooths her hair.

Paragraphs indent 5 to 7 spaces ($\frac{1}{2}$ inch).

This scenario, while generalized, is familiar: Our attraction to people—or lack of it—often depends on their physical traits. But why this attraction? Why does Jenny respond the way she does to her handsome lab partner? Why does she deem him handsome at all? Certainly Joey embodies the stereotypes of physical attractiveness prevalent in contemporary American society.

Advertisements, television shows, and magazine articles all provide Jenny with signals telling her what constitutes the ideal American man. Yet she is also attracted to Joey's new sports car even though she has a new car herself. Does Jenny find this man striking because of the influence of her culture, or does her attraction lie in a more fundamental part of her constitution? Evolutionary psychologists, who apply principles of evolutionary biology to research on the human mind, would say that Jenny's responses in this situation are due largely to mating strategies developed by her prehistoric ancestors. Driven by the need to reproduce and propagate the species, these ancestors of ours formed patterns of mate selection so effective in providing for

Sample Reference List, APA Style

IT'S IN OUR GENES   9

References •·· *Heading centered.*

Allman, W. F. (1993, July 19). The mating game. *U.S. News & World Report*, 115(3), 56–63.

Boyd, R., & Silk, J. B. (2000). *How humans evolved* (2nd ed.). New York, •··· *Alphabetized by authors' last names.*
    NY: Norton.

Buss, D. M., & Schmitt, D. P. (1993). Sexual strategies theory: An *All lines after the first line of each entry indented.*
    evolutionary perspective on human mating. *Psychological* •········
    Review, 100(2), 204–232.

Cosmides, L., & Tooby, J. (1997). Evolutionary psychology: A primer.
    Center for Evolutionary Psychology. Retrieved April 30, 2010,
    from http://www.psych.ucsb.edu/research/cep/primer.html

Cunningham, M. R., Roberts, A. R., Barbee, A. P., Druen, P. B., & Wu,
    C.-H. (1995). "Their ideas of beauty are, on the whole, the
    same as ours": Consistency and variability in the cross-
    cultural perception of female physical attractiveness. *Journal*
    of Personality and Social Psychology, 68, 261–279.

Frank, C. (2001, February). Why do we fall in—and out of—love? Dr.
    Helen Fisher unravels the mystery. *Biography*, 85–87, 112.

Sapolsky, R. M. (2001–2002, December–January). What do females
    want? *Natural History*, 18–21.

Singh, D. (1993). Adaptive significance of female physical
    attractiveness: Role of waist-to-hip ratio. *Journal of Personality*
    and Social Behavior, 65, 293–307.

Tattersall, I. (2001). Evolution, genes, and behavior. *Zygon: Journal of*
    Religion & Science, 36, 657–666. doi:10.1111/0591=2385.00389   *All sources listed are cited in the text.*

Weiten, W. (2001). *Psychology: Themes & variations* (5th ed.). San •··········
    Bernardino, CA: Wadsworth.

Chicago Style

The University of Chicago Press presents two systems of documentation. This chapter shows their notes-and-bibliography system, which calls for (1) a superscript number for each in-text citation, (2) a correspondingly numbered footnote or endnote, and (3) an end-of-paper bibliography. The models in this chapter draw on *The Chicago Manual of Style*, 16th edition (2010). Additional information about *Chicago* style is available at www.chicagomanualofstyle.org.

A DIRECTORY TO *CHICAGO* STYLE

Throughout this chapter, you'll find models that are color-coded to help you see how writers include source information in their notes and bibliographies: tan for author or editor, yellow for title, gray for publication information: place of publication, publisher, date of publication, page number(s), and so on.

CMS-a Citing with Notes and Bibliography

Put a superscript number in your text to indicate to your reader that you are citing material from a source. The superscript should follow the **QUOTATION**, **PARAPHRASE**, or **SUMMARY** of the source you are citing, as in the example below.

IN-TEXT CITATION

Kaplan insists that understanding power in the Near East requires "Western leaders who know when to intervene, and do so without illusions."[1]

The superscript number directs your reader to a footnote or endnote that gives more information about the source; these in-text citations are numbered sequentially throughout your text. Here is the note that documents the quote from Kaplan's book.

NOTE WHEN YOU FIRST CITE A SOURCE

1. Robert D. Kaplan, *Eastward to Tartary: Travels in the Balkans, the Middle East, and the Caucasus* (New York: Random House, 2000), 330.

If you cite the same source later in your paper, give a shorter form of the note that lists just the author's last name, an abbreviated title, and the page(s) cited.

SUBSEQUENT NOTES

4. Kaplan, *Eastward*, 332.

If you cite the same source in two consecutive notes, simply change the page number in the second note and use *Ibid.*, a Latin abbreviation meaning "in the same place." When your next citation is to the same page of that source, use just *Ibid.*

> 5. Ibid., 334.
>
> 6. Ibid.

BIBLIOGRAPHY

The bibliography at the end of your paper is an alphabetical list of the sources you've cited or consulted. Here is how Kaplan's book would appear in a bibliography.

> Kaplan, Robert D. *Eastward to Tartary: Travels in the Balkans, the Middle East, and the Caucasus.* New York: Random House, 2000.

If your bibliography includes all of the works cited in the notes, *Chicago* suggests providing only brief notes. Check your instructor's preference, however, before using this method.

CMS-b Note and Bibliography Models

Because *Chicago* style requires both notes and a bibliography for documentation, this chapter provides examples of both methods. See pages 199–200 for guidelines on preparing notes and a bibliography; for samples, see pages 203–204.

Books

For most books, you'll need to provide information about the author; the title and any subtitle; and the place of publication, publisher, and year of publication. Treat pamphlets and brochures like books, giving whatever information is available.

IMPORTANT DETAILS FOR CITING BOOKS

- AUTHORS: Include the author's middle name or initial, if any.
- TITLES: Capitalize the first and last words and all principal words of titles and subtitles. Italicize book titles. Use quotation marks around titles of chapters or other short works within books.

- **PUBLICATION PLACE:** If there's more than one city, use only the first. If a city may be unfamiliar or could be confused with another of the same name, give the state, province, or country. For the U.S. capital, use "Washington, DC." Do not list the state or country if that information is part of the publisher's name.

- **PUBLISHER:** Omit *The* at the start of a publisher's name, along with abbreviations such as *Inc.* If you shorten a publisher's name (e.g., *Wiley* for *John Wiley*), be consistent.

1. ONE AUTHOR

NOTE

> 1. Author's First Name Last Name, *Title* (Publication City: Publisher, Year of publication), Page(s).

> 1. Erik Larson, *The Devil in the White City: Murder, Mayhem, and Madness at the Fair That Changed America* (New York: Crown, 2003), 113.

BIBLIOGRAPHY

Author's Last Name, First Name. *Title.* Publication City: Publisher, Year of publication.

Larson, Erik. *The Devil in the White City: Murder, Mayhem, and Madness at the Fair That Changed America.* New York: Crown, 2003.

2. MULTIPLE AUTHORS

NOTE

> 2. First Author's First Name Last Name, Next Author's First and Last Names, and Third Author's First and Last Names, *Title* (Publication City: Publisher, Year of publication), Page(s).

> 2. Ronald W. Walker, Richard E. Turley Jr., and Glen M. Leonard, *Massacre at Mountain Meadows* (New York: Oxford University Press, 2008), 225.

Documentation Map (*Chicago*)

BOOK

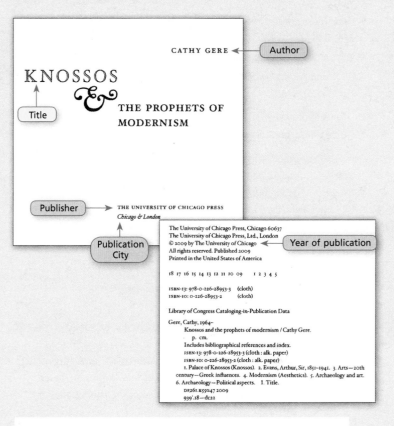

NOTE

1. Cathy Gere, *Knossos & the Prophets of Modernism*
(Chicago: University of Chicago Press, 2009), 18.

BIBLIOGRAPHY

Gere, Cathy. *Knossos & the Prophets of Modernism*. Chicago:
University of Chicago Press, 2009.

For more than three authors, give the first author's name followed by *et al.*, Latin for "and others."

> 2. David Goldfield et al., *Twentieth-Century America: A Social and Political History* (Upper Saddle River, NJ: Pearson Prentice Hall, 2005), 376.

BIBLIOGRAPHY

Give all authors' names for works with ten or fewer authors.

> First Author's Last Name, First Name, Next Author's First and Last Names, and Final Author's First and Last Names. *Title.* Publication City: Publisher, Year of publication.
>
> Goldfield, David, Carl E. Abbott, Jo Ann E. Argersinger, and Peter H. Argersinger. *Twentieth-Century America: A Social and Political History.* Upper Saddle River, NJ: Pearson Prentice Hall, 2005.

3. ORGANIZATION OR CORPORATION AS AUTHOR

NOTE

> 3. Organization Name, *Title* (Publication City: Publisher, Year of publication), Page(s).
>
> 3. Modern Humanities Research Association, *MHRA Style Guide: A Handbook for Authors, Editors, and Writers of Theses,* 2nd ed. (London: Modern Humanities Research Association, 2008), 21.

BIBLIOGRAPHY

> Organization Name. *Title.* Publication City: Publisher, Year of publication.
>
> Modern Humanities Research Association. *MHRA Style Guide: A Handbook for Authors, Editors, and Writers of Theses.* 2nd ed. London: Modern Humanities Research Association, 2008.

4. AUTHOR AND EDITOR

NOTE

4. Author's First Name Last Name, *Title*, ed. Editor's First Name Last Name (Publication City: Publisher, Year of publication), Page(s).

4. John P. Parker, *His Promised Land: The Autobiography of John P. Parker, Former Slave and Conductor on the Underground Railroad*, ed. Stuart Seely Sprague (New York: Norton, 1998), 218.

BIBLIOGRAPHY

Author's Last Name, First Name. *Title*. Edited by Editor's First Name Last Name. Publication City: Publisher, Year of publication.

Parker, John P. *His Promised Land: The Autobiography of John P. Parker, Former Slave and Conductor on the Underground Railroad.* Edited by Stuart Seely Sprague. New York: Norton, 1998.

5. EDITOR ONLY

NOTE

5. Editor's First Name Last Name, ed., *Title* (Publication City: Publisher, Year of publication), Page(s).

5. Eric Foner and John A. Garraty, eds., *The Reader's Companion to American History* (Boston: Houghton Mifflin, 1991), xix.

BIBLIOGRAPHY

Editor's Last Name, First Name, ed. *Title*. Publication City: Publisher, Year of publication.

Foner, Eric, and John A. Garraty, eds. *The Reader's Companion to American History.* Boston: Houghton Mifflin, 1991.

6. WORK IN AN EDITED COLLECTION OR ANTHOLOGY

NOTE

6. Author's First Name Last Name, "Title of Work," in *Title of Collection or Anthology*, ed. Editor's First Name Last Name (Publication City: Publisher, Year of publication), Page(s).

6. Lee Sandlin, "Losing the War," in *The New Kings of Nonfiction,* ed. Ira Glass (New York: Riverhead Books, 2007), 355.

BIBLIOGRAPHY

Author's Last Name, First Name. "Title of Work." In *Title of Collection or Anthology*, edited by Editor's First Name Last Name, Page range. Publication City: Publisher, Year of publication.

Sandlin, Lee. "Losing the War." In *The New Kings of Nonfiction,* edited by Ira Glass, 315–61. New York: Riverhead Books, 2007.

7. UNKNOWN AUTHOR

NOTE

7. *Title* (Publication City: Publisher, Year of publication), Page(s).

7. *All States Tax Handbook* (New York: Thomson Reuters, 2009), 5.

BIBLIOGRAPHY

Title. Publication City: Publisher, Year of publication.

All States Tax Handbook. New York: Thomson Reuters, 2009.

8. TRANSLATION

NOTE

8. Author's First Name Last Name, *Title*, trans. Translator's First Name Last Name (Publication City: Publisher, Year of publication), Page(s).

8. Norberto Fuentes, *The Autobiography of Fidel Castro*, trans. Anna Kushner (New York: Norton, 2009), 49.

BIBLIOGRAPHY

Author's Last Name, First Name. *Title*. Translated by Translator's First and Last Names. Publication City: Publisher, Year of publication.

Fuentes, Norberto. *The Autobiography of Fidel Castro*. Translated by Anna Kushner. New York: Norton, 2009.

9. EDITION OTHER THAN THE FIRST

NOTE

9. Author's First Name Last Name, *Title*, name or number of ed. (Publication City: Publisher, Year of publication), Page(s).

9. Michael D. Coe and Rex Koontz, *Mexico: From the Olmecs to the Aztecs,* 6th ed. (London: Thames & Hudson, 2008), 186–87.

BIBLIOGRAPHY

Author's Last Name, First Name. *Title*. Name or number of ed. Publication City: Publisher, Year of publication.

Coe, Michael D., and Rex Koontz. *Mexico: From the Olmecs to the Aztecs*. 6th ed. London: Thames & Hudson, 2008.

10. VOLUME OF A MULTIVOLUME WORK

NOTE

10. Author's First Name Last Name, *Title of Complete Work*, vol. number of individual volume, *Title of Individual Volume* (Publication City: Publisher, Year of publication), Page(s).

10. Bruce Catton, *The Army of the Potomac*, vol. 2, *Glory Road* (Garden City, NY: Doubleday, 1952), 169–70.

BIBLIOGRAPHY

Author's Last Name, First Name. *Title of Multivolume Work*. Vol. number, *Title of Individual Volume*. Publication City: Publisher, Year of publication.

Catton, Bruce. *The Army of the Potomac*. Vol. 2, *Glory Road*. Garden City, NY: Doubleday, 1952.

11. DICTIONARY OR ENCYCLOPEDIA ENTRY

Well-known reference works can be cited in a note without any publication information but do not need to be included in your bibliography. Use the abbreviation *s.v.*, meaning "under the word," before the name of the entry.

> 11. *Title,* edition number, s.v. "name of entry."

> 11. *The Random House Dictionary of the English Language*, 2nd ed., s.v. "ethos."

> 11. *The New Encyclopaedia Britannica*, 15th ed., s.v. "Paul Klee."

12. LETTER IN A PUBLISHED COLLECTION

NOTE

> 12. Sender's First Name Last Name to Recipient's First Name Last Name, Day Month Year, in *Title of Collection*, ed. Editor's First Name Last Name (Publication City: Publisher, Year of publication), Page(s).

> 12. Abigail Adams to John Adams, 14 August 1776, in *My Dearest Friend: Letters of Abigail and John Adams,* ed. Margaret A. Hogan and C. James Taylor (Cambridge, MA: Harvard University Press, 2007), 139–41.

BIBLIOGRAPHY

Sender's Last Name, First Name. Sender's First Name Last Name to Recipient's First Name Last Name, Month Day, Year. In *Title of Collection of Letters*, edited by Editor's First Name Last Name, Pages. Publication City: Publisher, Year.

Adams, Abigail. Abigail Adams to John Adams, August 14, 1776, In *My Dearest Friend: Letters of Abigail and John Adams,* edited by Margaret A. Hogan and C. James Taylor, 139–41. Cambridge, MA: Harvard University Press, 2007.

13. BOOK IN A SERIES

NOTE

13. Author's First Name Last Name, *Title of Book*, Title of Series (Publication City: Publisher, Year of publication), Page(s).

13. Karen Armstrong, *Buddha*, Penguin Lives (New York: Viking, 2004), 135.

BIBLIOGRAPHY

Author's Last Name, First Name. *Title of Book*. Title of Series. Publication City: Publisher, Year of publication.

Armstrong, Karen. *Buddha*. Penguin Lives. New York: Viking, 2004.

14. SACRED TEXT

Cite a sacred work in a note but not in your bibliography. Provide section information, such as book, chapter, and verse—but never a page number. If you are citing the Bible, identify the version. Translated texts should give the name of the version or translator.

14. Exod. 6:26–27 (New Revised Standard Version).

14. Qur'an 19:17–21.

15. SOURCE QUOTED IN ANOTHER SOURCE

Give the author, title, publication, and page information for the source quoted, followed by information on the source where you found it.

NOTE

15. John Gunther, *Inside USA* (New York: Harper and Brothers, 1947), 259, quoted in Thomas Frank, *What's the Matter with Kansas?* (New York: Henry Holt, 2004), 29.

BIBLIOGRAPHY

Gunther, John. *Inside USA*, 259. New York: Harper and Brothers, 1947. Quoted in Thomas Frank, *What's the Matter with Kansas?* (New York: Henry Holt, 2004), 29.

Periodicals

For most articles, you'll need to list the author; the article title and any subtitle; the periodical title; volume and issue numbers (for journals); and date information. Include page references only for journals and magazines.

IMPORTANT DETAILS FOR CITING PERIODICALS

- **AUTHORS:** If there is more than one author, follow the model for a book with multiple authors (see no. 2).

- **TITLES:** Capitalize article titles and subtitles as you would a work in an edited collection (see no. 6). Use quotation marks around article titles. Italicize periodical titles.

- **VOLUME, ISSUE, AND DATE:** Give Arabic numbers for the volume even if a journal uses roman numerals. If an issue number is given, there's no need to include the month or season in your citation. Magazines and newspapers are cited by date only.

- **PAGES:** Notes for journal and magazine articles should cite a specific page number; newspapers do not. Give the full page range of a journal article in your bibliography, but omit this information when citing magazines or newspapers.

16. ARTICLE IN A JOURNAL

NOTE

16. Author's First Name Last Name, "Title of Article," *Title of Journal* volume, no. issue (Year): Page(s).

16. Jeremy Adelman, "An Age of Imperial Revolutions," *American Historical Review* 113, no. 2 (2008): 336.

BIBLIOGRAPHY

Author's Last Name, First Name. "Title of Article." *Title of Journal* volume, no. issue (Year): Page range.

Adelman, Jeremy. "An Age of Imperial Revolutions." *American Historical Review* 113, no. 2 (2008): 319–40.

Documentation Map (*Chicago*)

ARTICLE IN A JOURNAL

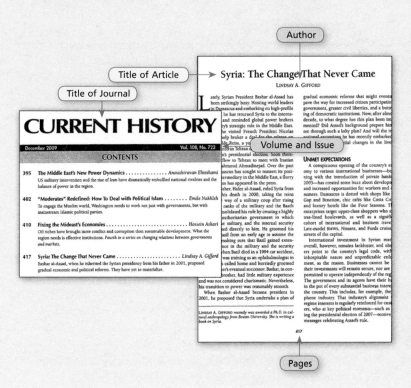

Author

Title of Article

Title of Journal

Volume and Issue

Pages

NOTE

16. Lindsay A. Gifford, "Syria: The Change That Never Came," *Current History* 108, no. 722 (2009): 417.

BIBLIOGRAPHY

Gifford, Lindsay A. "Syria: The Change That Never Came." *Current History* 108, no. 722 (2009): 417–23.

17. ARTICLE IN A MAGAZINE

Include the day for a weekly magazine. For a monthly magazine, give only the month and year with no comma in between.

NOTE

> 17. Author's First Name Last Name, "Title of Article," *Title of Magazine*, Month Day, Year, Page(s).
>
> 17. Jeffrey Toobin, "After Stevens: The Supreme Court's Liberal Leader," *New Yorker*, March 22, 2010, 40.

BIBLIOGRAPHY

Author's Last Name, First Name. "Title of Article." *Title of Magazine*, Month Day, Year, Page range.

Toobin, Jeffrey. "After Stevens: The Supreme Court's Liberal Leader," *New Yorker,* March 22, 2010, 38–47.

18. ARTICLE IN A NEWSPAPER

NOTE

> 18. Author's First Name Last Name, "Title of Article," *Title of Newspaper*, Month Day, Year, edition (if any), sec. (if any).
>
> 18. Stephanie Saul, "The Gift of Life, and Its Price," *New York Times,* October 11, 2009, early edition, sec. N.

BIBLIOGRAPHY

Author's Last Name, First Name. "Title of Article." *Title of Newspaper*, Month Day, Year, edition (if any), sec. (if any).

Saul, Stephanie. "The Gift of Life, and Its Price." *New York Times,* October 11, 2009, early edition, sec. N.

Documentation Map (*Chicago*)

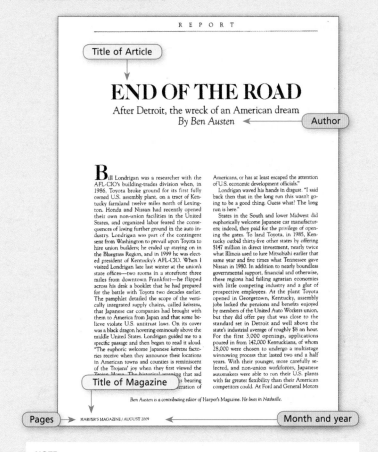

REPORT

Title of Article

END OF THE ROAD

After Detroit, the wreck of an American dream
By Ben Austen

Author

Bill Londrigan was a researcher with the AFL-CIO's building-trades division when, in 1986, Toyota broke ground for its first fully owned U.S. assembly plant, on a tract of Kentucky farmland twelve miles north of Lexington. Honda and Nissan had recently opened their own non-union facilities in the United States, and organized labor feared the consequences of losing further ground in the auto industry. Londrigan was part of the contingent sent from Washington to prevail upon Toyota to hire union builders; he ended up staying on in the Bluegrass Region, and in 1999 he was elected president of Kentucky's AFL-CIO. When I visited Londrigan late last winter at the union's state offices—two rooms in a storefront three miles from downtown Frankfort—he flipped across his desk a booklet that he had prepared for the battle with Toyota two decades earlier. The pamphlet detailed the scope of the vertically integrated supply chains, called *keiretsu*, that Japanese car companies had brought with them to America from Japan and that some believe violate U.S. antitrust laws. On its cover was a black dragon hovering ominously above the middle United States. Londrigan guided me to a specific passage and then began to read it aloud. "The euphoric welcome Japanese *keiretsu* factories receive when they announce their locations in American towns and counties is reminiscent of the Trojans' joy when they first viewed the Trojan Horse. The historical warning that and

Title of Magazine

Americans, or has at least escaped the attention of U.S. economic development officials."

Londrigan waved his hands in disgust. "I said back then that in the long run this wasn't going to be a good thing. Guess what? The long run is here."

States in the South and lower Midwest did euphorically welcome Japanese car manufacturers; indeed, they paid for the privilege of opening the gates. To land Toyota, in 1985, Kentucky outbid thirty-five other states by offering $147 million in direct investment, nearly twice what Illinois used to lure Mitsubishi earlier that same year and five times what Tennessee gave Nissan in 1980. In addition to nearly boundless governmental support, financial and otherwise, these regions had failing agrarian economies with little competing industry and a glut of prospective employees. At the plant Toyota opened in Georgetown, Kentucky, assembly jobs lacked the pensions and benefits enjoyed by members of the United Auto Workers union, but they did offer pay that was close to the standard set in Detroit and well above the state's industrial average of roughly $8 an hour. For the first 3,000 openings, applications poured in from 142,000 Kentuckians, of whom 28,000 were chosen to undergo a multistage winnowing process that lasted two and a half years. With their younger, more carefully selected, and non-union workforces, Japanese automakers were able to run their U.S. plants with far greater flexibility than their American competitors could. At Ford and General Motors

Ben Austen is a contributing editor of Harper's Magazine. He lives in Nashville.

Pages — HARPER'S MAGAZINE / AUGUST 2009 — **Month and year**

NOTE

17. Ben Austen, "End of the Road: After Detroit, the Wreck of an American Dream," *Harper's*, August 2009, 26.

BIBLIOGRAPHY

Austen, Ben. "End of the Road: After Detroit, the Wreck of an American Dream." *Harper's*, August 2009, 26–36.

19. UNSIGNED ARTICLE

When the author is unknown, put the article title first in notes. In the bibliography entry, put the name of the periodical first.

NOTE

> 19. "Title of Article," *Title of Newspaper*, Month Day, Year, edition (if any), sec. (if any).

> 19. "The Next Campaign," *New York Times*, November 8, 2010, New York edition, sec. A.

BIBLIOGRAPHY

> *Title of Newspaper*. "Title of Article." Month Day, Year, edition (if any), sec. (if any).

> *New York Times*. "The Next Campaign." November 8, 2010, New York edition, sec. A.

20. BOOK REVIEW

NOTE

> 20. Reviewer's First Name Last Name, review of *Title of Book*, by Author's First Name Last Name, *Title of Periodical* volume, no. issue (Year): Page(s).

> 20. Gary K. Waite, review of *The Path of the Devil: Early Modern Witch Hunts*, by Gary Jensen, *American Historical Review* 113, no. 2 (2008): 453.

BIBLIOGRAPHY

> Reviewer's Last Name, First Name. Review of *Title of Book*, by Author's First Name Last Name. *Title of Periodical* volume, no. issue (Year): Page range.

> Waite, Gary K. Review of *The Path of the Devil: Early Modern Witch Hunts*, by Gary Jensen. *American Historical Review* 113, no. 2 (2008): 453–54.

For a review in a magazine or newspaper, replace the volume and issue numbers with the publication date, as in nos. 17 and 18.

Online Sources

Citations for many online sources begin with the same elements you'd provide for a print source: author or editor; title of the work; publisher, place of publication, periodical title, publication date, and so on. Provide a DOI (Digital Object Identifier, a string of numbers that identifies an online document) or URL whenever possible. For websites you'll also need to include the site's title, sponsor, and a URL.

IMPORTANT DETAILS FOR CITING ONLINE SOURCES

- AUTHORS: When no person or separate organization is given as the author of a website, list the site's sponsor as the author. If there is more than one author, list subsequent authors as you would for a book with multiple authors (see no. 2).

- PAGES OR OTHER LOCATORS: When an online book or journal article has no page numbers, you may give another locator such as paragraph number or subsection heading. Be sure to make it clear (with an abbreviation such as *par.,* for example) that the locator you cite is not a page number. See no. 25 for an example that uses a subsection heading as a locator.

- ACCESS DATES: *Chicago* requires access dates only when a publication or revision date cannot be determined, or when a source is likely to be updated or removed without notice. However, some instructors require access dates for online sources, so the following models include them.

- DOI OR URL: *Chicago* prefers DOIs to URLs, as DOIs apply to a work in any medium. If no DOI is readily available, use the URL that appears in your browser's address bar; a shorter form is also acceptable if supplied with the work (known as a stable URL) or when citing a newspaper article. In general, break a URL that won't fit on one line before a slash or other punctuation mark—and do not add a hyphen or break the URL at one.

21. ARTICLE IN AN ONLINE JOURNAL

NOTE

21. Author's First Name Last Name, "Title of Article," *Title of Journal* volume, no. issue (Year): Page(s) or other locator, accessed Month Day, Year, DOI or URL.

21. Gary Gerstle, "A State Both Strong and Weak," *American Historical Review* 115, no. 3 (2010): 780, accessed October 7, 2010, doi:10.1086/ahr.115.3.779.

BIBLIOGRAPHY

Author's Last Name, First Name. "Title of Article." *Title of Journal* volume, no. issue (Year): Page(s) or other locator. Accessed Month Day, Year. DOI or URL.

Gerstle, Gary. "A State Both Strong and Weak." *American Historical Review* 115, no. 3 (2010): 778–85. Accessed October 7, 2010. doi:10.1086/ahr.115.3.779.

22. ARTICLE IN AN ONLINE MAGAZINE

NOTE

22. Author's First Name Last Name, "Title of Article," *Title of Magazine*, Month Day, Year, accessed Month Day, Year, DOI or URL.

22. Richard R. John, "The Selling of Samuel Morse," *AmericanHeritage.com*, October 1, 2010, accessed October 8, 2010, http://www.americanheritage.com/people/articles/web /100110-Samuel-Morse-Telegraph-Morse-Code-Patent-Office.shtml.

BIBLIOGRAPHY

Author's Last Name, First Name. "Title of Article." *Title of Magazine*, Month Day, Year. Accessed Month Day, Year. DOI or URL.

John, Richard R. "The Selling of Samuel Morse." *AmericanHeritage. com*, October 1, 2010. Accessed October 8, 2010. http://www

.americanheritage.com/people/articles/web/

100110-Samuel-Morse-Telegraph-Morse-Code-Patent-Office

.shtml.

23. ARTICLE IN AN ONLINE NEWSPAPER

Very lengthy newspaper URLs can be shortened to end after the first single forward slash.

NOTE

23. Author's First Name Last Name, "Title of Article," *Title of Newspaper*, Month Day, Year, accessed Month Day, Year. DOI or URL.

23. Andres Oppenheimer, "U.S. May Take New Look at 'War on Drugs,'" *Chicago Tribune*, December 10, 2009, accessed March 4, 2010, http://www.chicagotribune.com.

BIBLIOGRAPHY

Author's Last Name, First Name. "Title of Article." *Title of Newspaper*, Month Day, Year. Accessed Month Day, Year. DOI or URL.

Oppenheimer, Andres. "U.S. May Take New Look at 'War on Drugs.'"
    Chicago Tribune, December 10, 2009. Accessed March 4, 2010.
    http://www.chicagotribune.com.

24. ARTICLE ACCESSED THROUGH A DATABASE

For magazines and newspapers, add the appropriate information about the month, day, and year as shown in nos. 22 and 23. Give the URL of the article if the database supplies a stable one; if there's no stable URL, include the database name and article identification number. Supply an access date only if the work doesn't have a publication or revision date.

NOTE

24. Author's First Name Last Name, "Title of Article," *Title of Journal* volume, no. issue (Year): Pages(s), stable URL or Database Name (identification number).

24. David W. Galenson, "Analyzing Artistic Innovation,"

Documentation Map (Chicago)

ARTICLE ACCESSED THROUGH A DATABASE

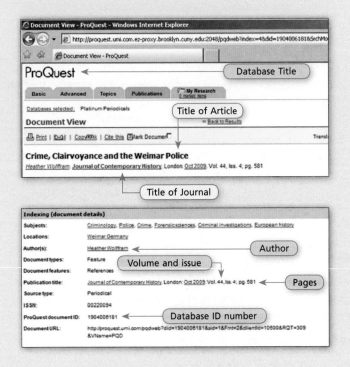

NOTE

24. Heather Wolffram, "Crime, Clairvoyance and the Weimar Police," *Journal of Contemporary History* 44, no. 4 (2009): 581, accessed February 22, 2010, ProQuest (1904006181).

BIBLIOGRAPHY

Wolffram, Heather. "Crime, Clairvoyance and the Weimar Police." *Journal of Contemporary History* 44, no. 4 (2009): 581–601. Accessed February 22, 2010. ProQuest (1904006181).

Historical Methods 41, no. 3 (2008): 114, accessed August 23, 2010, Academic Search Premier (34217664).

BIBLIOGRAPHY

Author's Last Name, First Name. "Title of Article." *Title of Journal*
 volume, no. issue (Year): Page range. Accessed Month Day, Year.
 Stable URL or Database Name (identification number).

Galenson, David W. "Analyzing Artistic Innovation." *Historical
 Methods* 41, no. 3 (2008): 111–20. Accessed August 23, 2010.
 Academic Search Premier (34217664).

25. EBOOK

Because pagination can vary depending on factors such as text size, indicate the chapter or section instead of a page reference.

NOTE

 25. Author's First Name Last Name, *Title* (Publication City:
 Publisher, Year of publication), Page(s) or other locator, DOI or URL.

 25. L. M. Cullen, *A History of Japan, 1582–1941: Internal and
 External Worlds* (Cambridge: Cambridge University Press, 2003),
 doi:10.2277/051107543X.

BIBLIOGRAPHY

Author's Last Name, First Name. *Title.* Publication City: Publisher,
 Year of publication. DOI or URL.

Cullen, L. M. *A History of Japan, 1582–1941: Internal and External
 Worlds*. Cambridge: Cambridge University Press, 2003.
 doi:10.2277/051107543X.

To cite a downloaded ebook of a print work, follow the setup for a print book but indicate the format of the ebook at the end of your citation (*PDF ebook, Kindle edition*). Note that the publisher and year may be different from the print version. (See page 193 for examples.)

Documentation Map (*Chicago*)

WORK FROM A WEBSITE

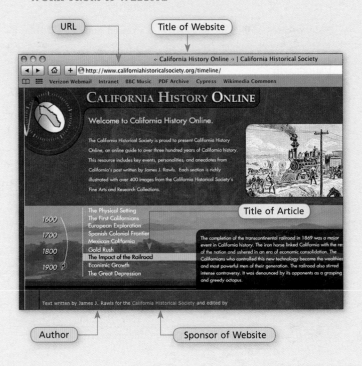

URL

Title of Website

Title of Article

Author

Sponsor of Website

NOTE

26. James J. Rawls, "The Impact of the Railroad," California History Online, California Historical Society, accessed February 22, 2010, http://www.californiahistoricalsociety.org/timeline/.

BIBLIOGRAPHY

Rawls, James J. "The Impact of the Railroad." California History Online. California Historical Society. Accessed February 22, 2010. http://www.californiahistoricalsociety.org/timeline/.

NOTE

25. Erik Larson, *The Devil in the White City: Murder, Mayhem, and Madness at the Fair That Changed America* (New York: Vintage, 2004), Kindle edition, pt. 2, under "Convocation."

BIBLIOGRAPHY

Larson, Erik. *The Devil in the White City: Murder, Mayhem, and Madness at the Fair That Changed America*. New York: Vintage, 2004. Kindle edition.

26. WORK FROM A WEBSITE

If no author is given, list the sponsor as the author and do not repeat its name after the title of the website.

NOTE

26. Author's First Name Last Name or Organization Name, "Title of Work," Title of Site, Sponsor, Month Day, Year of publication or modification, accessed Month Day, Year, URL.

26. David P. Silverman and Zahi Hawass, "The Story of King Tut," The Field Museum, accessed August 5, 2010, http://www.fieldmuseum .org/tut/story.asp.

BIBLIOGRAPHY

Author's Last Name, First Name or Organization Name. "Title of Work." Title of Site. Sponsor. Month Day, Year of publication or modification. Accessed Month Day, Year. URL.

Silverman, David P., and Zahi Hawass. "The Story of King Tut." The Field Museum. 2010. Accessed August 5, 2010. http://www .fieldmuseum.org/tut/story.asp.

27. BLOG ENTRY

If a blog is sponsored by a larger publication, include the publication's title in italics. Omit *(blog)* if that word is included in the title, as in the example on page 194.

NOTE

27. Author's First Name Last Name, "Title of Entry," *Title of Blog* (blog), Month Day, Year, accessed Month Day, Year, URL.

27. Gary Locke, "The Presidential Summit on Entrepreneurship," *The White House Blog*, November 3, 2009, accessed March 3, 2010, http://www.whitehouse.gov/blog/2009/11/02/presidential-summit-entrepreneurship.

BIBLIOGRAPHY

Author's Last Name, First Name. "Title of Entry." *Title of Blog* (blog). Month Day, Year. Accessed Month Day, Year. URL.

Locke, Gary. "The Presidential Summit on Entrepreneurship." *The White House Blog*. November 3, 2009. Accessed March 3, 2010. http://www.whitehouse.gov/blog/2004/11/02/presidential-summit-entrepreneurship.

28. PODCAST

If you're citing an interview, use the model for a broadcast interview (no. 29) and insert the medium (*podcast audio, podcast video*) before the date.

NOTE

28. Author's or Speaker's First Name Last Name, "Title of Podcast," *Title of Site*, Sponsor, medium, Month Day, Year of posting, URL.

28. Marideth Sisco, "Safety in the Middle of the Road," *These Ozark Hills,* Ozarks Public Radio (KSMU), podcast audio, July 30, 2009, http://www.ksmu.org/index.php?option=com_content&task=view&id=4927&Itemid=74.

BIBLIOGRAPHY

Author's or Speaker's Last Name, First Name. "Title of Podcast." *Title of Site*. Sponsor. Medium. Month Day, Year of posting. URL.

Sisco, Marideth. "Safety in the Middle of the Road." *These Ozark Hills.* Ozarks Public Radio (KSMU). Podcast audio. July 30, 2009. http://www.ksmu.org/index.php?option=com_content &task=view&id=4927&Itemid=74.

29. EMAIL OR POSTING TO AN ONLINE FORUM

Include these sources in notes, but not in a bibliography.

EMAIL

29. Writer's First Name Last Name, email message to author, Month Day, Year.

29. Ana Cooke, email message to author, January 10, 2010.

POSTING TO AN ELECTRONIC FORUM

29. Writer's First Name Last Name to Name of Forum, Month Day, Year, accessed Month Day, Year, URL.

29. David Elbert to New American Folk Music Listserv, July 3, 1998, accessed March 3, 2010, http://www.folkmusic.org/archives /fm/0492.html.

Other Kinds of Sources

30. BROADCAST INTERVIEW

NOTE

30. Subject's First Name Last Name, interview by First Name Last Name, *Title of Program*, Network, Month Day, Year.

30. Gerald Stern, interview by Linda Wertheimer, *All Things Considered,* NPR, April 10, 2010.

BIBLIOGRAPHY

Subject's Last Name, First Name. Interview by Interviewer's First Name Last Name. *Title of Program.* Network, Month Day, Year.

Stern, Gerald. Interview by Linda Wertheimer. *All Things Considered.* NPR, April 10, 2010.

31. SOUND RECORDING

NOTE

> 31. Composer's First Name Last Name, *Title of Work*, other appropriate information about the performer, conductor, recording, etc., Recording Company identifying number of recording, year of release, medium.

> 31. Giuseppe Verdi, *Rigoletto*, London Symphony Orchestra, conducted by Richard Bonynge, with Joan Sutherland, Luciano Pavarotti, Sherrill Milnes, et al., recorded at Kingsway Hall, June 1971, London 414269, 1990, MP3 file.

BIBLIOGRAPHY

Composer's Last Name, First Name. *Title of Work*. Other appropriate information about the performer, conductor, recording, etc. Recording Company identifying number of recording, year of release, medium.

Verdi, Giuseppe. *Rigoletto*. London Symphony Orchestra. Richard Bonynge. With Joan Sutherland, Luciano Pavarotti, Sherrill Milnes, et al. Recorded at Kingsway Hall, June 1971. London 414269, 1990, MP3 file.

To cite a particular person's work, start with that name.

> 31. Bruce Springsteen, vocal performance of "Shenandoah," by Pete Seeger, on *We Shall Overcome: The Seeger Sessions*, Columbia 82867, 2006, compact disc.

32. VIDEO OR DVD

To cite a particular person's work, start with that name.

NOTE

> 32. Writer's First Name Last Name, *Title*, directed by First Name Last Name (Original release year; City: Studio, Year of recording release), Medium.

32. Diablo Cody, *Juno,* directed by Jason Reitman (2007; Los Angeles: Fox Searchlight, 2008), DVD.

BIBLIOGRAPHY

Writer's Last Name, First Name. *Title.* Directed by First Name Last Name. Original release year. City: Studio, Year of recording release. Medium.

Cody, Diablo. *Juno.* DVD. Directed by Jason Reitman. 2007. Los Angeles: Fox Searchlight, 2008.

33. VIDEO CLIP

The information you provide will vary according to what you're citing. Here's an example of a video clip on YouTube.

NOTE

33. "Michael Lewis: Wall Street Can't Control Itself," YouTube video, 9:57, posted by CBS, April 19, 2010. http://www.youtube.com /watch?v=M93YUdbAVDA&feature=fvst.

BIBLIOGRAPHY

"Michael Lewis: Wall Street Can't Control Itself." YouTube video, 9:57. Posted by CBS. April 19, 2010. http://www.youtube.com /watch?v=M93YUdbAVDA&feature=fvst.

34. GOVERNMENT PUBLICATION

Most government publications can be cited like a work by an organization or corporation (no. 3) or a work by an unknown author (no. 7).

NOTE

34. *The 9/11 Commission Report: Final Report of the National Commission on Terrorist Attacks Upon the United States*, official government edition (Washington, DC: U.S. Government Printing Office, 2004), 33.

BIBLIOGRAPHY

The 9/11 Commission Report: Final Report of the National
 Commission on Terrorist Attacks Upon the United States,
 official government edition. Washington, DC: U.S. Government
 Printing Office, 2004.

Citing Sources Not Covered by *Chicago*

To cite a source for which *Chicago* does not provide guidelines, look for models similar to the source you are citing. Give any information readers will need in order to find your source themselves—author; title; publisher; date of publication; information about electronic retrieval (such as the URL and date of access); and any other pertinent information. You might want to try out your citation yourself, to be sure it will lead others to your source.

CMS-c Formatting a Paper

Name, course, title. Type the title of your paper about halfway down a page; capitalize it as you would the title of a book. Place your name on the line below the title. At the bottom of the page, give the title of your course, your instructor's name, and the date. Center each element on the title page on a separate line.

Page numbers. Insert a page number, preceded by either your name or a short form of the title, in the upper right-hand corner of each page; number pages consecutively, but do not put a page number on the title page.

Spacing and margins. Double-space the entire paper, including endnotes and bibliography; single-space any footnotes. Set one-inch margins on all sides.

Long quotations. When quoting more than a hundred words (at least six lines) or two or more paragraphs, set off the quotation as a block, indenting it one-half inch (or five spaces) from the left margin. Block quotations should not be enclosed in quotation marks.

Bruce Catton describes the end of the U.S. Civil War:

> The end of the war was like the beginning, with the
> army marching down the open road under the spring sky,
> seeing a far light on the horizon. Many lights had died in
> the windy dark but far down the road there was always
> a gleam, and it was as if a legend had been created to
> express some obscure truth that could not otherwise be
> stated. Everything had changed, the war and the men
> and the land they fought for, but the road ahead had not
> changed. It went on through the trees and past the little
> towns and over the hills, and there was no getting to the
> end of it.[1]

Poetry should be set off when you're quoting two or more lines.

> By referring to him as both "Captain" and "father," Walt
> Whitman makes clear the strong sense of identification he has
> felt with the now-fallen Lincoln:
>
> > My Captain does not answer, his lips are pale and still,
> > My father does not feel my arm, he has no pulse nor will.[2]

Illustrations. You may wish to include figures and tables. Figures include charts, diagrams, graphs, maps, photographs, and other illustrations. Figures and tables should be numbered and given a title (Figure 1. A Map of Columbus, Ohio, 2010; Table 1. Telephone Ownership, 1900–20). Any illustration that comes from another source should include a short citation—*Source:* David Siegel, *Creating Killer Web Sites* (Indianapolis, IN: Hayden Books, 1996), 72.—along with full source information in your bibliography. Put the title above the illustration and any source note below. Position illustrations as soon as possible after they are discussed in your text—and be sure to explain how they relate to your point.

Notes. You may choose to give notes as footnotes at the bottom of the page on which you cite the source, or as endnotes that are grouped at the end of your text under the heading *Notes*. For both footnotes and endnotes, indent the first line one-half inch (five spaces); do not indent subsequent lines. Footnotes should be single-spaced with an extra line between notes; endnotes should be double-spaced.

Bibliography. Start your list on a new page at the end of your paper, following any notes. Center the heading. Each entry should begin at the left margin, and subsequent lines should be indented one-half inch (or five spaces). Alphabetize the list by authors' or editors' last names; for works with no author or editor, or for multiple works by the same author, use the first important words of titles. If you include multiple works by the same author, use a three-em dash (or three hyphens) in place of the author's name in every entry after the first.

CMS-d Sample Pages

The following sample pages are from "History at Home: Leighton House, Sambourne House, and the Heritage Debate," written by Erika Graham for a museum studies course and internship during a study-abroad program in London. They are formatted according to the guidelines of the *Chicago Manual of Style*, 16th edition. To read Graham's complete research paper, go to **wwnorton.com/write/ little-seagull-handbook**.

Sample Title Page, *Chicago* Style

History at Home:

Leighton House, Sambourne House, and the Heritage Debate

Title and name.

Erika Graham

Professors Strauber and Vinter

Grinnell-in-London Internship

December 3, 2008

Instructors' names, course title, and date.

Sample Page of Research Paper, *Chicago* Style

Graham   2

Double-spaced throughout.

Last name and page number.

In the Royal Borough of Kensington and Chelsea, many Victorian houses remain standing, for this part of London was favored by many artists of the day. Two of these buildings have since become museums: Leighton House, home to Frederic Lord Leighton, P.R.A., and Linley Sambourne House, residence of the premier cartoonist for *Punch* magazine and his family. Though managed by the same team of curators and staff, the houses have distinct characters, which stem from the finery of their interiors— Sambourne House sports almost entirely original furnishings and decor, while Leighton House has been painstakingly restored to its intended grandeur as a "palace of art."

But although it might not be apparent to an average visitor overwhelmed by these displays, both museums are unavoidably involved in the fierce debate that surrounds all sites that present "the past." This debate is multifaceted, but all strands return eventually to the issue of whether or not such presentations can educate the visitor—the key role of the museum. As museum-studies scholar Eilean Hooper-Greenhill observes, "Knowledge is now well understood as the commodity that museums offer."[1] The details of this knowledge vary by museum; we will here be focusing on the transmission of historical knowledge. The history museum, however, has an interesting place in the discourse on museum education, for not everyone accepts that these institutions fulfill their didactic role. The accusation runs that some history museums have abandoned their educational duties by moving beyond the glass case format to display history in context through reconstruction, preservation, and, most feared of all, living history

1"

Author in signal phrase; superscript number to cite source.

1"

1"

1"

Sample Endnotes, *Chicago* Style

Notes •·············

Heading centered.

1. Eilean Hooper-Greenhill, *Museums and the Shaping of* •·········
Knowledge, Heritage: Care-Preservation-Management (London:
Routledge, 1992), 2.

First line indented; subsequent lines flush left.

2. Emma Barker, "Heritage and the Country House," in
Contemporary Cultures of Display, ed. Emma Barker (New Haven,
CT: Yale University Press, 1999), 206.

Double-spaced.

3. G. Ellis Burcaw, *Introduction to Museum Work,* 3rd ed.
(London: AltaMira Press, 1997), 177; Beth Goodacre and Gavin •··········
Baldwin, *Living the Past: Reconstruction; Recreation, Re-Enactment, and
Education at Museums and Historical Sites* (London: Middlesex
University Press, 2002), 44.

Multiple sources in a note separated by semicolons.

4. Kevin Walsh, *The Representation of the Past: Museums and
Heritage in the Post-Modern World,* Heritage: Care-Preservation-
Management (London: Routledge, 1992), 102; Paul Greenhalgh,
"Education, Entertainment and Politics: Lessons from the Great
International Exhibitions," in *The New Museology,* ed. Peter Vergo
(London: Reaktion Books, 1989). •·······························

Page number omitted in a reference to the source as a whole.

5. Though a criticism here, not everyone believes this is a
bad thing. For example, see Kevin Moore, *Museums and Popular
Culture,* Contemporary Issues in Museum Culture (London: Cassell,
1997).

6. Goodacre and Baldwin, *Living,* 9 (italics added). •···············

Shortened note for second citation.

7. Walsh, *Representation,* 94; Peter J. Fowler, *The Past in
Contemporary Society: Then. Now,* Heritage: Care-Preservation-
Management (London: Routledge, 1992), 5.

8. Walsh, *Representation,* 102.

Sample Bibliography, *Chicago* Style

Bibliography ●┈┈┈┈┈┈┈┈┈┈┈┈ *Heading centered.*

Alphabetized by author's last name.
┈┈ Barker, Emma. "Heritage and the Country House." *Contemporary Cultures of Display,* edited by Emma Barker, 200–28. New Haven, CT: Yale University Press, 1999.

First line flush left; subsequent lines indented.
Burcaw, G. Ellis. *Introduction to Museum Work.* 3rd ed. London: AltaMira Press, 1997.

Fowler, Peter J. *The Contemporary Society: Then, Now.* Heritage: Care-Preservation-Management. London: Routledge, 1992.

Double-spaced.
Goodacre, Beth, and Gavin Baldwin. *Living the Past: Reconstruction, Recreation, Re-Enactment and Education at Museums and Historical Sites.* London: Middlesex University Press, 2002.

Greenhalgh, Paul. "Education, Entertainment and Politics: Lessons from the Great International Exhibitions." In *The New Museology,* edited by Peter Vergo, 74–98. London: Reaktion Books, 1989.

Handler, Richard. "Authenticity." *Anthropology Today* 2, no. 1 (1986):
DOI.
●┈┈┈ 2–4. Accessed September 30, 2008. doi:10.2307/3032899.

3-em dash replaces author's name for subsequent works by the same author.
●┈┈ ———. "Heritage and Hegemony: Recent Works on Historic Preservation and Interpretation." *Anthropological Quarterly* 60, no. 3 (1987): 137–41. Accessed October 22, 2008. http://www .jstor.org/stable/i274779.

Hooper-Greenhill, Eilean. *Museums and the Shaping of Knowledge.* Heritage: Care-Preservation-Management. London: Routledge, 1992.

James, Simon. "Imag(in)ing the Past: The Politics and Practicalities of Reconstructions in the Museum Gallery." In *Making Early*

CSE Style

The Council of Science Editors (CSE) offers three systems of documentation—citation-sequence, citation-name, and name-year; this chapter provides guidelines on all three. The models in this chapter draw on *Scientific Style and Format: The CSE Manual for Authors, Editors, and Publishers*, 7th edition (2006).

A DIRECTORY TO CSE STYLE

Throughout this chapter, you'll find models that are color-coded to help you see how writers include source information in their texts and in reference lists: tan for author or editor, yellow for title, gray for publication information: place of publication, publisher, date of publication, page number(s), and so on.

CSE-a In-Text Documentation

In CSE style, either a numeral or brief documentation in your text indicates to your reader that you are citing material from a source. You can use one of three formats:

Citation-Sequence Format calls for you to put a number (either a superscript or a number in parentheses) after any mention of a source. Once you number a source, use that same number each time the source is mentioned: if your first reference to something written by Christopher Gillen is Gillen[1], every subsequent citation of the same work by this author will also be Gillen[1]. Number sources in the order you mention them—the first source you refer to is numbered 1, the second one is numbered 2, and so on.

Citation-Name Format calls for you first to alphabetize your list of references and then number the sources consecutively in the order they appear on the list: the first source on the list is number 1, the second is number 2, and so on. Then put the appropriate number (either a superscript or a number in parentheses) after each mention of a source. So if Zuefle is the tenth source cited on your alphabetical list of references, every citation of the same work by this author will be Zuefle[10].

Name-Year Format calls for you to give the author's last name and the year of publication in parentheses after any mention of a source. If you mention the author's name in a signal phrase, you need put only the year in parentheses. For instance:

> Atherosclerosis seems to predate our modern lifestyles (Singer 2009[8]).

> Singer (2009)[8] questions whether atherosclerosis is inevitable.

If a work has two authors, give both names: Davidson and Lyon 1987[14]. For three or more authors, give only the first author, followed by *et al.*, a Latin abbreviation meaning "and others" (Rathus et al. 2010[15]). If you include more than one work in parentheses, separate them with a semicolon (Gilder 2008; Singer 2009[6,8]).

CSE-b List of References

The in-text documentation corresponds to the sources you list at the end of your paper in a list of references. The way you sequence sources in your References, whether you number them, and where you put publication dates depends on which format you use.

- *In citation-sequence format,* arrange and number the sources in the order in which they are first cited in your text. Put the date for a book at the end of the publication information; put the date for a periodical article after the periodical's title.

- *In citation-name format,* arrange and number the sources in alphabetical order. Put the date for a book at the end of the publication information; put the date for a periodical article after the periodical's title.

- *In name-year format,* arrange the sources alphabetically, and do not number them. Put the date after the name(s) of the author(s).

Because citation-sequence and citation-name present information in the same way (the differences lie in the organization of
the in-text superscripts and list of references), these two formats
are combined under a single heading (SEQUENCE/NAME) in the following models. See page 225 for guidelines on preparing a list of
references; for samples from a paper using citation-sequence style,
see pages 226–228.

Books

For most books, you'll need to provide information about the author;
the title and any subtitle; and the place of publication, publisher, and
year of publication.

IMPORTANT DETAILS FOR CITING BOOKS

- **AUTHORS:** Put each author's last name first, and list initials for
  first and middle names. Do not add space between initials, and
  omit punctuation except a period after the final initial.

- **TITLES:** For book and chapter titles, capitalize only the first word,
  any acronyms, or proper nouns or adjectives. For periodical titles,
  capitalize all major words, even if abbreviated. Do not italicize,
  underline, or put quotation marks around any title.

- **PUBLICATION PLACE:** Place the two-letter abbreviation for state,
  province, or country after cities within parentheses.

- **PUBLISHER:** You may shorten a publisher's name by omitting *the*
  and abbreviations such as *Inc.*

1. ONE AUTHOR

SEQUENCE/NAME

1. Author's Last Name Initials. Title. Publication City (State):
   Publisher; Year of publication.

1. Singh S. Big bang: the origin of the universe. New York (NY):
   Fourth Estate; 2004.

Documentation Map (CSE)

BOOK

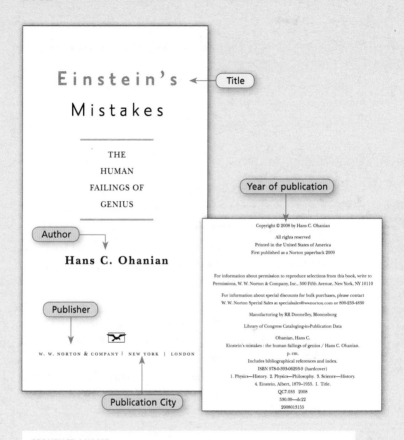

SEQUENCE / NAME

1. Ohanian HC. Einstein's mistakes: the human failings of genius.
   New York (NY): Norton; 2008.

NAME-YEAR

Ohanian HC. 2008. Einstein's mistakes: the human failings of genius.
New York (NY): Norton.

NAME-YEAR

Author's Last Name Initials. Year of publication. Title. Publication City (State): Publisher.

Singh S. 2004. Big bang: the origin of the universe. New York (NY): Fourth Estate.

2. MULTIPLE AUTHORS

List up to ten authors, separating them with commas.

SEQUENCE / NAME

2. First Author's Last Name Initials, Next Author's Last Name Initials, Final Author's Last Name Initials. Title. Publication City (State): Publisher; Year of publication.

2. Gaines SM, Eglinton G, Rullkotter J. Echoes of life: what fossil molecules reveal about Earth history. New York (NY): Oxford University Press; 2009.

NAME-YEAR

First Author's Last Name Initials, Next Author's Last Name Initials, Final Author's Last Name Initials. Year of publication. Title. Publication City (State): Publisher.

Gaines SM, Eglinton G, Rullkotter J. 2009. Echoes of life: what fossil molecules reveal about Earth history. New York (NY): Oxford University Press.

For a work by eleven or more authors, list the first ten, followed by *et al.* or *and others.*

3. ORGANIZATION OR CORPORATION AS AUTHOR

SEQUENCE / NAME

3. Organization Name. Title. Publication City (State): Publisher; Year of publication.

3. National Research Council. Black and smokeless powders:
   technologies for finding bombs and the bomb makers.
   Washington (DC): National Academy Press; 1998.

NAME-YEAR

Begin with the group's abbreviation, if any, and use it in the in-text
citation; however, alphabetize the entry by the first word of the
group's actual name, not by its abbreviation.

[Abbreviation if any] Organization Name. Year of publication. Title.
Publication City (State): Publisher.

[NRC] National Research Council. 1998. Black and smokeless powders:
technologies for finding bombs and the bomb makers. Washington
(DC): National Academy Press.

4. EDITOR, NO AUTHOR

SEQUENCE / NAME

4. Editor's Last Name Initials, editor. Title. Publication City (State):
   Publisher; Year of publication.

4. Wood RA, editor. The weather almanac. 11th ed. New York (NY):
   Wiley; 2007.

NAME-YEAR

Editor's Last Name Initials, editor. Year of publication. Title.
Publication City (State): Publisher.

Wood RA, editor. 2007. The weather almanac. 11th ed. New York
(NY): Wiley.

5. WORK IN AN EDITED COLLECTION

SEQUENCE / NAME

5. Author's Last Name Initials. Title of work. In: Editor's Last Name
   Initials, editor. Title of book. Publication City (State): Publisher;
   Year of publication, p. Pages.

5. Bonning BC. Biotechnology and insects. In: Resh VH, Cardé RT, editors. Encyclopedia of insects. 2nd ed. San Diego (CA): Academic Press; 2009. p. 120-122.

NAME-YEAR

Author's Last Name Initials. Year of publication. Title of work. In: Editor's Last Name Initials, editor. Title of book. Publication City (State): Publisher, p. Pages.

Bonning BC. 2009. Biotechnology and insects. In: Resh VH, Cardé RT, editors. Encyclopedia of insects. 2nd ed. San Diego (CA): Academic Press, p. 120-122.

6. CHAPTER OF A BOOK

SEQUENCE / NAME

6. Author's Last Name Initials. Title of book. Publication City (State): Publisher; Year of publication. Chapter number, Title of chapter; p. Pages.

6. Gilder L. The age of entanglement: when quantum physics was reborn. New York (NY): Knopf; 2008. Chapter 13, Solvay 1927; p. 110-127.

NAME-YEAR

Author's Last Name Initials. Year of publication. Title. Publication City (State): Publisher. Chapter number, Title of chapter; p. Pages.

Gilder L. 2008. The age of entanglement: when quantum physics was reborn. New York (NY): Knopf. Chapter 13, Solvay 1927; p. 110-127.

7. PAPER OR ABSTRACT FROM PROCEEDINGS OF A CONFERENCE

If you cite an abstract of a paper rather than the paper itself, place *[abstract]* after the paper's title but before the period.

SEQUENCE / NAME

7. Author's Last Name Initials. Title of paper. In: Editor's Last Name
   Initials, editor. Title of book. Number and Name of Conference;
   Date of Conference; Place of Conference. Publication City (State):
   Publisher; Year of publication. p. Pages.

7. Polivy J. Physical activity, fitness, and compulsive behaviors. In:
   Bouchard C, Shephard RJ, Stephens T, editors. Physical activity,
   fitness, and health: international proceedings and consensus
   statement. 2nd International Consensus Symposium on Physical
   Activity, Fitness, and Health; 1992 May 5-9; Toronto,
   Canada. Champaign (IL): Human Kinetics Publishers; 1994.
   p. 883-897.

NAME-YEAR

Author's Last Name Initials. Year of publication. Title of paper. In:
Editor's Last Name Initials, editor. Title of book. Number and Name
of Conference; Date of Conference; Place of Conference. Publication
City (State): Publisher. p. Pages.

Polivy J. 1994. Physical activity, fitness, and compulsive behaviors. In:
Bouchard C, Shephard RJ, Stephens T, editors. Physical activity,
fitness, and health: international proceedings and consensus
statement. 2nd International Consensus Symposium on Physical
Activity, Fitness, and Health; 1992 May 5-9; Toronto, Canada.
Champaign (IL): Human Kinetics Publishers. p. 883-897.

Periodicals

For most journal articles, you'll need to list the author; the title and
any subtitle of the article; the title of the periodical; volume and issue
numbers; year; and the inclusive page numbers of the article. Articles
in newspapers and some magazines have different requirements.

Documentation Map (CSE)

ARTICLE IN A JOURNAL

Year of publication

Pages

Title of Journal

Title of article

Volume and issue

Authors

Ecology, 88(8), 2007, pp. 1917–1923
© 2007 by the Ecological Society of America

SPECIES DIVERSITY MODULATES PREDATION

PAVEL KRATINA,[1,3] MATTHIJS VOS,[1,2] AND BRADLEY R. ANHOLT[1]

[1]*Department of Biology, University of Victoria, P.O. Box 3020, Victoria, British Columbia V8W 3N5 Canada*
[2]*Netherlands Institute of Ecology (NIOO-KNAW), Centre for Estuarine and Marine Ecology, P.O. Box 140, 4400 AC Yerseke, The Netherlands*

Abstract. Predation occurs in a context defined by both prey and non-prey species. At present it is largely unknown how species diversity in general, and species that are not included in a predator's diet in particular, modify predator–prey interactions.

Therefore we studied how both the density and diversity of non-prey species modified predation rates in experimental microcosms. We found that even a low density of a single non-prey species depressed the asymptote of a predator's functional response. Increases in the density and diversity of non-prey species further reduced predation rates to very low levels. Controls showed that this diversity effect was not due to the identity of any of the non-prey species. Our results establish that both the density and diversity of species outside a predator's diet can significantly weaken the strength of predator–prey interactions. These results have major implications for ecological theory on species interactions in simple vs. complex communities. We discuss our findings in terms of the relationship between diversity and stability.

Key words: biodiversity; functional response; interaction modification; microcosms; non-prey species; Paramecium aurelia; predator–prey model; predatory flatworm; Stenostomum virginianum.

INTRODUCTION

A predator's intake rate as a function of prey density is known as its functional response (Solomon 1949, Holling 1959). This relationship is an important component of community and food web models that are central to theoretical ecology and its applications in conservation biology, fisheries management, and biological control. However, experimental studies of functional responses are usually carried out in simplified systems in which predators only encounter a single prey species (e.g., Hassell 1978, Gross et al. 1993). Much of the structural complexity and diversity of non-prey species in the food web are often excluded from experimental set ups, even though these may have substantial effects on a predator's ability to locate and pursue prey in nature. Nearly all functional responses published in the literature suffer from this simplification. As a result, much of current predator–prey theory may contribute more to understanding trophic interactions in relatively contrived laboratory settings than give insight into predation and food web dynamics in realistic natural environments.

Naturally, there is good reason to exclude much of the complexity observed in the real world when modeling or performing experiments. Most of the non-prey species in a food web are irrelevant to particular predator–prey interactions. However, for each specific predator, a

subset of species will modify its interaction with any given prey. This may occur for a variety of reasons. Some non-prey species provide structural complexity that allows prey to avoid and evade predators more easily (Mayer et al. 2001, Grabowski 2004). Other species provide a masking background in terms of infochemical cues or a cryptic background in terms of visual cues that make prey less detectable (Wootton 1992, Vos et al. 2001). Some non-prey may be similar to prey in one or more aspects of their shapes, colors, sounds, or odors, and these similarities may cause confusion in predators. All of the above effects force predators to spend increasing amounts of time on information processing as the diversity of "relevant" non-prey and the ratio of such non-prey to prey in the environment increase (Vos et al. 2001).

These kinds of effects are a form of interaction modification (Abrams 1983, Wootton 1993), where one species alters the interaction between individuals of two other species. There is a growing recognition that interaction modifications are likely to be important in nature (e.g., Anholt and Werner 1995, 1998, Peckarsky and McIntosh 1998, Cardinale et al. 2003, Polomo et al. 2003). However, few studies have started to address consequences of interaction modifications in communities caused by species diversity (but see Vos et al. 2001, Thébault and Loreau 2006).

Empirical studies across many taxa (Drutz 1976, Kareiva 1985, Stachowicz and Hay 1999, Mayer et al. 2001, Vos et al. 2001, Grabowski 2004, van Veen et al. 2005) show that a non-prey species may interfere with the foraging behavior of predators and parasitoids and

Manuscript received 6 September 2006; revised 16 January 2007; accepted 22 March 2007. Corresponding Editor: D. K. Skelly.
[3] E-mail: pavelk@uvic.ca

1917

SEQUENCE / NAME

8. Kratina P, Vos M, Anholt BR. Species diversity modulates predation. Ecology. 2007;88(8):1917-1923.

NAME-YEAR

Kratina P, Vos M, Anholt BR. 2007. Species diversity modulates predation. Ecology. 88(8):1917-1923.

IMPORTANT DETAILS FOR CITING PERIODICALS

- **TITLES:** Capitalize article titles as you would a book chapter. Abbreviate the title of scholarly journals; capitalize all the abbreviated words in the title.
- **DATE:** For periodicals with no volume or issue numbers, provide the year, month, and day. Abbreviate months to the first three letters: *Jan, Feb, Mar,* and so on.

8. ARTICLE IN A JOURNAL

SEQUENCE / NAME

8. Author's Last Name Initials. Title of article. Title of Journal. Year;Volume(issue):Pages.

8. Mitchell SL, Teno JM, Kiely DK, Shaffer ML, Jones RN, Prigerson HG, Volicer L, Givens JL, Hamel MB. The clinical course of advanced dementia. New Engl J Med. 2009;361(16):1529-1538.

NAME-YEAR

Author's Last Name Initials. Year. Title of article. Title of Journal. Volume(issue):Pages.

Mitchell SL, Teno JM, Kiely DK, Shaffer ML, Jones RN, Prigerson HG, Volicer L, Givens JL, Hamel MB. 2009. The clinical course of advanced dementia. New Eng J Med. 361(16):1529-1538.

9. ARTICLE IN A WEEKLY JOURNAL OR MAGAZINE

SEQUENCE / NAME

9. Author's Last Name Initials. Title of article. Title of Magazine. Year Month Day:Pages.

9. Wiberg K. Envisioning the ecocity. World Watch. 2010 Mar-Apr:10-19.

NAME-YEAR

Author's Last Name Initials. Year. Title of article. Title of Magazine. Month Day:Pages.

Wiberg K. 2010. Envisioning the ecocity. World Watch. Mar-Apr:10-19.

If a magazine has volume and issue numbers, cite them as you would for a journal.

SEQUENCE / NAME

9. Millius S. Virus makes liars of squash plants. Science News.
   2010;177(2):8.

NAME-YEAR

Millius S. 2010. Virus makes liars of squash plants. Science News.
177(2):8.

10. ARTICLE IN A NEWSPAPER

SEQUENCE / NAME

10. Author's Last Name Initials. Title of article. Title of Newspaper
    (Edition). Year Month Day;Sect. section letter or number:first
    page of article (col. column number).

10. Singer N. Artery disease in some very old patients: doctors test
    mummies at a Cairo museum and find signs of atherosclerosis.
    New York Times (New England Ed.). 2009 Nov 24;Sect. D:6 (col. 3).

NAME-YEAR

Author's Last Name Initials. Year Month Day. Title of article. Title of
Newspaper (Edition). Sect. section letter or number:first page of
article (col. column number).

Singer N. 2009 Nov 24. Artery disease in some very old patients:
doctors test mummies at a Cairo museum and find signs of
atherosclerosis. New York Times (New England Ed.). Sect. D:6 (col. 3).

Online Sources

Many citations for Internet sources begin with basic elements—author of work; title of work; and publication information. In addition, you usually need to include several other items, such as the title of the website, medium, access date, and URL.

IMPORTANT DETAILS FOR CITING ONLINE SOURCES

- **TITLES**: Format the titles of books, journals, and articles on the Web as you would for print sources. For titles of other Web materials, including home pages, reproduce the wording, capitalization, and punctuation as they appear on the site.

- **MEDIUM**: Indicate that a book, journal, magazine, or newspaper is online by writing *[Internet]*.

- **PUBLICATION CITY**: If you cannot identify the city of publication, write *[place unknown]*.

- **PUBLISHER**: List the person or organization that sponsors the website as the publisher. If you cannot identify the publisher, write *[publisher unknown]*.

- **DATES**: Whenever possible, cite three dates: the date a work was first published on the Internet or the copyright date; the date of its latest update; and the date you accessed it.

- **PAGES, DOCUMENT NUMBERS, LENGTH**: For online articles with a document number instead of page numbers, include the document number. If there are no page numbers and no document number, indicate the length in brackets: *[2 screens]*, *[8 paragraphs]*.

- **URL**: Break URLs that won't fit on one line after a slash, but do not add a hyphen. If the URL ends with a slash, follow it with a period (as in no. 16). If a DOI (Digital Object Identifier) is available, list it after the URL; CSE does not consider DOIs essential.

11. ONLINE BOOK

SEQUENCE / NAME

11. Author's Last Name Initials. Title [Medium]. Publication City: Publisher; Year of publication [cited Year Month Day]. Available from: URL

11. Dean L. Blood groups and red cell antigens [Internet]. Bethesda (MD): National Library of Medicine; 2005 [cited 2009 Nov 25].

Available from: http://www.ncbi.nlm.nih.gov/bookshelf/
br.fcgi?book=rbcantigen

NAME-YEAR

Author's Last Name Initials. Year of publication. Title [Medium].
Publication City: Publisher; [cited Year Month Day]. Available from:
URL

Dean L. 2005. Blood groups and red cell antigens [Internet].
Bethesda (MD): National Library of Medicine; [cited 2009 Nov 25].
Available from: http://www.ncbi.nlm.nih.gov/bookshelf/
br.fcgi?book=rbcantigen

To cite a chapter of an online book, include the title of the part after
the publication information.

12. ARTICLE ACCESSED THROUGH A DATABASE

CSE does not provide specific guidelines for citing articles from an
online database. This model is based on its guidelines for citing an
online journal article. Include the document number if the database
assigns one.

SEQUENCE / NAME

12. Author's Last Name Initials. Title of article. Title of Periodical
    [Medium]. Date of publication [updated Year Month Day; cited
    Year Month Day]; Volume(issue):Pages or length. Name of
    Database. Available from: URL of database. Database Doc No
    number.

12. Kemker BE, Stierwalt JAG, LaPointe LL, Heald GR. Effects of a cell
    phone conversation on cognitive processing performances. J
    Amer Acad Audiol [Internet]. 2009 [cited 2009 Nov 29];20(9):582-
    588. Academic Search Premier. Available from: http://web.
    ebscohost.com. Database Doc No 45108388.

Documentation Map (CSE)

ARTICLE ACCESSED THROUGH A DATABASE

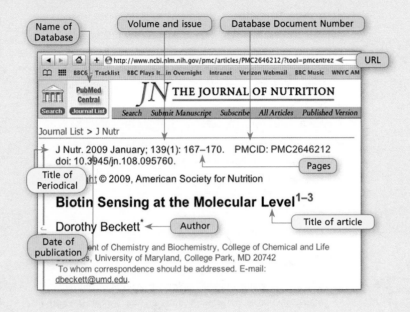

SEQUENCE / NAME

12. Beckett D. Biotin sensing at the molecular level. J Nutr [Internet].
    2009 [cited 2010 Mar 2];139(1):167-170. PubMed Central.
    Available from: http://www.ncbi.nlm.nih.gov/pmc. Database Doc
    No PMC2646212.

NAME-YEAR

Beckett D. 2009. Biotin sensing at the molecular level. J Nutr
[Internet]. [cited 2010 Mar 2];139(1):167-170. PubMed Central.
Available from: http://www.ncbi.nlm.nih.gov/pmc. Database Doc
No PMC2646212.

NAME-YEAR

Author's Last Name Initials. Date of publication. Title of article. Title of Periodical [Medium]. [updated Year Month Day; cited Year Month Day];Volume(issue):Pages or length. Name of Database. Available from: URL of database. Database Doc No number.

Kemker BE, Stierwalt JAG, LaPointe LL, Heald GR. 2009. Effects of cell phone conversation on cognitive processing performances. J Amer Acad Audiol [Internet]. [cited 2009 Nov 29];20(9):582-588. Academic Search Premier. Available from: http://web.ebscohost .com. Database Doc No 45108388.

13. ARTICLE IN AN ONLINE JOURNAL

SEQUENCE / NAME

13. Author's Last Name Initials. Title of article. Title of Journal [Medium]. Year of publication [updated Year Month Day; cited Year Month Day];Volume(issue):Pages or length. Available from: URL

13. Voelker R. Medical simulation gets real. JAMA [Internet]. 2009 [cited 2009 Nov 25];302(20):2190–2192. Available from: http:// jama.ama-assn.org/cgi/content/full/302/20/2190

NAME-YEAR

Author's Last Name Initials. Year of publication. Title of article. Title of Journal [Medium]. [updated Year Month Day; cited Year Month Day];Volume(issue):Pages or length. Available from: URL

Voelker R. 2009. Medical simulation gets real. JAMA [Internet]. [cited 2009 Nov 5];302(20):2190-2192. Available from: http:// jama.ama-assn.org/cgi/content/full/302/20/2190

14. ARTICLE IN AN ONLINE NEWSPAPER

SEQUENCE / NAME

14. Author's Last Name Initials. Title of article. Title of Newspaper [Medium]. Publication City (State): Publisher; Year Month Day [cited Year Month Day];Pages or length. Available from: URL

14. Sohn E. Omega-3 fatty acids are key to a healthier life. Los Angeles Times [Internet]. Los Angeles (CA): Tribune; 2010 Apr 26 [cited 2010 May 2];[about 8 screens]. Available from: http://articles.latimes.com/2010/apr/26/health/la-he-omega-3s-20100426

NAME-YEAR

Author's Last Name Initials. Year Month Day. Title of article. Title of Newspaper [Medium]. Publication City (State): Publisher; [cited Year Month Day];Pages or length. Available from: URL

Sohn E. 2010 Apr 26. Omega-3 fatty acids are key to healthier life. Los Angeles Times [Internet]. Los Angeles (CA): Tribune; [cited 2010 May 2];[about 8 screens]. Available from: http://articles.latimes.com/2010/apr/26/health/la=he=omega=3s=20100426

15. WEBSITE

If no individual is identified as author, begin with the title of the site. If an organization is the only author given, begin with the title of the site and give the organization's name as the publisher.

SEQUENCE / NAME

15. Author's Last Name Initials. Title of Site [Medium]. Publication City (State): Publisher; Year of publication [updated Year Month Day; cited Year Month Day]. Available from: URL

15. American Wind Energy Association [Internet]. Washington (DC): American Wind Energy Association; c1996-2010 [cited 2010 Mar 17]. Available from: http://www.awea.org

NAME-YEAR

If there is no individual author and you begin with the title of the site, give the year of publication after the title and medium.

> Author's Last Name Initials. Year of publication. Title of Site
> [Medium]. Publication City (State): Publisher; [updated Year Month
> Day; cited Year Month Day]. Available from: URL

> American Wind Energy Association [Internet]. 1996-2010.
> Washington (DC): American Wind Energy Association; [cited 2010
> Mar 17]. Available from: http://www.awea.org

16. PART OF A WEBSITE

When citing a government website, include the country's abbreviation in parentheses if it is not part of the name.

SEQUENCE / NAME

> 16. Title of Site [Medium]. Publication City: Publisher; Year of site
>   publication. Title of part; Year Month Day of part publication
>   [updated Year Month Day; cited Year month Day];[length of
>   part]. Available from: URL of part

> 16. U.S. Environmental Protection Agency [Internet]. Research
>   Triangle Park (NC): U.S. Environmental Protection Agency, Office
>   of Air Quality Planning and Standards. Our nation's air: status
>   and trends through 2008; 2010 Feb [updated 2010 Apr 1; cited
>   2010 Nov 15];[54 p.]. Available from: http://www.epa.gov/
>   airtrends/2010/.

NAME-YEAR

> Title of Site [Medium]. Year of site publication. Publication City
> (State): Publisher. Title of part; Year Month day of part publication
> [updated Year Month Day; cited Year Month Day];[length of part].
> Available from: URL of part.

> U.S. Environmental Protection Agency [Internet]. 2010 Feb. Research
> Triangle Park (NC): U.S. Environmental Protection Agency, Office of

Air Quality Planning and Standards. Our nation's air: status and
trends through 2008 [updated 2010 Apr 1; cited 2010 Nov 15];
[54 p.]. Available from: http://www.epa.gov/airtrends/2010/.

If the author of the part you are citing is different from the author
of the site, begin with the former author's name and the title of the
part, and do not not give the title of the complete website.

SEQUENCE / NAME

16. Author's Last Name Initials. Title of part. [Medium]. Publication
    City (State): Publisher; Year Month Day of part publication
    [updated Year Month Day; cited Year Month Day]. [Length of
    part]. Available from: URL of part

16. Macklin SA. PICES metadata federation [Internet]. Sidney (BC):
    PICES North Pacific Marine Science Organization; 2008 Nov [cited
    2010 May 2]. [15 paragraphs]. Available from: http://
    www.pices.int/projects/npem/default.aspx

NAME-YEAR

Author's Last Name Initials. Year Month Day of part publication.
Title of part [Medium]. Publication City (State): Publisher; [updated
Year Month Day; cited Year Month Day]. [Length of part]. Available
from: URL of part

Macklin SA. 2008 Nov. PICES metadata federation [Internet].
Sidney (BC): PICES North Pacific Marine Science Organization;
[cited 2010 May 2]. [15 paragraphs]. Available from: http://
www.pices.int/projects/npem/default.aspx

Citing Sources Not Covered by CSE

To cite a source for which CSE does not provide guidelines, look for
models similar to the source you are citing. Give any information
readers will need in order to find your source themselves—author;
title; publisher, date of publication, information about electronic
retrieval (such as the medium, URL, and date of citation), and any

other pertinent information. You might want to try your citation your-self, to be sure it will lead others to your source.

CSE-c Formatting a Paper

Title page. CSE does not provide guidelines for college papers. Check to see if your instructor prefers a separate title page; if so, include your name, the title of your paper, your instructor's name, the name of the course, and the date.

Page numbers and running head. Put the page number and a short version of your title in the top right-hand corner of each page except for the title page.

Margins and line spacing. Leave one-inch margins all around the page; double-space your text but single-space your list of references, leaving a line space between entries.

Headings. Especially when your paper is long, or when it has clear parts, headings can help readers to follow your argument. Center headings but without adding any extra space above or below.

Abstract. If you are required to include an **ABSTRACT**, put it on its own page after the title page, with the word *Abstract* centered at the top of the page.

Long quotations. When you are quoting forty or more words, set them off from your text, indented slightly from the left margin. Do not enclose such quotations in quotation marks. Indicate the source in a **SIGNAL PHRASE** before the quotation or in parentheses at the end, after any final punctuation. In either case, include a superscript note number to the full source citation as well.

Interpreting data from NASA probes, Edward Bell[9] described sunrise on Mercury.

> Sunrise and sunset on Mercury are spectacles to behold. Two and one half times larger in the sky than seen on Earth, the sun appears to rise and set twice during a Mercurian day. It rises, then arcs across the sky, stops, moves back toward the rising

horizon, stops again, and finally restarts its journey toward the setting horizon. These aerial maneuvers occur because Mercury rotates three times for every two orbits around the sun and because Mercury's orbit is very elliptical.

Illustrations. Insert each illustration close to where it is referred to. Number and label each one (Table 1, Figure 3) and provide a descriptive title (Figure 5 Structure and bonding in ethylene). Titles use sentence-style capitalization. Figures include charts, graphs, maps, photographs, and other types of illustrations. Number tables and figures consecutively, using separate numbering for tables and figures.

References. Start your list of sources on a new page at the end of your paper; center the heading *References* at the top of the page. CSE single-spaces entries and separates them with a line space. For citation-sequence and citation-name format, number each entry and align subsequent lines of each entry below the first word of the first line. For name-year format, begin each line of the entry at the left margin.

CSE-d Sample Pages

The following sample pages are from "Guppies and Goldilocks: Models and Evidence of Two Types of Speciation," a paper written by Pieter Spealman for an undergraduate biology course. They are formatted in the citation-sequence format according to the guidelines of *Scientific Style and Format: The CSE Manual for Authors, Editors, and Publishers*, 7th edition (2006). To read the complete paper, go to **wwnorton.com/write/little-seagull-handbook.**

Sample Title Page, CSE Style

Title and name centered.

Guppies and Goldilocks: Models and Evidence

of Two Types of Speciation

Pieter Spealman

Course title, instructor's name, date.

Biology 38

Professor Lipke

February 17, 2010

Sample Page of Research Paper, CSE Style

1"   Two Types of Speciation   1

Brief title and page number.

Determining how a given species has arisen is a central question for any field biologist. There are two competing models of speciation: allopatric and sympatric. In 1859, Charles Darwin[1] asserted that speciation could be sympatric, saying, "I believe that many perfectly defined species have been formed on strictly continuous areas." One hundred years later, Ernst Mayr[2] contested Darwin's assertion, saying, "All the evidence that has accumulated since Darwin indicates that this assumption [that species have been formed on strictly continuous areas] is unwarranted as far as higher animals are concerned." Was Mayr right to condemn Darwin for failing to assess correctly the lessons of nature that he observed in the Galapagos archipelago? The difficulty of determining the provenance of a species—whether it arose through sympatric or allopatric speciation—lies in knowing what to look for. And while recent research employing computer simulations[3] suggests a solution to the problem by providing a set of criteria necessary for sympatric speciation, the results predicted by those simulations did not actually arise in the field study that provides the most comprehensive data available to test the model. Rather than *1"* invalidating the model, however, this research points to the challenges that complex natural environments pose to the isolation of observable criteria for distinguishing the two types of speciation.

Superscript number to cite source.

Double-spaced text.

Words added to a quotation are enclosed in brackets.

1"

Allopatric and Sympatric: Conditions and Examples

The two types of speciation differ in their view of what conditions are crucial in determining whether speciation can occur. Allopatric speciation, which Mayr[2] championed, explains the divergence of species by physical isolation, as when a population

Headings help organize the paper.

In citation-sequence style, source previously cited uses same number as first citation.

1"

Sample Page of Reference List, CSE Style

Heading centered. .... References

Entries are single-spaced with a line space between each. Subsequent lines of entries align below the first.

1. Darwin C. On the origin of species. In: Wilson EO, editor. From so simple a beginning. New York (NY): Norton; 2006. p. 441-760.

2. Mayr E. Isolation as an evolutionary factor. Proc Am Philos Soc. 1959;103(2):221-230.

3. van Doorn GS, Edelaar P, Weissing FJ. On the origin of species by natural and sexual selection. Science. 2009;326(5960):1704-1707.

4. Schilthuizen M. Frogs, flies, and dandelions: speciation—the evolution of new species. New York (NY): Oxford University Press; 2001.

5. Grant BR, Grant PR. Darwin's finches: population variation and sympatric speciation. Proc Nat Acad Sci USA. 1979;76(4):2359-2363.

6. Endler JA. Natural selection on color patterns in *Poecilia reticulata*. Evolution [Internet]. 1980 [cited 2010 Feb 7];34(1):76-91. Available from: http://jstor.org/stable/2408316

7. Weiner J. The beak of the finch. New York (NY): Vintage; 1994.

8. Smith JM. Sympatric speciation. Am Nat [Internet]. 1966 [cited 2010 Feb 7];100(916):637-650. Available from: http://jstor.org/stable/2459301

9. Stewart P. Galapagos: islands that changed the world. New Haven (CT): Yale University Press; 2006.

Citation-sequence format: Sources numbered in the sequence they appear in the text.

Edit

We edit to let the fire show through
the smoke.

—ARTHUR PLOTNIK

S-1   Complete Sentences

In casual situations, we often use a kind of shorthand, because we know our audience will fill in the gaps. When we say to a dinner guest, "Coffee?" he knows we mean, "Would you like some coffee?" When we email a friend, "7:00 at Starbucks?" our friend will understand that we are asking, "Should we meet at 7:00 at Starbucks?" In more formal writing or speaking situations, though, our audience may not share the same context, so to be sure we're understood we usually need to present our ideas in complete sentences. This section reviews the parts of a sentence.

S-1a Elements of a Sentence

Subjects and predicates

A sentence contains a subject and a predicate. The subject, usually a **NOUN** or **PRONOUN**, names the topic of the sentence; the predicate, which always includes a **VERB**, says what the subject is or does.

> s p
> ▶ Birds fly.

> s ┌────────p────────┐
> ▶ Birds are feathered vertebrates.

The subject and the predicate each may contain only one word. Usually, however, both the subject and the predicate contain more than one word.

> ┌──────────s──────────┐┌──────────p──────────┐
> ▶ Birds of many kinds fly south in the fall.

A sentence may contain more than one subject or verb.

> s s v
> ▶ Birds and butterflies fly south in the fall.

> s v v
> ▶ Birds fly south in the fall and return north in the spring.

At times, the subject comes after the verb.

▶ Here comes the sun.

Expressing subjects explicitly

English requires an explicit subject in every **CLAUSE**, even if all of the clauses in a sentence are about the same subject.

> *it*
▶ Although the dinner cost too much, impressed my guests.
                                      ^

The only exception is commands, in which the subject is understood to be *you*.

▶ Eat smaller portions at each meal.

Sentences beginning with *there* or *it*. In some cases the subject comes after the verb and an **EXPLETIVE**—*there* or *it*—comes before the verb.

> *There is*
▶ Is no place like home.
   ^

> *It is*
▶ Is both instructive and rewarding to work with young children.
   ^

You can also rephrase the sentence to avoid using the expletive.

> *Working with young children is*
▶ Is both instructive and rewarding, ~~to work with young children~~.
   ^   ^

If English is not your first language, be aware that English does not emphasize a subject by repeating it in the same clause.

▶ My friend Jing Jing ~~she~~ changed her name to Jane.

▶ The students who visited ~~they~~ were detained at the airport.

Clauses

A clause is a group of words containing a subject and predicate. An independent clause can function alone as a sentence: *Birds fly*. A subordinate clause begins with a **SUBORDINATING WORD** such as *as, because,* or *which* and cannot stand alone as a sentence: *because birds fly.*

┌─INDEPENDENT CLAUSE─┐ ┌─────────SUBORDINATE CLAUSE─────────┐
▶ My yard is now quiet because most of the birds flew south.

Phrases

A phrase is a word group that lacks a subject, a verb, or both and thus cannot stand alone as a sentence. Some common ones are prepositional, appositive, participial, gerund, and infinitive phrases.

A prepositional phrase starts with a **PREPOSITION** such as *at, from, of,* or *in* and usually ends with a noun: *at school, from home, in bed.*

▶ The day *after the World Series* San Francisco celebrated.

An appositive phrase follows and gives additional information about a noun or pronoun. Appositives function as nouns.

▶ I knew I was in the right house because my daddy's only real possession, *a velvet-covered board pinned with medals,* sat inside a glass cabinet on a table.   —Rick Bragg, "All Over But the Shoutin'"

A participial phrase contains the present or past participle of a verb plus any **OBJECTS**, **MODIFIERS**, and **COMPLEMENTS**.

▶ *Brimming with optimism,* I headed over to the neighborhood watering hole and waited.   —Hal Niedzviecki, "Facebook in a Crowd"

▶ A study from Princeton *issued at the same time as the Duke study* showed that women in the sciences reported less satisfaction in their jobs and less of a sense of belonging than their male counterparts.
        —Anna Quindlen, "Still Needing the F Word"

A gerund phrase includes the *-ing* form of a verb plus any objects, modifiers, and complements. It functions as a noun.

▶ For roller coasters, *being the star of summer amusement park rides* certainly has its ups and downs.
        —Cathi Eastman and Becky Burrell, "The Science of Screams"

An infinitive phrase includes an infinitive verb: *to read, to write*) and any objects, modi...

▶ *To commit more troops* seemed crazy when we co...

▶ The point of ribbon decals is *to signal that we support*

S-2 Sentence Fragments

Sentence fragments often show up in advertising: "Got milk?" "Good to the last drop." "Not bad for something that tastes good too." We use them in informal speech and text messages as well. But some readers consider fragments too informal, and in many academic writing situations it's better to avoid them altogether. This section helps you identify and edit out fragments.

S-2a Identifying Fragments

A sentence fragment is a group of words that is capitalized and punctuated as a sentence but is not a sentence. A sentence needs at least one **INDEPENDENT CLAUSE**, which contains a **SUBJECT** and **VERB** and does not start with a **SUBORDINATING WORD**.

NO SUBJECT   The catcher batted fifth. Fouled out, ending the inning.
    Who fouled out?

NO VERB   The first two batters walked. Manny Ramirez again.
    What did Ramirez do again?

SUBORDINATE CLAUSE   Although the Yankees loaded the bases.
    There is a subject (Yankees) and a verb (loaded), but although makes this into a subordinate clause. What happened after the Yankees loaded the bases?

A list of common subordinating words appears on the next page.

SOME SUBORDINATING WORDS

after	because	so that	until	while
although	before	that	when	who
as	if	though	where	which
as if	since	unless	whether	why

Writers often use sentence fragments for emphasis or to be informal.

> **FOR EMPHASIS**   Throughout my elementary and middle school years, I was a strong student, always on the honor roll. I never had a GPA below 3.0. I was smart, and I knew it. *That is, until I got the results of the proficiency test.*
> —Shannon Nichols, " 'Proficiency' "

> **TO BE INFORMAL**   The SAT writing test predicts how successful a student will be in college. *Since when?*

S-2b Editing Fragments

Since some readers regard fragments as errors, it's generally better to write complete sentences. Here are four ways to make fragments into sentences.

Remove the subordinating word

▶ I'm thinking about moving to a large city. ~~Because~~ I dislike the lack of privacy in my country town of three thousand.

Add a subject

        He fouled
▶ The catcher batted fifth. ~~Fouled~~ out, ending the inning.

Add a verb

                   walked
▶ The first two batters walked. Manny Ramirez again.

Sometimes a fragment contains a verb form, such as a present or past participle, that cannot function as the main verb of a sentence.

230 - 235

In these cases, you can either substitute an appropriate verb form or add a **HELPING VERB**.

▶ As the game progressed, the fans' excitement diminished. The pitcher's arm ~~weakening,~~ *weakened,* and the fielders ~~making~~ *made* a number of errors.

▶ The media influence the election process. Political commercials *are* appearing on television more frequently than in years past.

Attach the fragment to a nearby sentence

▶ Some candidates spread nasty stories, *about* ~~About~~ their opponents.

▶ These negative stories can deal with many topics, *, such* ~~Such~~ as marital infidelity, sources of campaign funds, and drug use.

▶ Put off by negative campaigning, *, some* ~~Some~~ people decide not to vote at all.

S-3   Comma Splices, Fused Sentences

When you join two independent clauses using only a comma, you've created a comma splice: "He dropped the bucket, the paint spilled on his feet." Without the comma—"He dropped the bucket the paint spilled on his feet"—it's a fused sentence. You'll sometimes see comma splices and fused sentences in ads or literary works, but they're generally regarded as errors in academic writing. This section shows how to recognize comma splices and fused sentences and edit them out of your writing.

S-3a Identifying Comma Splices and Fused Sentences

A comma splice occurs when an **INDEPENDENT CLAUSE** follows another independent clause with only a comma between them.

COMMA SPLICE	T. S. Eliot is best known for his poetry, he also wrote and produced several plays.

A fused sentence occurs when one independent clause follows another with no punctuation in between.

FUSED SENTENCE	The school board debated the issue for three days they were unable to reach an agreement.

S-3b Editing Comma Splices and Fused Sentences

There are several ways to edit comma splices and fused sentences.

Make the clauses two sentences

▶ T. S. Eliot is best known for his poetry, he also wrote several plays.

Add a comma and a **COORDINATING CONJUNCTION**

▶ The school board debated the issue for three days they were unable to reach an agreement.

Add a semicolon

If the relationship between the two clauses is clear without a coordinating conjunction, you can simply join them with a semicolon.

▶ Psychologists study individuals' behavior, sociologists focus on group-level dynamics.

When clauses are linked by a **TRANSITION** such as *therefore* or *as a result*, the transition needs to be preceded by a semicolon and followed by a comma.

▶ The hill towns experienced heavy spring and summer rain, therefore, the fall foliage fell far short of expectations.

Recast one clause as a subordinate clause

Add a SUBORDINATING WORD to clarify the relationship between the two clauses.

▶ ~~Initial~~ critical responses to *The Waste Land* were mixed, the poem
  Although initial
  has been extensively anthologized, read, and written about.

S-4 Verbs

Verbs are the engines of sentences, giving energy, action, and life to writing. "I Googled it" is much more vivid than "I found it on the Internet"—and the difference is the verb. Sometimes our use of verbs can obscure meaning, however, as when a politician avoids taking responsibility by saying, "Mistakes were made." Our choice of verbs shapes our writing in important ways, and this section reviews ways of using verbs appropriately and effectively.

S-4a Verb Tenses

To express time, English verbs have three simple tenses—present, past, and future. In addition, each of these verb tenses has perfect and progressive forms that indicate more complex time frames. The present perfect, for example, indicates an action that began in the past but is continuing into the present. The lists that follow show each of these tenses for the regular verb *talk* and the irregular verb *write*.

Simple tenses

PRESENT	PAST	FUTURE
I talk	I talked	I will talk
I write	I wrote	I will write

Use the simple present to indicate actions that take place in the present or that occur habitually. Use the simple past to indicate actions that were completed in the past. Use the simple future to indicate actions that will take place in the future.

▶ Every few years the Republicans *propose* a tax cut.
　　　　　—David Brooks, "The Triumph of Hope over Self-Interest"

▶ One day my mother *came* home from Coffee Dan's with an awful story.
　　　　　—Mike Rose, "Potato Chips and Stars"

▶ Prohibiting English *will do* for the language what Prohibition *did* for liquor.　—Dennis Baron, "Don't Make English Official—Ban It Instead"

Use the present tense to express scientific or general facts even when the rest of the sentence is in the past tense.

▶ Agatston showed that South Beach dieters l̶o̶s̶t̶ *lose* about ten pounds in the first two weeks.

In general, use the present tense to write about literature.

▶ In *The Bluest Eye*, Pecola *evokes* the theme of vision when she says that she wishes for blue eyes that will be seen as beautiful and earn her the respect of the cruel people in her life.

▶ As in many fantasy novels and fairy tales, the central character *is* on a quest; however, the narrative of Harry's quest *unfolds* more like a classic mystery.　—Philip Nel, "Fantasy, Mystery, and Ambiguity"

In APA style, use the past tense or the present perfect to report results of an experiment and the present tense to give your own insights into or conclusions about the results.

▶ The bulk of the data collected in this study *validated* the research of Neal Miller; the subjects *appeared* to undergo operant conditioning of their smooth muscles in order to relax their frontalis muscles and increase their skin temperatures. Subjects 3 and 6 each *failed* to do this in one session; subject 7 *failed* to do this several times. This finding *is* difficult to explain precisely.
　　　　　—Sarah Thomas, "The Effect of Biofeedback Training on Muscle Tension and Skin Temperature"

Perfect tenses

PRESENT PERFECT	PAST PERFECT	FUTURE PERFECT
I have talked	I had talked	I will have talked
I have written	I had written	I will have written

Use the present perfect to indicate actions that took place at no specific time in the past or that began in the past and continue into the present.

▶ As a middle-class black I *have* often *felt* myself contriving to be "black."   —Shelby Steele, "On Being Black and Middle Class"

Use the past perfect for an action that was completed before another past action began.

▶ By the time I was born, the Vietnam War ~~already~~ ended.
        had

   The war ended before the writer was born.

Use the future perfect to indicate actions that will be completed at a specific time in the future.

▶ By this time next year, you *will have graduated*.

Progressive tenses

PRESENT PROGRESSIVE	PAST PROGRESSIVE	FUTURE PROGRESSIVE
I am talking	I was talking	I will be talking
I am writing	I was writing	I will be writing

PRESENT PERFECT PROGRESSIVE	PAST PERFECT PROGRESSIVE	FUTURE PERFECT PROGRESSIVE
I have been talking	I had been talking	I will have been talking
I have been writing	I had been writing	I will have been writing

Use progressive tenses to indicate continuing action.

▶ Congress *is considering*, and may soon pass, legislation making English the official language of the United States.
        —Dennis Baron, "Don't Make English Official—Ban It Instead"

▶ The night after Halloween, we *were watching* TV when the doorbell
  rang.   —David Sedaris, "Us and Them"

▶ As they do every year on the Friday before exams, the Kenyon
  Kokosingers *will be singing* next Friday evening in Rosse Hall.

▶ Willie joined the Grace Church Boy Choir when he was ten, and he *has
  been singing* ever since.

S-4b Verb Forms

There are four forms of a verb: the base form, the past, the past participle, and the present participle. Samples of each appear in the lists below. All of the various tenses are generated with these four forms.

The past tense and past participle of all regular verbs are formed by adding *-ed* or *-d* to the base form (*talked, lived*). Irregular verbs are not as predictable; see the list of some common ones below. The present participle consists of the base form plus *-ing* (*talking, living*).

BASE FORM	On Thursdays, we *visit* a museum.
PAST TENSE	Last week, we *visited* the Museum of Modern Art.
PAST PARTICIPLE	I have also *visited* the Metropolitan Museum, but I've not yet *been* to the Cloisters.
PRESENT PARTICIPLE	We will be *visiting* the Cooper-Hewitt Museum tomorrow to see the cutlery exhibit.

Some common irregular verbs

BASE FORM	PAST TENSE	PAST PARTICIPLE	PRESENT PARTICIPLE
be	was/were	been	being
choose	chose	chosen	choosing
do	did	done	doing
eat	ate	eaten	eating
fall	fell	fallen	falling
give	gave	given	giving
go	went	gone	going

BASE FORM	PAST TENSE	PAST PARTICIPLE	PRESENT PARTICIPLE
hang (suspend)	hung	hung	hanging
have	had	had	having
know	knew	known	knowing
lay	laid	laid	laying
lie (recline)	lay	lain	lying
make	made	made	making
prove	proved	proved, proven	proving
rise	rose	risen	rising
set	set	set	setting
sit	sat	sat	sitting
teach	taught	taught	teaching
write	wrote	written	writing

It's easy to get confused about when to use the past tense and when to use a past participle. One simple guideline is to use the past tense if there is no helping verb and to use a past participle if there is one.

▶ For vacation last spring, my family ~~gone~~ *went* to Turkey.

▶ After two weeks in Istanbul, we had ~~ate~~ *eaten* a lot of Turkish delight.

Helping verbs

Do, *have*, *be*, and **MODALS** such as *can* and *may* all function as helping verbs that work with main verbs to express certain verb **TENSES** and **MOODS**. Do, *have*, and *be* change form to indicate tenses; modals do not.

FORMS OF *DO*   do, does, did

FORMS OF *HAVE*   have, has, had

FORMS OF *BE*   be, am, is, are, was, were, been

MODALS   can, could, may, might, must, should, will, would, ought to

Do, *does*, and *did* require the base form of the main verb.

▶ That professor *did take* class participation into account when calculating grades.

▶ Sometimes even the smartest students *do* not *like* to answer questions out loud in class.

Have, has, and *had* require the past participle of the main verb.

▶ I *have written* to my senator to express my views on global warming.

▶ When all of the visitors *had gone,* the security guards locked the building for the night.

Forms of *be* are used with a present participle to express a continuing action or with a past participle to express the PASSIVE VOICE .

CONTINUING ACTION

▶ The university *is considering* a change in its policy on cell phone use.

▶ I *was studying* my notes from last week as I walked to class.

PASSIVE VOICE

▶ Six classes per semester *is considered* a heavy course load.

▶ Ancient Greek *was studied* by many university students in the early twentieth century, but it is not a popular major today.

Modals are used with the base form of the main verb.

▶ After each class, small groups *will meet* for focused discussion.

▶ Each student *should participate* in every group session.

Gerunds and infinitives

A gerund is a verb form ending in *-ing* that functions as a noun: *hopping, skipping, jumping.*

▶ Although many people like *driving,* some prefer *walking.*

An infinitive is *to* plus the base form of a verb: *to hop, to skip, to jump.*

▶ Although many people like *to drive,* some prefer *to walk.*

In general, use infinitives to express intentions or desires, and use gerunds to express plain facts.

▶ I planned *to learn* Spanish, Japanese, and Arabic.

▶ I also wanted *to know* Russian.

▶ Unfortunately, I ended up *studying* only Spanish and Arabic—and *speaking* only Spanish.

▶ Just in time for Thanksgiving, the painters finished ~~to put~~ up the wallpaper.
  putting

With several verbs—*forget, remember, stop,* and a few others—the choice of an infinitive or gerund changes the meaning.

▶ I stopped *to eat* lunch.

  In other words, I took a break so that I could eat lunch.

▶ I stopped *eating* lunch.

  In other words, I no longer ate lunch.

Always use a gerund after a **PREPOSITION**.

▶ The water is too cold for ~~to swim.~~
  swimming.

S-4c Active and Passive Voice

Verbs can be active or passive. When a verb is in the active voice, the subject performs the action (*she threw the ball*). When a verb is in the passive voice, the subject receives the action (*the ball was thrown to her*).

ACTIVE   The wealthiest 1 percent of the American population
holds 38 percent of the total national wealth.
—Gregory Mantsios, "Class in America—2003"

PASSIVE   By the 1970s, Leslie had developed a distinctive
figural style in which subjects *are shown* in frontal,
confrontational poses, at close range.
—David S. Rubin, "It's the Same Old Song"

Active verbs tend to be more direct and easier to understand, but the passive voice can be useful when you specifically want to emphasize the recipient of the action.

▶ In a sense, little girls *are urged* to please adults with a kind of coquettishness, while boys *are enjoined* to behave like monkeys toward each other.   —Paul Theroux, "Being a Man"

The passive voice is also appropriate in scientific writing when you wish to emphasize the research itself, not the researchers.

▶ The treatment order was random for each subject, and it *was reversed* for his or her second treatment.
                    —Sarah Thomas, "The Effect of Biofeedback Training
                    on Muscle Tension and Skin Temperature"

S-4d Mood

There are three moods in English: indicative, imperative, and subjunctive. The indicative is used to state facts, opinions, or questions.

▶ Thanks to its many volunteers, Habitat for Humanity *has built* twelve houses in the region this year.

▶ What other volunteer opportunities *does* Habitat *offer*?

The imperative is used to give commands or directions.

▶ *Sit* up straight, and *do* your work.

The subjunctive is used to indicate hypothetical or unlikely conditions or to express wishes or requests.

▶ She would be happier if she *had* less pressure at work.

▶ My mother wishes my brother *were* more responsible with his money.

Conditional sentences   2 4 5 - 2 5 0

The subjunctive is used most often in conditional sentences, ones that include a clause beginning with *if* or another word that states a condition. Use the indicative to show you are confident the condition can be met and the subjunctive to show it's doubtful or impossible.

If it's a fact. When there's no doubt that the information in the *if* clause is true or possible, use the same tense in both clauses.

▶ If an earthquake *strikes* that region, forecasters *expect* a tsunami.

▶ A century ago, if a hurricane *hit*, residents *had* very little warning.

If it's a possibility. When the information in the *if* clause is probably possible, use the present tense in the *if* clause and a modal such as *will* or *might* + the base form of the verb in the other clause.

▶ If you faithfully *follow* the South Beach Diet for two weeks, you *will lose* about ten pounds.

If it's hypothetical, or unlikely. When the information in the *if* clause is not likely to be possible, use the past form in the *if* clause and *would* (or *could* or *might*) + the base form of the verb in the other clause. For *be*, use *were* in the *if* clause, not *was*.

▶ If doctors *discovered* a cure for cancer, they *could save* millions of lives.

▶ If Martin Luther King Jr. *were* alive, he *would acknowledge* progress in race relations, but he *would* also *ask* significant questions.

When the *if* clause is about an event in the past that never happened, use the past perfect in the *if* clause and *would have* (or *could have* or *might have*) + a past participle in the other clause.

▶ If the police officer *had separated* the witnesses, their evidence *would have been* admissible in court.

Requests and demands

Use the subjunctive in *that* clauses following verbs such as *ask, insist,* or *suggest* in order to express a request, a demand, or a recommendation. Use the base form of the verb in the *that* clause.

▶ I recommend that Hannah *study* French as an undergraduate.

▶ The CEO will insist that you *be* at your desk before nine each morning.

S-5   Subject-Verb Agreement

Subjects and verbs should agree: if the subject is in the third-person singular, the verb should be in the third-person singular—"Dinner is on the table." Yet sometimes context affects subject-verb agreement, as when we say that "macaroni and cheese *are* available in most grocery stores" but that "macaroni and cheese *is* our family's favorite comfort food." This section focuses on subject-verb agreement.

S-5a Agreement in Number and Person

Subjects and verbs should agree with each other in number (singular or plural) and person (first, second, or third). To make a present-tense verb agree with a third-person singular subject, add *-s* or *-es* to the base form.

▶ A 1922 *ad* for Resinol soap *urges* women to "make that dream come true" by using Resinol.   —Doug Lantry, "'Stay Sweet As You Are'"

To make a present-tense verb agree with any other subject, simply use the base form without any ending.

▶ *I listen* to NPR every morning while I brush my teeth.

▶ *Drunk drivers cause* thousands of preventable deaths each year.

Be and *have* have irregular forms (shown on pp. 240 and 241) and so do not follow the -s/-es rule.

▶ The test of all knowledge *is* experiment.
—Richard Feynman, "Atoms in Motion"

▶ The scientist *has* a lot of experience with ignorance and doubt and uncertainty, and this experience is of great importance.
—Richard Feynman, "The Value of Science"

S-5b Subjects and Verbs Separated

A verb should agree with its subject, not with another word that falls in between.

▶ In the backyard, the *leaves* of the apple tree *rattle* across the lawn.
—Gary Soto, "The Guardian Angel"

▶ The *price* of soybeans ~~fluctuate~~ according to demand.
  fluctuates
  ^

S-5c Compound Subjects

Two or more subjects joined by *and* are generally plural.

▶ Obviously, safety and security *are* important issues in American life.
—Andie McDonie, "Airport Security"

However, if the parts of the subject form a single unit, they take a singular verb.

▶ Forty acres and a mule ~~are~~ what General William T. Sherman promised each freed slave.
  is
  ^

If the subjects are joined by *or* or *nor*, the verb should agree with the closer subject.

▶ Either you or she ~~are~~ mistaken.
  is
  ^

▶ Neither the teacher nor his students ~~was~~ able to solve the equation.
  were
  ^

S-5d Subjects That Follow the Verb

English verbs usually follow their subjects. Be sure the verb agrees with the subject even when the subject follows the verb, such as when the sentence begins with *there is* or *there are*.

▶ There *is* too many unresolved problems for the project to begin.
     are

▶ In the middle of the baby pool *is* a hot tub, just for little kids.
                        —Michael Lewis, *Home Game*

S-5e Collective Nouns

Collective nouns such as *group, team, audience,* or *family* can take singular or plural verbs, depending on whether the noun refers to the group as a single unit or to the individual members of the group.

▶ The choir *sing* The *Messiah* every Christmas.
       sings

▶ Gregor's family *keep* reassuring themselves that things will be just fine again.   —Scott Russell Sanders, "Under the Influence"

The individual members of the family reassure one another.

S-5f *Everyone* and Other Indefinite Pronouns

Most **INDEFINITE PRONOUNS**, such as *anyone, anything, each, either, everybody, everything, neither, nobody, no one, one, somebody, someone,* and *something,* take a singular verb.

▶ But . . . no one *is* selling the content that gets shared on P2P services.
                        —Lawrence Lessig, "Some Like It Hot"

▶ Each of the candidates *agree* with the president.
              agrees

Both, few, many, others, and *several* are always plural.

▶ Already, few *know* how to read a serious book.
> —Paul West, "Borrowed Time"

All, any, enough, more, most, none, and *some* are singular when they refer to a singular noun, but they are plural whenever they refer to a plural noun.

▶ Don't assume that all of the members of a family ~~votes~~ the same way.
> vote

▶ None of the music we heard last night ~~come~~ from the baroque period.
> comes

S-5g   *Who, That,* or *Which*

The **RELATIVE PRONOUNS** *who, that,* and *which* take a singular verb when they come after a singular noun and a plural verb when they come after a plural noun.

▶ I find it refreshing to have work that *rewards* initiative and effort.
> —Lars Eighner, "On Dumpster Diving"

▶ We fell in with some other hippie-groupie types who *were* obsessed with Hendrix, the Doors, Janis Joplin, and Zeppelin as well as the Stones.   —Susan Jane Gilman, "Mick Jagger Wants Me"

One of the is always followed by a plural noun, and the verb should be plural.

▶ Jaime is one of the speakers who ~~asks~~ provocative questions.
> ask

Several speakers ask provocative questions. Jaime is one. Who refers to speakers, so the verb is plural.

The only one, however, takes a singular verb.

▶ Jaime is the only one of the speakers who ~~ask~~ provocative questions.
> asks

Only one speaker asks provocative questions: Jaime. Who thus refers to one, so the verb is singular.

S-5h Singular Words Such as *News* and *Physics*

Words like *news*, *athletics*, and *politics* seem plural but are in fact singular in meaning and take singular verb forms.

▶ The *news* of widespread dismissals *alarms* everyone in the company.

Nouns such as *economics*, *mathematics*, *politics*, and *statistics* are often singular but have plural meanings in some uses.

▶ For my roommate, mathematics *is* an endlessly stimulating field.

▶ The complex mathematics involved in this proof *are* beyond the scope of this lecture.

S-5i Titles and Words Used as Words

Titles and words that you discuss as words are singular.

▶ *The Royal Tenenbaums* ~~depict~~ *depicts* three talented siblings who are loosely based on characters created by J. D. Salinger.

▶ *Man-caused disasters* ~~are~~ *is* a term favored by some political analysts as a substitute for the term *terrorist attacks.*

S-6 Pronouns

We use pronouns to take the place of nouns so that we don't have to write or say the same word or name over and over. Imagine how repetitive our writing would be without pronouns: *Little Miss Muffet sat on a tuffet eating Little Miss Muffet's curds and whey.* Luckily, we have pronouns, and this section demonstrates how to use them clearly.

S-6a Pronoun-Antecedent Agreement

A pronoun must agree with its antecedent in gender and number.

IN GENDER   *Grandma* took *her* pie out of the oven.

IN NUMBER   *My grandparents* spent weekends at *their* cabin on
White Bear Lake.

Generic nouns

A noun that is used as a typical example of the members of a group
can be either singular or plural; make sure that your pronoun agrees
with the noun antecedent.

▶ A lab technician should always wear goggles to protect ~~their~~ *his or her* eyes
while working with chemicals.

▶ ~~A lab technician~~ *Lab technicians* should always wear goggles to protect their eyes
while working with chemicals.

Indefinite pronouns

INDEFINITE PRONOUNS such as *anyone, each, either, everyone, neither, no
one, someone,* and *something* take a singular pronoun.

▶ Everyone in the class did ~~their~~ *his or her* best.

If you find *his or her* awkward, you can rewrite the sentence.

▶ ~~Everyone~~ *All of the students* in the class did their best.

Collective nouns

Collective nouns such as *audience, committee,* or *team* take a singular
pronoun when they refer to the group as a whole and a plural pronoun when they refer to members of the group as individuals.

▶ The winning team drew ~~their~~ *its* inspiration from the manager.

▶ The winning team threw ~~its~~ *their* gloves in the air.

He, his, and other masculine pronouns

To avoid **SEXIST LANGUAGE**, use *he*, *him*, *his*, or *himself* only when you know that the antecedent is male.

▶ Before meeting a new doctor, many people worry about not liking him *or her*.

S-6b Pronoun Reference

A pronoun needs to have a clear antecedent, a specific word to which the pronoun points.

▶ My grandmother spent a lot of time reading to me. She mostly read the standards, like *The Little Engine That Could*.

      —Richard Bullock, "How I Learned about the Power of Writing"

Ambiguous reference

A pronoun is ambiguous if it could refer to more than one antecedent.

▶ After I plugged the printer into the computer, ~~it~~ *the printer* sputtered and died.

What sputtered and died—the computer or the printer? The edit makes the reference clear.

Implied reference

If a pronoun does not refer clearly to a specific word, rewrite the sentence to omit the pronoun, or insert an antecedent.

Unclear reference of *this, that,* and *which*. These three pronouns must refer to specific antecedents.

▶ Ultimately, the Justice Department did not insist on the breakup of Microsoft, ~~which~~ *an oversight that* set the tone for a liberal merger policy.

Indefinite use of *they*, *it*, and *you*.   *They* and it should be used only to refer to people or things that have been specifically mentioned. *You* should be used only to address your reader.

▶ ~~In many~~ European countries, ~~they~~ don't allow civilians to carry handguns.
   Many ^

▶ ~~On the~~ weather station, ~~it~~ said that storms would hit Key West today.
   The ^

▶ Many doctors argue that age should not be an impediment to
   physical exercise ~~if you~~ have always been active.
                   for people who ^

S-6c Pronoun Case

The pronouns in the list below change case according to how they function in a sentence. There are three cases: subjective, objective, and possessive. Pronouns functioning as subjects or subject complements are in the subjective case; those functioning as objects are in the objective case; those functioning as possessives are in the possessive case.

SUBJECTIVE   *We* lived in a rented house three blocks from the school.

OBJECTIVE   I went to my room and shut the door behind *me*.

POSSESSIVE   All *my* life chocolate has made me ill.

—David Sedaris, "Us and Them"

SUBJECTIVE	OBJECTIVE	POSSESSIVE
I	me	my / mine
we	us	our / ours
you	you	your / yours
he / she / it	him / her / it	his / her / hers / its
they	them	their / theirs
who / whoever	whom / whomever	whose

In subject complements

Use the subjective case for pronouns that follow **LINKING VERBS** such as *be, seem, become,* and *feel.*

▶ In fact, Li was not the one who broke the code; it was ~~me~~.
   I.

   If It was I *sounds awkward, revise the sentence further:* I broke it.

In compound structures

When a pronoun is part of a compound subject, it should be in the subjective case. When it's part of a compound object, it should be in the objective case.

▶ On our vacations, my grandfather and ~~me~~ went fishing together.
   I

▶ There were never any secrets between ~~he~~ and ~~I~~.
   him   me.

After than *or* as

Often comparisons with *than* or *as* leave some words out. When such comparisons include pronouns, your intended meaning determines the case of the pronoun.

▶ You trust John more than *me.*

   This sentence means You trust John more than you trust me.

▶ You trust John more than *I.*

   This sentence means You trust John more than I trust him.

Before or after infinitives

Pronouns that come before or after an **INFINITIVE** are usually in the objective case.

▶ The professor asked Scott and ~~I~~ to act the scene for ~~she~~ and the class.
   me   *her*

Before gerunds

Pronouns that come before a **GERUND** are usually in the possessive.

▶ Savion's fans loved ~~him~~ tap dancing to classical music.
   his

With who *and* whom

Use *who* (and *whoever*) where you would use *he* or *she*, and use *whom* (and *whomever*) where you would use *him* or *her*. These words appear most often in questions and in **SUBORDINATE CLAUSES**.

In questions. It can be confusing when one of these words begins a question. To figure out which case to use, try answering the question using *she* or *her*. If *she* works, use *who*; if *her* works, use *whom*.

Whom
▶ ~~Who~~ do the critics admire most?
     ^
They admire her, *so change* who *to* whom.

Who
▶ ~~Whom~~ will begin the discussion on this thorny topic?
       ^
She will begin the discussion, so change whom *to* who.

In subordinate clauses. To figure out whether to use *who* or *whom* in a subordinate clause, you need to determine how it functions in the clause. If it functions as a subject, use *who*; if it functions as an object, use *whom*.

whomever
▶ You may invite ~~whoever~~ you like.
                ^
Whomever is the object of you like.

who
▶ I will invite Josh, ~~whom~~ likes dancing.
                     ^
Who is the subject of likes dancing.

When we *or* us *precedes a noun*

If you don't know whether to use *we* or *us* before a noun, choose the pronoun that you would use if the noun were omitted.

▶ *We* students object to the recent tuition increases.

Without students, *you would say* We object, *not* Us object.

▶ The state is solving its budget shortfall by unfairly charging *us* students.

Without students, *you would say* unfairly charging us, *not* unfairly charging we.

S-7   Parallelism

Been there, done that. Eat, drink, and be merry. For better or for worse. Out of sight, out of mind. All of these common sayings are parallel in structure, putting related words in the same grammatical form. Parallel structure emphasizes the connection between the elements and can make your writing rhythmic and easy to read. This section offers guidelines for maintaining parallelism in your writing.

S-7a In a Series or List

Use the same grammatical form for all items in a series or list—all nouns, all gerunds, all prepositional phrases, and so on.

▶ The seven deadly sins—*avarice*, *sloth*, *envy*, *lust*, *gluttony*, *pride*, and *wrath*—were all committed Sunday during the twice-annual bake sale at St. Mary's of the Immaculate Conception Church.   —*The Onion*

▶ After fifty years of running, biking, swimming, weight lifting, and *playing squash* ~~on the squash court~~ to stay in shape, Aunt Dorothy was unhappy to learn she had a knee problem requiring arthroscopic surgery.

S-7b With Paired Ideas

One way to emphasize the connection between two ideas is to put them in identical grammatical forms. When you connect ideas with *and*, *but*, or another COORDINATING CONJUNCTION, make the ideas parallel in structure, and when you link ideas with *either . . . or* or another CORRELATIVE CONJUNCTION, use the same grammatical structure after each part.

▶ Many rural residents are voting on conservation issues and *agreeing* ~~agree~~ to pay higher taxes in order to keep community land undeveloped.

▶ General Electric paid millions of dollars to dredge the river and *to remove* ~~for removing~~ carcinogens from backyards.

▶ Sweet potatoes are highly nutritious, providing both dietary fiber and ~~as a good source of~~ vitamins A and C.

▶ Information on local cleanup efforts can be obtained not only from the town government but also ~~by going to~~ ^{at} the public library.

S-7c On PowerPoint Slides

PowerPoint and other presentation tools present most information in lists. Entries on these lists should be in parallel grammatical form.

During the 1946 presidential race, Truman
- Conducted a whistle-stop campaign
- Made hundreds of speeches
- Spoke energetically
- Connected personally with voters

S-7d On a Résumé

Entries on a résumé should be grammatically and typographically parallel. Each entry in the example below has the date on the left; the job title in bold followed by the company on the first line; the city and state on the second line; and the duties performed on the remaining lines, each starting with a verb.

2010–present   **INTERN**, Benedetto, Gartland, and Company
New York, NY
Assist in analyzing data for key accounts.
Design PowerPoint slides and presentations.

2009, summer   **SALES REPRESENTATIVE**, Vector Marketing Corporation
New York, NY
Sold high-quality cutlery, developing client base.

2008, summer   **TUTOR**, Grace Church Opportunity Project
New York, NY
Tutored children in math and reading.

S-7e In Headings

When you add headings to a piece of writing, put them in parallel form—all nouns, all prepositional phrases, and so on. Consider, for example, the following three headings in R-4 .

Taking Notes
Integrating Sources
Acknowledging Sources

S-7f With All the Necessary Words

Be sure to include all the words necessary to make your meaning clear and your grammar parallel.

▶ Voting gained urgency in cities, *in* suburbs, and on farms.

▶ She loved her son more than *she loved* her husband.

> *The original sentence was ambiguous; it could also mean that she loved her son more than her husband did.*

S-8 Coordination and Subordination

When we combine two or more ideas in one sentence, we can use coordination to give equal weight to each idea or subordination to give emphasis to one of the ideas. Assume, for example, that you're writing about your Aunt Irene. Aunt Irene made great strawberry jam. She did not win a blue ribbon at the Iowa State Fair.

COORDINATION Aunt Irene made great strawberry jam, but she did not win the blue ribbon at the Iowa State Fair.

SUBORDINATION Though Aunt Irene made great strawberry jam, she did not win the blue ribbon at the Iowa State Fair.

S-8a Linking Equal Ideas

To link ideas that you consider equal in importance, use a coordinating conjunction, a pair of correlative conjunctions, or a semicolon.

COORDINATING CONJUNCTIONS

and	or	so	yet
but	nor	for	

▶ The line in front of Preservation Hall was very long, *but* a good tenor sax player was wandering up and down the street, *so* I took my place at the end of the line.   —Fred Setterberg, "The Usual Story"

▶ New models of coursework may need to be developed, *and* instructors may need to be hired.
          —Megan Hopkins, "Training the Next Teachers for America"

Be careful not to overuse *and*. Try to use the coordinating conjunction that best expresses your meaning.

▶ Mosquitoes survived the high-tech zapping devices, ~~and~~ *but* bites were a small price for otherwise pleasant evenings in the country.

CORRELATIVE CONJUNCTIONS

either . . . or	not only . . . but also	whether . . . or
neither . . . nor	just as . . . so	

▶ *Just as* the summer saw endless rain, *so* the winter brought many snowstorms.

While a semicolon alone can signal equal importance, you might use a **TRANSITION** such as *therefore* or *however* to make the relationship between the ideas especially clear.

▶ Second, reading and spelling require much more than just phonics; spelling strategies and word-analysis skills are equally important.
—Debra Johnson, "Balanced Reading Instruction"

▶ As in many fantasy novels and fairy tales, the central character is on a quest; *however*, the narrative of Harry's quest unfolds more like a classic mystery.   —Philip Nel, "Fantasy, Mystery, and Ambiguity"

S-8b Emphasizing One Idea over Others

To emphasize one idea over others, put the most important one in an **INDEPENDENT CLAUSE** and the less important ones in **SUBORDINATE CLAUSES** or **PHRASES**.

▶ Because storytelling lies at the heart of Pueblo culture, it is absurd to attempt to fix the stories in time.
—Leslie Marmon Silko, "Language and Literature from a Pueblo Indian Perspective"

▶ Even ignoring the extreme poles of the economic spectrum, we find enormous class differences in the life-styles among the haves, the have-nots, and the have-littles.
—Gregory Mantsios, "Class in America—2003"

S-9   Shifts

You're watching the news when your brother grabs the remote and changes the channel to a cartoon. The road you're driving on suddenly changes from asphalt to gravel. These shifts are jarring and sometimes disorienting. Similarly, shifts in writing—from one tense to another, for example—can confuse your readers. This section explains how to keep your writing consistent in verb tense and point of view.

S-9a Shifts in Tense

Only when you want to emphasize that actions took place at different times should you shift verb TENSE.

▶ My plane *will arrive* in Albuquerque two hours after it *leaves* Portland.

Otherwise, keep tenses consistent.

▶ As the concert ended, several people ~~are~~ already on their way up the aisle, causing a distraction.
   were

In writing about literary works, use the present tense. Be careful not to shift to the past.

▶ The two fugitives start down the river together, Huck fleeing his abusive father and Jim running away from his owner. As they ~~traveled~~, they ~~met~~ with many colorful characters, including the Duke and King, two actors and con artists who involve Huck and Jim in their schemes.
   travel,
   meet

S-9b Shifts in Point of View

Do not shift between first person (*I*, *we*), second person (*you*), and third person (*he*, *she*, *it*, *they*, *one*).

▶ When ~~one has~~ a cold, you should stay home to avoid exposing others.
   you have

S-9c Shifts in Number

Unnecessary shifts between singular and plural subjects can confuse readers.

▶ Because of late frosts, oranges have risen dramatically in price. But since ~~the orange is~~ such a staple, they continue to sell.
   oranges are

L-1 Appropriate Words

Cool. Sweet. Excellent. These three words can mean the same thing, but each has a different level of formality. We usually use informal language when we're talking with friends, and we use slang and abbreviations when we send text messages, but we choose words that are more formal for most of our academic and professional writing. Just as we wouldn't wear an old T-shirt to most job interviews, we wouldn't write in a college essay that *Beloved* is "an awesome book." This section offers you help in choosing words that are appropriate for different audiences and purposes.

L-1a Formal and Informal Words

Whether you use formal or informal language depends on your
PURPOSE and **AUDIENCE**.

FORMAL   Four score and seven years ago our fathers brought forth on this continent, a new nation, conceived in Liberty, and dedicated to the proposition that all men are created equal.   —Abraham Lincoln, Gettysburg Address

INFORMAL   Our family, like most, had its ups and downs.
                                      —Judy Davis, "Ours Was a Dad"

Abraham Lincoln delivered the first, more formal sentence in 1863 to 20,000 people, including many officials and prominent citizens. The second, less formal sentence was spoken in 2004 by a woman to a small gathering of family and friends at her father's funeral.

Colloquial language (*What's up? No clue*) and slang (*A-list, S'up?*) are not appropriate for formal speech and may be too informal for most academic and professional writing.

▶ ~~A lot of~~ _{Many} drivers are ~~hot~~ _{excited} about the fuel efficiency of the new hybrid cars.

▶ We ~~wolfed down~~ _{ate} our lunch and then ~~hit the books.~~ _{went to the library.}

262

L-1b Pretentious Language

Long or complicated words might seem to lend authority to your writing, but often they make it sound pretentious and stuffy. Use such words sparingly and only when they best capture your meaning and suit your WRITING CONTEXT.

> *After*   *claimed*
> ► ~~Subsequent to~~ adopting the new system, managers ~~averred~~ that their
>   ^   ^
>   *together*   *better than expected.*
>   staff worked ~~synergistically in a way that exceeded parameters.~~
>   ^   ^

L-1c Jargon

Jargon is a specialized vocabulary of a profession, trade, or field and should be used only when you know your audience will understand what you are saying. The following paragraph might be easily understood by a computer enthusiast, but most readers would not be familiar with terms like *HDMI*, *DVI*, and *1080p*.

> ► HDMI is the easiest and most convenient way to go about high-def.
>   Why? Because you get audio and sound in a single, USB-like cable,
>   instead of a nest of component cables or the soundless garden hose of
>   DVI. Also, unless you're trying to run 1080p over 100 feet or somesuch,
>   stay away from premium brands. Any on-spec cheapie HDMI cable will
>   be perfect for standard living room setups.
>   —Rob Beschizza, "Which Is Better, HDMI or Component?"

When you are writing for an audience of nonspecialists, resist the temptation to use overly technical language.

> *small incision*   *breastbone preserved*
> ► The ~~mini-sternotomy~~ at the lower end of the ~~sternum resulted in~~
>   ^   ^
>   *her appearance.*
>   ~~satisfactory cosmesis.~~
>   ^

L-1d Clichés

Steer clear of clichés, expressions so familiar that they have become trite (*white as snow, the grass is always greener*).

▶ The company needs a recruiter who thinks *unconventionally.* ~~outside the box.~~
^

▶ After canoeing all day, we all slept *soundly.* ~~like logs.~~
^

▶ Nita *collaborates well,* ~~is a team player,~~ so we hope she will be assigned to the project.
^

L-2 Precise Words

Serena Overpowers Zvonareva. Nadal Triumphs Over Berdych. In each case, the writer could have simply used the word *defeats*. But at least to tennis fans, these newspaper headlines are a bit more precise and informative as a result of the words chosen. This section offers guidelines for editing your own writing to make it as precise as it needs to be.

L-2a *Be* and *Do*

Try not to rely too much on *be* or *do*. Check your writing to see if you can replace forms of these words with more precise verbs.

▶ David Sedaris's essay "Us and Them" *focuses on* ~~is about~~ his love/hate relationship
^
with his family.

▶ Some doctors no longer believe that *solving* ~~doing~~ crossword puzzles can
^
delay the onset of senility and even Alzheimer's disease.

Sometimes using a form of *be* or *do* is unavoidable, such as when you are describing someone or something.

▶ Barnes *is* a legend among southern California Met lovers—an icon, a beacon, and a font of useful knowledge and freely offered opinions.
                                                              —Bob Merlis, "Foster Cars"

L-2b Balancing General and Specific Words

Abstract words refer to general qualities or ideas (*truth, beauty*), whereas concrete words refer to specific things we can perceive with our senses (*books, lipstick*). You'll often need to use words that are general or abstract, but remember that specific, concrete words can make your writing more precise and more vivid—and can make the abstract easier to understand.

▶ In Joan Didion's work, there has always been a fascination with what she once called "the unspeakable peril of the everyday"—the coyotes by the interstate, the snakes in the playpen, the fires and Santa Ana winds of California.

　　　　　　　—Michiko Kakutani, "The End of Life As She Knew It"

The concrete coyotes, snakes, fires, *and* winds *help explain the abstract* peril of the everyday.

L-2c Prepositions

Prepositions are words like *at, in,* and *on* that express relationships between words. Do you live *in* a city, *on* an island, or *at* the beach? In each case, you need to use a certain preposition. You'll often need to check a dictionary to decide which preposition to use. Here are some guidelines for using *in, on,* and *at* to indicate place and time.

Prepositions of place

IN

a container, room, or area: in the mailbox, *in* my office, *in* the woods

a geographic location: in San Diego, *in* the Midwest

a printed work: in the newspaper, *in* chapter 3

ON

a surface: on the floor, *on* the grass

a street: on Ninth Street, *on* Western Avenue

an electronic medium: on DVD, *on* the radio

public transportation: on the bus, *on* an airplane

AT

a specific address or business: at 33 Parkwood Street, *at* McDonald's
a public building or unnamed business: at the courthouse, *at* the bakery
a general place: at home, *at* work

Prepositions of time

IN

a defined time period: in an hour, *in* three years
a month, season, or year: in June, *in* the fall, *in* 2011
a part of the day: in the morning, *in* the evening

ON

a day of the week: on Friday
an exact date: on September 12
a holiday: on Thanksgiving, *on* Veteran's Day

AT

a specific time: at 4:30 p.m., *at* sunset, *at* lunchtime, *at* night

L-2d Figurative Language

Figures of speech such as SIMILES and METAPHORS are words used imaginatively rather than literally. They can help readers understand an abstract point by comparing it to something they are familiar with or can easily imagine.

SIMILE His body is in almost constant motion—rolling those cigarettes, rubbing an elbow, reaching for a glass—but the rhythm is tranquil and fluid, *like a cat licking its paw.*
—Sean Smith, "Johnny Depp: Unlikely Superstar"

METAPHOR And so, before the professor had even finished his little story, *I had become a furnace of rage.*
—Shelby Steele, "On Being Black and Middle Class"

L-3   Words Often Confused

When you're tired, do you *lay* down or *lie* down? After dinner, do you eat *desert* or *dessert*? This section's purpose is to alert you to everyday words that can trip you up and to help you understand the differences between certain words people tend to confuse.

accept, except   *Accept* means "to receive willingly": *accept an award.* *Except* as a preposition means "excluding": *all languages except English.*

adapt, adopt   *Adapt* means "to adjust": *adapt the recipe to be dairy free.* *Adopt* means "to take as one's own": *adopt a pet from a shelter.*

advice, advise   *Advice* means "recommendation": *a lawyer's advice.* *Advise* means "to give advice": *We advise you to learn your rights.*

affect, effect   *Affect* as a verb means "to produce a change in": *Stress can affect health.* *Effect* as a noun means "result": *cause and effect.*

all right, alright   *All right* is the preferred spelling.

allusion, illusion   *Allusion* means "indirect reference": *an allusion to Beowulf.* *Illusion* means "false appearance": *an optical illusion.*

a lot   Always two words, *a lot* means "a large number or amount" or "to a great extent": *a lot of voters; he misses her a lot.* The phrase is too informal for most academic writing.

among, between   Use *among* for three or more items: *among the fifty states.* Use *between* for two items: *between you and me.*

amount, number   Use *amount* for items you can measure but not count: *a large amount of water.* Use *number* for things you can count: *a number of books.*

as, as if, like   *Like* introduces a noun or noun phrase: *It feels like silk.* To begin a subordinate clause, use *as* or *as if: Do as I say, not as I do; it seemed as if he had not prepared at all for the briefing.*

bad, badly   Use *bad* as an adjective following a linking verb: *I feel bad.* Use *badly* as an adverb following an action verb: *I play piano badly.*

capital, capitol A *capital* is a city where the government of a state, province, or country is located: *Kingston was the first state capital of New York*. A *capitol* is a government building: *the dome of the capitol*.

cite, sight, site *Cite* means "to give information from a source by quoting, paraphrasing, or summarizing": *Cite your sources*. *Sight* is the act of seeing or something that is seen: *an appalling sight*. A *site* is a place: *the site of a famous battle*.

compose, comprise The parts *compose* the whole: *Fifty states compose the Union*. The whole *comprises* the parts: *The Union comprises fifty states*.

could of In writing, use *could have* (*could've*).

council, counsel *Council* refers to a body of people: *the council's vote*. *Counsel* means "advice" or "to advise": *her wise counsel*; *she counseled victims of domestic abuse*.

criteria, criterion *Criteria* is the plural of *criterion* and takes a plural verb: *certain criteria have been established*.

data *Data*, the plural of *datum*, technically should take a plural verb (*The data arrive from many sources*), but some writers treat it as singular (*The data is persuasive*).

desert, dessert *Desert* as a noun means "arid region": *Mojave Desert*. As a verb it means "to abandon": *he deserted his post*. *Dessert* is a sweet served toward the end of a meal.

disinterested, uninterested *Disinterested* means "fair" or "unbiased": *a disinterested jury*. *Uninterested* means "bored" or "indifferent": *uninterested in election results*.

emigrate (from), immigrate (to) *Emigrate* means "to leave one's country": *emigrate from Slovakia*. *Immigrate* means "to move to another country": *immigrate to Canada*.

etc. The abbreviation *etc.* is short for the Latin *et cetera*, "and other things." *Etc.* is fine in notes and bibliographies, but avoid using it in your writing in general. Substitute *and so on* if necessary.

everyday, every day *Everyday* is an adjective meaning "ordinary": *After the holidays, we go back to our everyday routine.* *Every day* means "on a daily basis": *Eat three or more servings of fruit every day.*

fewer, less Use *fewer* when you refer to things that can be counted: *fewer calories.* Use *less* when you refer to an amount of something that cannot be counted: *less fat.*

good, well *Good* is an adjective: *She looks good in that color; a good book.* *Well* can be an adjective indicating physical health after a linking verb *(She looks well despite her recent surgery)* or an adverb following an action verb *(He speaks Spanish well).*

hopefully In academic writing, avoid *hopefully* to mean "it is hoped that"; use it only to mean "with hope": *to make a wish hopefully.*

imply, infer *Imply* means "to suggest": *What do you mean to imply? Infer* means "to conclude": *We infer that you did not enjoy the trip.*

its, it's *Its* is a possessive pronoun: *The movie is rated R because of its language. It's* is a contraction of "it is" or "it has": *It's an action film.*

lay, lie *Lay,* meaning "to put" or "to place," always takes a direct object: *She lays the blanket down. Lie,* meaning "to recline" or "to be positioned," never takes a direct object: *She lies on the blanket.*

lead, led The verb *lead* (rhymes with *bead*) means "to guide": *I will lead the way. Led* is the past tense and past participle of *lead: Yesterday I led the way.* The noun *lead* (rhymes with *head*) is a type of metal: *Use copper pipes instead of lead.*

literally Use *literally* only when you want to stress that you don't mean *figuratively: While sitting in the grass, he realized that he literally had ants in his pants.*

loose, lose *Loose* means "not fastened securely" or "not fitting tightly": *a pair of loose pants. Lose* means "to misplace" or "to not win": *lose an earring; lose the race.*

man, mankind Use *people, human,* or *humankind* instead.

may of, might of, must of In writing, use *may have, might have,* or *must have.*

media   *Media*, a plural noun, takes a plural verb: *The media report another shooting.* The singular form is *medium*: *Television is a popular medium for advertising.*

percent, percentage   Use *percent* after a number: *80 percent.* Use *percentage* after an adjective or article: *an impressive percentage*; *the percentage was impressive.*

principal, principle   As a noun, *principal* means "a chief official" or "a sum of money": *in the principal's office*; *raising the principal for a down payment.* As an adjective, it means "most important": *the principal cause of death.* *Principle* means "a rule by which one lives" or "a basic truth or doctrine": *Lying is against her principles*; *the principles of life, liberty, and the pursuit of happiness.*

raise, rise   Meaning "to grow" or "to cause to move upward," *raise* always takes a direct object: *He raised his hand.* Meaning "to get up," *rise* never takes a direct object: *The sun rises at dawn.*

the reason . . . is because   Use *because* or *the reason . . . is (that)*, but not both: *The reason for the price increase was a poor growing season* or *prices increased because of a poor growing season.*

reason why   Instead of this redundant phrase, use *the reason* or *the reason that*: *Psychologists debate the reasons that some people develop depression and others do not.*

respectfully, respectively   *Respectfully* means "full of respect": *Speak to your elders respectfully.* *Respectively* means "in the order given": *George H. W. Bush and George W. Bush were the forty-first president and the forty-third president, respectively.*

sensual, sensuous   *Sensual* suggests sexuality: *a sensual caress.* *Sensuous* involves pleasing the senses through art, music, and nature: *the violin's sensuous solo.*

set, sit   *Set*, meaning "to put" or "to place," takes a direct object: *Please set the table.* *Sit*, meaning "to take a seat," does not take a direct object: *She sits on the bench.*

should of   In writing, use *should have* (*should've*).

stationary, stationery   Stationary means "staying put": *a stationary lab table*. Stationery means "writing paper": *the college's official stationery*.

than, then   Than is a conjunction used for comparing: *She is taller than her mother.* Then is an adverb used to indicate a sequence: *Finish your work, and then reward yourself.*

that, which   Use *that* to add information that is essential for identifying something: *The horses that live on this island are endangered.* Use *which* to give additional but nonessential information: *Abaco Barb horses, which live on an island in the Bahamas, are endangered.*

their, there, they're   Their signifies possession: *their canoe.* There tells where: *Put it there.* They're is a contraction of they are: *They're busy.*

to, too, two   To is either a preposition that tells direction (*Give it to me*) or part of an infinitive (*To err is human*). Too means "also" or "excessively": *The younger children wanted to help, too; too wonderful for words.* Two is a number: *tea for two*.

unique   Because *unique* suggests that something is the only one of its kind, avoid adding comparatives or superlatives (*more, most, less, least*), intensifiers (such as *very*), or hedges (such as *somewhat*).

weather, whether   Weather refers to atmospheric conditions: *dreary weather.* Whether refers to a choice between options: *whether to stay home or go out.*

who's, whose   Who's is a contraction for *who is* or *who has*: *Who's the best candidate for the job?* Whose refers to ownership: *Whose keys are these? Tom, whose keys were on the table, had left.*

would of   In writing, use *would have* (*would've*).

your, you're   Your signifies possession: *your diploma.* You're is a contraction for you are: *You're welcome.*

L-4   Unnecessary Words

At this point in time. Really unique. In a manner of speaking. Each of these phrases includes words that are unnecessary or says something that could be said more concisely. This section shows you how to edit your own writing to make every word count.

L-4a   *Quite, Very,* and Other Empty Words

Intensifiers such as *quite* and *very* are used to strengthen what we say. Hedges such as *apparently, possibly,* and *tend* are a way to qualify what we say. It's fine to use words of this kind when they are necessary. Sometimes, however, they are not. You shouldn't say something is "very unique," because things either are unique or they're not; there's no need to add the intensifier. And why say someone is "really smart" when you could say that he or she is "brilliant"?

▶ Accepted by five colleges, Jackson ~~seems to be facing an apparently very~~ *is facing a* difficult decision.

L-4b   *There Is, It Is*

The **EXPLETIVE** constructions *there* is and it is are useful ways to introduce and emphasize an idea, but often they add unnecessary words and can be replaced with stronger, more precise verbs.

▶ ~~It is necessary for~~ Americans today ~~to~~ *must* learn to speak more than one language.

▶ *Four* ~~There are four~~ large moons and more than thirty small ones ~~that~~ orbit Jupiter.

In certain contexts, *there* is and it is can be the best choices. Imagine the ending of *The Wizard of Oz* if Dorothy were to say *No place is like home* instead of the more emphatic (and sentimental) *There's no place like home.*

L-4c **Wordy Phrases**

Many common phrases use several words when a single word will do.
Editing out such wordy phrases will make your writing more concise
and easier to read.

WORDY	CONCISE
as far as . . . is concerned	concerning
at the time that	when
at this point in time	now
in spite of the fact that	although, though
in the event that	if
in view of the fact that	because, since

▶ ~~Due to the fact that~~ ^{*Because*} Professor Lee retired, the animal sciences
department now lacks a neurology specialist.

L-4d **Redundancies**

Eliminate words and phrases that are unnecessary for your meaning.

▶ Painting the house purple ~~in color~~ will make it stand out from the
many white houses in town.

▶ Dashing ~~quickly~~ into the street to retrieve the ball, the young girl was
almost hit by a car.

▶ How much wood is ~~sufficient~~ enough for the fire to burn all night?

L-5   Adjectives and Adverbs

Adjectives and adverbs are words that describe other words, adding
important information and detail. When Dave Barry writes that the
Beatles "were the *coolest* thing you had ever seen" and that "they were

smart; they were *funny*; they didn't take themselves *seriously*," the adjectives and adverbs (italicized here) make clear why he "wanted *desperately* to be a Beatle." This section will help you use adjectives and adverbs in your own writing.

L-5a When to Use Adjectives and Adverbs

Adjectives are words used to modify **NOUNS** and **PRONOUNS**. They usually answer one of these questions: which? what kind? how many?

▶ *Parallel* rows of *ancient oak* trees lined the *narrow* driveway.

▶ Years of testing will be needed to prove whether geneticists' theories are *correct*.

▶ If you are craving something *sweet,* have a piece of fruit.

Adverbs are words used to modify **VERBS**, adjectives, and other adverbs. They usually answer one of these questions: how? when? where? why? under what conditions? to what degree? Although many adverbs end in -ly (*tentatively*, *immediately*), many do not (*now*, *so*, *soon*, *then*, *very*).

▶ Emergency personnel must respond *quickly* when an ambulance arrives.

▶ Environmentalists are *increasingly* worried about Americans' consumption of fossil fuels.

▶ If the senator had known that the news cameras were on, she would not have responded *so angrily*.

Well *and* good

Use *well* as an adjective to describe physical health; use *good* to describe emotional health or appearance.

▶ Some herbs can keep you feeling ~~good~~ *well* when everyone else has the flu.

▶ Staying healthy can make you feel *good* about yourself.

Good should not be used as an adverb; use *well*.

▶ Because both Williams sisters play tennis so ~~good,~~ *well,* they frequently

compete against each other in major tournaments.

Bad *and* badly

Use the adjective *bad* after a LINKING VERB to describe an emotional state or feeling. In such cases, the adjective describes the subject.

▶ Arguing with your parents can make you feel *bad*.

Use the adverb *badly* to describe an ACTION VERB.

▶ Arguing with your parents late at night can make you sleep *badly*.

L-5b Comparatives and Superlatives

Most adjectives and adverbs have three forms: the positive, the comparative, and the superlative. The comparative is used to compare two things, and the superlative is used to compare three or more things.

COMPARATIVE   Who's the *better* quarterback, Eli Manning or his brother?

SUPERLATIVE   Many Colts fans consider Peyton Manning to be the
               greatest quarterback ever.

The comparative and superlative of most adjectives are formed by adding the endings *-er* and *-est*: *slow, slower, slowest*. Longer adjectives and most adverbs use *more* and *most* (or *less* and *least*): *helpful, more helpful, most helpful*. If you add *-er* or *-est* to an adjective or adverb, do not use *more, most, less,* or *least*.

▶ The ~~most~~ lowest point in the United States is in Death Valley.

L-5c Modifier Placement

Place adjectives, adverbs, and other MODIFIERS close to the words they describe.

▶ The doctor *at the seminar* explained advances in cancer treatment to the families of
patients. ~~at the seminar.~~

The doctor, not the patients, is at the seminar.

▶ *Before the anesthesiologist arrived, the*
~~The~~ doctors assured the patient that they intended to make only two
small incisions. ~~before the anesthesiologist arrived~~.

*The original sentence suggests that the incisions will be made without
anesthesia, surely not the case.*

To avoid ambiguity, position limiting modifiers such as *almost, even,
just, merely,* and *only* next to the word or phrase they modify—and
be careful that your meaning is clear. See how the placement of *only*
results in two completely different meanings.

▶ A triple-threat athlete, Martha ~~only~~ played soccer *only* in college.

▶ A triple-threat athlete, Martha ~~only~~ played *only* soccer in college.

Be careful that your placement of *not* doesn't result in a meaning
you don't intend.

▶ When I attended college, every student was ~~not~~ *not* using a laptop.

Dangling modifiers

Modifiers are said to be dangling when they do not clearly modify
any particular word in the sentence. You can fix a dangling modifier
by adding the **SUBJECT** that the modifier is intended to describe to the
main clause or by adding a subject to the modifier itself.

▶ Speaking simply and respectfully, *the doctor comforted* many people ~~felt comforted by the~~
~~doctor's~~ *with his* presentation.

The doctor was speaking, not the other people.

▶ *I was*
While running to catch the bus, the shoulder strap on my fake
Balenciaga bag broke.
^

Split infinitives

When a modifier comes between *to* and the verb in an **INFINITIVE**,
you create a split infinitive: *to deliberately avoid.* When a split infinitive
is awkward or makes a sentence difficult to follow, put the modifier
elsewhere in the sentence.

rigorously
▶ Professional soccer players are expected to ~~rigorously~~ train every day.
^

Sometimes, however, a split infinitive is easier to follow.

▶ One famous split infinitive appears in the opening sequence of
Star Trek: "to boldly go where no man has gone before."

L-6   Articles

A, an, and *the* are articles, words that tell whether something is indefinite or definite. Use *a* or *an* with nouns whose specific identity is not
known to your audience—for example, when you haven't mentioned
them before: *I'm reading a great book.* Use *the* with nouns whose specific identity is known to your audience—for instance, a noun that
describes something specific, as in *the book on the table,* or something
that you've mentioned before, as in *Francesca finally finished writing
her book. The book will be published next year.*

L-6a When to Use *A* or *An*

Use *a* or *an* with singular count nouns whose identity is not known
to your audience. Count nouns refer to things that can be counted:

one book, two books. Use *a* before a consonant sound: *a tangerine;* use *an* before a vowel sound: *an orange.*

▶ Do you want to see *a movie* this afternoon?

▶ Yesterday we went to see *a fascinating* documentary about World War II.

▶ There was *an article* about the film in last Saturday's newspaper.

▶ I'd like to watch *an amusing* movie today rather than a serious one.

Do not use *a* or *an* before a noncount noun. Noncount nouns refer to abstractions or masses that can be quantified only with certain modifiers or units: *too much information, two cups of coffee.*

▶ These students could use *some encouragement* from their teacher.

▶ The last thing Portland needs this week is *more rain.*

L-6b When to Use *The*

Use *the* before nouns whose identity is clear to your audience and before superlatives.

▶ Our teacher warned us that *the poem she had assigned* had multiple levels of meaning.

▶ *The Secretary-General of the United Nations* will speak later this morning about *the military crackdown in Myanmar.*

▶ Some of *the fastest runners in the country* compete at *the Penn Relays.*

Do not use *the* with most singular PROPER NOUNS (*Judge Judy, Lake Titicaca*), but do use it with most plural proper nouns (*the Adirondack Mountains, the Philippines*).

Do use *the* before singular proper nouns in the following categories.

LARGER BODIES OF WATER   the Arctic Ocean, the Mississippi River

GOVERNMENT BODIES   the U.S. Congress, the Canadian Parliament

HISTORICAL PERIODS   the Renaissance, the Tang Dynasty

LANDMARKS   the Empire State Building, the Taj Mahal

REGIONS   the East Coast, the Middle East, the Mojave Desert

RELIGIOUS ENTITIES, TEXTS, AND LEADERS   the Roman Catholic Church, the Qur'an, the Dalai Lama

L-7 Words That Build Common Ground

A secretary objects to being called one of "the girls." The head of the English department finds the title "chairman" offensive. Why? The secretary is male, the department head is a woman, and those terms don't include them. We can build common ground—or not—by the words we choose, by including others or leaving them out. This section offers tips for using language that is positive and inclusive and that will build common ground with those we wish to reach.

L-7a Avoiding Stereotypes

Stereotypes are generalizations about groups of people and as such can offend because they presume that all members of a group are the same. The writer Geeta Kothari explains how she reacts to a seemingly neutral assumption about Indians: "Indians eat lentils. I understand this as an absolute, a decree from an unidentifiable authority that watches and judges me."

We're all familiar with stereotypes based on sex or race, but stereotypes exist about other characteristics: age, body type, education, income, occupation, physical ability, political affiliation, region, religion, sexual orientation, and more. Be careful not to make any broad generalizations about any group—even neutral or positive ones (that Asian students work hard, for example, or that Republicans are patriotic).

Also, be careful not to call attention to a person's group affiliation if that information is not relevant.

▶ The ~~gay~~ physical therapist who worked the morning shift knew when to let patients rest and when to push them.

L-7b Using Preferred Terms

When you are writing about a group of people, try to use terms that members of that group use themselves. This advice is sometimes easier said than done, because language changes—and words that were commonly used ten years ago may not be in wide use today. Americans of African ancestry, for example, were referred to many years ago as "colored" or "Negro" and then as "black"; today the preferred terminology is "African American."

When you are referring to ethnicities, it's usually best to be as specific as possible. Instead of saying someone is Latin or Hispanic, for instance, it's better to say he or she is Puerto Rican or Dominican or Cuban, as appropriate. The same is true of religions; it's better to specify a religion when you can (Sunni Muslims, Episcopalians, Orthodox Jews). And while "Native American" and "American Indian" are both acceptable as general terms, the only truly accurate method is to refer to particular tribal nations (Dakota, Chippewa).

L-7c Editing Out Sexist Language

Sexist language is language that stereotypes or ignores women or men—or that gratuitously calls attention to someone's gender. Try to eliminate such language from your writing.

Default he

Writers once used *he, him,* and other masculine pronouns as a default to refer to people whose sex was unknown to them. Today such usage is not widely accepted—and is no way to build common ground. Here are some alternatives.

Use both masculine and feminine pronouns joined by *or*. (Note, however, that using this option repeatedly may become awkward.)

▶ Before anyone can leave the country, he *or she* must have a passport or other
documentation.

Replace a singular noun or pronoun with a plural noun.

▶ Before ~~anyone~~ *travelers* can leave the country, ~~he~~ *they* must have a passport or other
documentation.

Eliminate the pronoun altogether.

▶ Before ~~anyone can leave~~ *leaving* the country, ~~he~~ *a traveler* must have a passport or other
documentation.

You should also avoid nouns that include *man* when you're referring
to people who may be either men or women.

INSTEAD OF	USE
man, mankind	humankind, humanity, humans
salesman	salesperson
fireman	firefighter
congressman	representative, Member of Congress
male nurse	nurse
female truck driver	truck driver

P-1   Commas

Commas matter. Consider the title of the best-selling book *Eats, Shoots & Leaves*. The cover shows two pandas, one with a gun in its paw, one whitewashing the comma. Is the book about a panda that dines, then fires a gun and exits? Or about the panda's customary diet? In fact, it's a book about punctuation; the ambiguity of its title illustrates how commas affect meaning. This section shows when and where to use commas in your writing.

P-1a To Join Independent Clauses with *and, but,* and Other Coordinating Conjunctions

Put a comma before the COORDINATING CONJUNCTIONS *and, but, for, nor, or, so,* and *yet* when they connect two INDEPENDENT CLAUSES. The comma signals that one idea is ending and another is beginning.

▶ I do not love Shakespeare, but I still have those books.
　　　　　　　　　　—Rick Bragg, "All Over But the Shoutin'"

▶ Most people think the avocado is a vegetable, yet it is actually a fruit.

▶ The blue ribbon went to Susanna, and Sarah got the red ribbon.

　Without the comma, readers might first think both girls got blue ribbons.

Although some writers omit the comma, especially with short independent clauses, you'll never be wrong to include it.

▶ I was smart, and I knew it.　　　—Shannon Nichols, "'Proficiency'"

No comma is needed between the verbs when a single subject performs two actions—but you need commas when a third verb is added.

▶ Many fast-food restaurants now give calorie counts on menus and offer a variety of healthy meal options.

▶ Augustine wrote extensively about his mother but mentioned his father only briefly.

▶ Kim bought the sod, delivered it, and rolled it out for us.

P-1b To Set Off Introductory Words

Use a comma after an introductory word, PHRASE, or CLAUSE to mark
the end of the introduction and the start of the main part of the
sentence.

▶ Consequently, our celebration of Howard Stern, Don Imus, and other
  heroes of "shock radio" might be evidence of a certain loss of moral
  focus.   —Stephen L. Carter, "Just Be Nice"

▶ On the other hand, opponents of official English remind us that
  without legislation we have managed to get over ninety-seven percent
  of the residents of this country to speak the national language.
                —Dennis Baron, "Don't Make English Official—Ban It Instead"

▶ Even ignoring the extreme poles of the economic spectrum, we find
  enormous class differences in the life-styles among the haves, the
  have-nots, and the have-littles.
                          —Gregory Mantsios, "Class in America—2003"

▶ When Miss Emily Grierson died, our whole town went to her funeral.
                          —William Faulkner, "A Rose for Emily"

Some writers don't use a comma after a short introductory word,
phrase, or clause, but it's never wrong to include one.

P-1c To Separate Items in a Series

Use a comma to separate the items in a series.

▶ I spend a great deal of time thinking about the power of language
  —the way it can evoke an emotion, a visual image, a complex idea, or
  a simple truth.   —Amy Tan, "Mother Tongue"

Though some writers leave out the comma between the final two
items in a series, this omission can confuse readers. It's never wrong
to include the final comma.

▶ Nadia held a large platter of sandwiches—egg salad, peanut butter,
  ham, and cheese.
     ^
  Without the last comma, it's not clear whether there are three or four kinds
  of sandwiches on the platter.

P-1d To Set Off Nonessential Elements

A nonessential (or nonrestrictive) element is one that could be deleted without changing the basic meaning of the sentence; it should be set off with commas. An essential (or restrictive) element is one that is needed to understand the sentence and therefore should not be set off with commas.

NONESSENTIAL

▶ Spanish, which is a Romance language, is one of six official languages at the United Nations.

The detail about being a Romance language adds information, but it is not essential to the meaning of the sentence and so is set off with a comma.

ESSENTIAL

▶ Navajo is the Athabaskan language that is spoken in the Southwest by the Navajo people.

The detail about where Navajo is spoken is essential: Navajo is not the only Athabaskan language; it is the Athabaskan language that is spoken in the Southwest.

Essential and nonessential elements can be clauses, phrases, or words.

CLAUSES

▶ He always drove Chryslers, which are made in America.

▶ He always drove cars that were made in America.

PHRASES

▶ I fumble in the dark, trying to open the mosquito netting around my bed.

▶ I see my mother clutching my baby sister.
                                    —Chanrithy Him, "When Broken Glass Floats"

WORDS

▶ At 8:59, Flight 175 passenger Brian David Sweeney tried to call his wife, Julie.

▶ At 9:00, Lee Hanson received a second call from his son Peter.
                    —The 9/11 Commission, "The Hijacking of United 175"

Sweeney had only one wife, so her name provides extra but nonessential information. Hanson presumably had more than one son, so it is essential to specify which son called.

P-1e To Set Off Parenthetical Information

Information that interrupts the flow of a sentence needs to be set off with commas.

▶ Bob's conduct, most of us will immediately respond, was gravely
  wrong.   —Peter Singer, "The Singer Solution to World Poverty"

▶ With as little as two servings of vegetables a day, it seems to me,
  you can improve your eating habits.

P-1f To Set Off Transitional Expressions

TRANSITIONS such as *thus, nevertheless, for example,* and *in fact* help connect sentences or parts of sentences. They are usually set off with commas. When a transition connects two **INDEPENDENT CLAUSES** in the same sentence, it is preceded by a semicolon and is followed by a comma.

▶ [S]torytelling always includes the audience, the listeners. *In fact,*
  a great deal of the story is believed to be inside the listener; the
  storyteller's role is to draw the story out of the listeners.
                    —Leslie Marmon Silko, "Language and Literature
                                from a Pueblo Indian Perspective"

▶ There are few among the poor who speak of themselves as lower class;
  instead, they refer to their race, ethnic group, or geographic location.
                    —Gregory Mantsios, "Class in America—2003"

P-1g To Set Off Direct Quotations

Use commas to set off quoted words from the speaker or source.

▶ Pa shouts back, "I just want to know where the gunfire is coming
   from."   —Chanrithy Him, "When Broken Glass Floats"

▶ "You put a slick and a con man together," she said, "and you have
   predatory lenders."
      —Peter Boyer, "Eviction: The Day They Came for Addie Polk's House"

▶ "Death and life are in the power of the tongue," says the proverb.

P-1h To Set Off Direct Address, *Yes* or *No*, Interjections, and Tag Questions

DIRECT ADDRESS	"Yes, Virginia, there really is a Santa Claus."
YES OR NO	No, you cannot replace the battery on your iPhone.
INTERJECTION	Oh, a Prius. How long did you have to wait to get it?
TAG QUESTION	That wasn't so hard, was it?

P-1i With Addresses, Place Names, and Dates

▶ Send contributions to Human Rights Campaign, 1640 Rhode Island
   Ave., Washington, DC 20036.

▶ Athens, Georgia, is famous for its thriving music scene.

▶ On July 2, 1937, the aviator Amelia Earhart disappeared over the
   Pacific Ocean while trying to make the first round-the-world flight at
   the equator.

   *Omit the commas, however, if you invert the date (on 2 July 1937) or if
   you give only the month and year (in July 1937).*

P-1j Checking for Unnecessary Commas

Commas have so many uses that it's easy to add them unnecessarily. Here are some situations when you should not use a comma.

Between subject and verb

▶ What the organizers of the 1969 Woodstock concert did not anticipate, was the turnout.

▶ The event's promoters, turned down John Lennon's offer to play with his Plastic Ono Band.

Between verb and object

▶ Pollsters wondered, how they had so poorly predicted the winner of the 1948 presidential election.

▶ Virtually every prediction indicated, that Thomas Dewey would defeat Harry Truman.

After a coordinating conjunction

▶ The College Board reported a decline in SAT scores and, attributed the decline to changes in "student test-taking patterns."

▶ The SAT was created to provide an objective measure of academic potential, but, studies in the 1980s found racial and socioeconomic biases in some test questions.

After *like* or *such as*

▶ Many American-born authors, such as, Henry James, Ezra Pound, and F. Scott Fitzgerald, lived as expatriates in Europe.

With a question mark or an exclamation point

▶ Why would any nation have a monarch in an era of democracy?, you might ask yourself.

▶ "O, be some other name!," exclaims Juliet.

P-2 Semicolons

Semicolons offer one way to connect two closely related thoughts. Look, for example, at Martha Stewart's advice about how to tell if fruit is ripe: "A perfectly ripened fruit exudes a subtle but sweet fragrance from the stem end, appears plump, and has deeply colored skin; avoid those that have wrinkles, bruises, or tan spots." Stewart could have used a period, but the semicolon shows the connection between what to look for and what to avoid when buying peaches or plums.

P-2a Between Independent Clauses

Closely related independent clauses are most often joined with a comma plus *and* or another COORDINATING CONJUNCTION. If the two clauses are closely related and don't need a conjunction to signal the relationship, they may be linked with a semicolon.

▶ The silence deepened; the room chilled.
　　　　　　　　　　　—Wayson Choy, "The Ten Thousand Things"

▶ The life had not flowed out of her; it had been seized.
　　　　　　　　　　　—Valerie Steiker, "Our Mother's Face"

A period would work in either of the examples above, but the semicolon suggests a stronger connection between the two independent clauses.

Another option is to use a semicolon with a TRANSITION that clarifies the relationship between the two independent clauses. Put a comma after the transition.

▶ There are few among the poor who speak of themselves as lower class; instead, they refer to their race, ethnic group, or geographic location.
　　　　　　　　　　　—Gregory Mantsios, "Class in America—2003"

P-2b In a Series with Commas

Use semicolons to separate items in a series when one or more of the items contain commas.

▶ There are images of a few students: Erwin Petschaur, a muscular German boy with a strong accent; Dave Sanchez, who was good at math; and Sheila Wilkes, everyone's curly-haired heartthrob.
—Mike Rose, "Potato Chips and Stars"

P-2c Checking for Mistakes with Semicolons

Use a comma, not a semicolon, to set off an introductory clause.

▶ When the sun finally sets⁄, everyone gathers at the lake to watch the fireworks.

Use a colon, not a semicolon, to introduce a list.

▶ Every American high school student should know that the U.S. Constitution contains three sections⁄: preamble, articles, and amendments.

P-3 End Punctuation

She married him. She married him? She married him! In each of these three sentences, the words are the same, but the end punctuation completely changes the meaning, from a simple statement to a bemused question to an emphatic exclamation. This section will help you use periods, question marks, and exclamation points in your writing.

P-3a Periods

Use a period to end a sentence that makes a statement.

▶ Rose Emily Meraglio came to the United States from southern Italy as a little girl in the early 1920s and settled with her family in Altoona, Pennsylvania.   —Mike Rose, "The Working Life of a Waitress"

An indirect question, which reports something someone else has asked, ends with a period, not a question mark.

▶ Presidential candidates are often asked how they will address the ballooning national debt?.
                                    ^

When a sentence ends with an abbreviation that has its own period, do not add another period.

▶ The Rat Pack included Frank Sinatra and Sammy Davis Jr./

See **P-10** for more on periods with abbreviations.

P-3b Question Marks

Use a question mark to end a direct question.

▶ Did I think that because I was a minority student jobs would just come looking for me? What was I thinking?
                                    —Richard Rodriguez, "None of This Is Fair"

Use a period rather than a question mark to end an indirect question.

▶ Aunt Vivian often asked what Jesus would do?.
                                    ^

P-3c Exclamation Points

Use an exclamation point to express strong emotion or add emphasis to a statement or command. Exclamation points should be used sparingly, however, or they may undercut your credibility.

▶ "Keith," we shrieked as the car drove away, "Keith, we love you!"
                                    —Susan Jane Gilman, "Mick Jagger Wants Me"

When the words themselves are emotional, an exclamation point is often unnecessary, and a period is sufficient.

▶ It was so close, so low, so huge and fast, so intent on its target that I swear to you, I swear to you, I felt the vengeance and rage emanating from the plane.   —Debra Fontaine, "Witnessing"

P-4   Quotation Marks

"Girls Just Want to Have Fun" "Two thumbs up!" "Frankly, my dear, I don't give a damn." These are just some of the ways that quotation marks are used—to indicate a song title, to cite praise for a movie, to set off dialogue. In college writing, you will use quotation marks frequently to acknowledge when you've taken words from others. This chapter will show you how to use quotation marks correctly and appropriately.

P-4a Direct Quotations

Use quotation marks to enclose words spoken or written by others.

▶ "Nothing against Tom, but Johnny may be the bigger star now," says director John Waters. —Sean Smith, "Johnny Depp: Unlikely Superstar"

▶ Newt Gringrich and Jesse Jackson have both pounded nails and raised funds for Habitat for Humanity. This is what Millard Fuller calls the "theology of the hammer."
                                    —Diana George, "Changing the Face of Poverty"

When you introduce quoted words with *he said*, *she claimed*, or the like, use a comma between the verb and the quote. When you follow a quote with such an expression, use a comma before the closing quotation mark (unless the quote is a question or an exclamation).

▶ When my mother reported that Mr. Tomkey did not believe in television, my father said, "Well, good for him. I don't know that I believe in it either."
     "That's exactly how I feel," my mother said, and then my parents watched the news, and whatever came on after the news.
                                    —David Sedaris, "Us and Them"

You do not need any punctuation between *that* and a quotation.

▶ We were assigned to write one essay agreeing or disagreeing with George Orwell's statement that, "the slovenliness of our language makes it easier for us to have foolish thoughts."

In dialogue, insert a new pair of quotation marks to signal each change of speaker.

▶ "What's this?" the hospital janitor said to me as he stumbled over my right shoe.
"My shoes," I said.
"That's not a shoe, brother," he replied, holding it to the light. "That's a brick."   —Henry Louis Gates Jr., "A Giant Step"

P-4b Long Quotations

Long quotations should be set off without quotation marks as **BLOCK QUOTATIONS** . Each documentation style has distinct guidelines for the length and formatting of block quotations; you'll find more on long quotations in **MLA-d**, **APA-d**, **CMS-c**, and **CSE-c**. The following example uses MLA style, which calls for setting off quotations of five or more typed lines of prose by indenting them ten spaces (or one inch) from the left margin. Note that in the following example, the period precedes the parenthetical citation.

Biographer David McCullough describes Truman's railroad campaign as follows:

No president in history had ever gone so far in quest of support from the people, or with less cause for the effort, to judge by informed opinion. . . . As a test of his skills and judgment as a professional politician, not to say his stamina and disposition at age sixty-four, it would be like no other experience in his long, often difficult career, as he himself understood perfectly. (655)

P-4c Titles of Short Works

Use quotation marks to enclose the titles of articles, chapters, essays, short stories, poems, songs, and episodes of television series. Titles of books, films, newspapers, and other longer works should be in italics rather than enclosed in quotation marks.

▶ In "Unfriendly Skies Are No Match for El Al," Vivienne Walt, a writer
   for *USA Today,* describes her experience flying with this airline.
                                    —Andie McDonie, "Airport Security"

   Note that the title of the newspaper is italicized, whereas the newspaper
   article title takes quotation marks.

▶ With every page of Edgar Allan Poe's story "The Tell-Tale Heart," my
   own heart beat faster.

▶ Rita Dove's poem "Dawn Revisited" contains vivid images that appeal
   to the senses of sight, sound, smell, and taste.

P-4d Single Quotation Marks

When you quote a passage that already contains quotation marks,
whether they enclose a quotation or a title, change the inner ones
to single quotation marks.

▶ Debra Johnson notes that according to Marilyn J. Adams, "effective
   reading instruction is based on 'direct instruction in phonics, focusing
   on the orthographic regularities of English.' "

▶ Certain essays are so good (or so popular) that they are included
   in almost every anthology. *The Norton Reader* notes, for example,
   "Some essays—Martin Luther King Jr.'s 'Letter from Birmingham Jail'
   and Jonathan Swift's 'Modest Proposal,' for example—are constant
   favorites" (xxiii).

P-4e With Other Punctuation

The following examples show how to use other punctuation marks
inside or outside quotation marks.

Commas and periods

Put commas and periods inside closing quotation marks.

▶ "On the newsstand, the cover is acting as a poster, an ad for what's
   inside," she said. "The loyal reader is looking for what makes the
   magazine exceptional."
                           —Katharine Q. Seelye, "Lurid Numbers on Glossy Pages!"

When there is parenthetical **DOCUMENTATION** after an end quotation mark, the period goes after the parentheses.

▶ Dewey himself said, "When you're leading, don't talk" (qtd. in McCullough 672).   —Dylan Borchers, "Against the Odds"

Semicolons and colons

Put semicolons and colons outside closing quotation marks.

▶ No elder stands behind our young to say, "Folks have fought and died for your right to pierce your face, so do it right"; no community exists that can model for a young person the responsible use of the "right"; for the right, even if called self-expression, comes from no source other than desire.   —Stephen L. Carter, "Just Be Nice"

▶ According to James Garbarino, author of *Lost Boys: Why Our Sons Turn Violent and How We Can Save Them*, it makes no sense to talk about violent media as a direct cause of youth violence. Rather, he says, "it depends": Media violence is a risk factor that, working in concert with others, can exacerbate bad behavior.
                    —Maggie Cutler, "Whodunit—The Media?"

Question marks and exclamation points

Put question marks and exclamation points inside closing quotation marks if they are part of the quotation but outside if they apply to the whole sentence.

▶ Then she began to talk more loudly. "What he want, I come to New York tell him front of his boss, you cheating me?"
                    —Amy Tan, "Mother Tongue"

▶ How many people know the words to "Louie, Louie"?

If there's a parenthetical citation at the end, it immediately follows the closing quotation mark, and any punctuation that's part of your sentence comes after it.

▶ An avid baseball fan, Tallulah Bankhead once said, "There have been only two geniuses in the world: Willie Mays and Willie Shakespeare" (183).

P-4f Checking for Mistakes with Quotation Marks

Avoid using quotation marks to identify slang, to indicate irony, or to emphasize a word. Remove the quotation marks or substitute a better word.

SLANG   Appearing ⁊hip⁊ is important to many parents in New York.

                                          delegating tasks

IRONY   Natalie was more interested in ~~"facilitating"~~ than in doing work herself.

EMPHASIS   The woman explained that she is ⁊only⁊ the manager, not the owner, of the health club.

Do not enclose indirect quotations in quotation marks.

▶ Even before winning her fourth Wimbledon singles title, Venus Williams said that ⁊she expected to play well.⁊

P-5 Apostrophes

McDonald's: "I'm lovin' it" proclaims a recent advertisement, demonstrating two common uses of the apostrophe: to show ownership (*McDonald's*) and to mark missing letters (*I'm, lovin'*). This section offers guidelines on these and other common uses for apostrophes.

P-5a Possessives

Use an apostrophe to make a word possessive: *Daniel Craig's eyes, someone else's problem, the children's playground.*

Singular nouns

To make most singular nouns possessive, add an apostrophe and -s.

▶ Some bloggers are getting press credentials for this summer**'s**
Republican Convention. —Lev Grossman, "Meet Joe Blog"

▶ The magical thinking of denial became Ms. Didion**'s** companion.
—Michiko Kakutani, "The End of Life As She Knew It"

▶ Bill Gates**'s** philanthropic efforts focus on health care and education.

If adding -'s makes a word hard to pronounce, use only an apostrophe.

▶ Euripides**'** plays are more realistic than those of Aeschylus.

Plural nouns

To form the possessive of a plural noun not ending in -s, add an apostrophe and -s. For plural nouns that end in -s, add only an apostrophe.

▶ Are women**'s** minds different from men**'s** minds?
—Evelyn Fox Keller, "Women in Science"

▶ The surrounding neighbors**'** complaints about noise led the club owner to install soundproof insulation.

▶ Did you hear that Laurence Strauss is getting married? The reception will be at the Strauses**'** home.

Something, everyone, *and other indefinite pronouns*

To form the possessive of an **INDEFINITE PRONOUN**, add an apostrophe and -s.

▶ Clarabelle was everyone**'s** favorite clown.

Joint possession

To show that two or more individuals possess something together, use the possessive form for the last noun only.

▶ Carlson and Ventura**'s** book is an introduction to Latino writers for English-speaking adolescents.

To show individual possession, make each noun possessive.

▶ Jan's and Stuart's heart transplants inspired me to become an organ donor.

Compound nouns

For compound nouns, make the last word possessive.

▶ The surgeon general's report persuaded many people to stop smoking.

P-5b Contractions

An apostrophe in a contraction indicates where letters have been omitted.

▶ "Let's do it, Susie," she said. "We're really going to do it."
                              —Susan Jane Gilman, "Mick Jagger Wants Me"

Let's *is a contraction of* let us; we're *is a contraction of* we are.

P-5c Plurals

Most writers add an apostrophe and -s to pluralize numbers, letters, and words discussed as words, but usage is changing and some writers now leave out the apostrophe. Either way is acceptable, as long as you are consistent. Notice that you need to italicize the number, letter, or word but not the plural ending.

▶ The resolution passed when there were more *aye*'s than *nay*'s.

▶ The winning hand had three *7*'s.

▶ The admissions officers at Brown spoke enthusiastically about their no-grades option—and then told us we needed mostly *A*'s to get in.

Most writers omit the apostrophe when pluralizing decades.

▶ During the 1950s, the civil rights movement and environmentalism began to develop in the United States.

To make an abbreviation plural, add only an -s.

▶ How many TV**s** does the average American family have in its home?

▶ The United States has been seeking comprehensive free trade
agreements (FTA**s**) with the Middle Eastern nations most firmly on the
path to reform.   —The 9/11 Commission,
"Prevent the Continued Growth of Islamist Terrorism"

P-5d Checking for Mistakes with Apostrophes

Do not use an apostrophe in the following situations.

With plural nouns that are not possessive

    cellists
▶ Both ~~cellist's~~ played encores.

With his, hers, ours, yours, and theirs

       Ours   *yours?*
▶ Look at all the lettuce. ~~Our's~~ is organic. Is ~~your's?~~

With the possessive its

    its
▶ It's an unusual building; ~~it's~~ style has been described as postmodern,
but it fits beautifully with the Gothic buildings on our campus.

It's *is a contraction meaning* "it is"; its *is the possessive form of it.*

P-6   Other Punctuation

Some carpenters can do their jobs using only a hammer and a saw,
but most rely on additional tools. The same is true of writers: you can
get along with just a few punctuation marks, but having some others

in your toolbox—colons, dashes, parentheses, brackets, ellipses, and slashes—can help you say what you want to say in your writing and can help readers follow what you write. This section can help you use these other punctuation marks effectively.

P-6a Colons

Colons are used to direct attention to words that follow the colon: an explanation or elaboration, a list, a quotation, and so on.

▶ What I remember best, strangely enough, are the two things I couldn't understand and over the years grew to hate: grammar lessons and mathematics.   —Mike Rose, "Potato Chips and Stars"

▶ I sized him up as fast as possible: tight black velvet pants pulled over his boots, black jacket, a red-green-yellow scarf slashed around his neck.   —Susan Jane Gilman, "Mick Jagger Wants Me"

▶ She also voices some common concerns: "The product should be safe, it should be easily accessible, and it should be low-priced."
                    —Dara Mayers, "Our Bodies, Our Lives"

▶ Fifteen years after the release of the Carnegie report, College Board surveys reveal data are no different: test scores still correlate strongly with family income.   —Gregory Mantsios, "Class in America—2003"

Colons are also used after the salutation in a business letter, in ratios, between titles and subtitles, between city and publisher in bibliographies, between chapter and verse in biblical references, and between numbers that indicate hours, minutes, and seconds.

▶ Dear President Michaels:

▶ For best results, add water to the powder in a 3:1 ratio.

▶ *The Last Campaign: How Harry Truman Won the 1948 Election*

▶ New York: Norton, 2008.

▶ "Death and life are in the power of the tongue" (Proverbs 18:21).

▶ The morning shuttle departs at 6:52 a.m.

P-6b Dashes

You can create a dash by typing two hyphens (--) with no spaces before or after or by selecting the em dash from the symbol menu of your word-processing program.

Use dashes to set off material you want to emphasize. Unlike colons, dashes can appear not only after an independent clause but also at other points in a sentence. To set off material at the end of a sentence, place a dash before it; to set off material in the middle of the sentence, place a dash before and after the words you want to emphasize.

▶ After that, the roller coaster rises and falls, slowing down and speeding up—all on its own.
  —Cathi Eastman and Becky Burrell, "The Science of Screams"

▶ It did not occur to me—possibly because I am an American—that there could be people anywhere who had never seen a Negro.
  —James Baldwin, "Stranger in the Village"

Dashes are often used to signal a shift in tone or thought.

▶ The best way to keep children home is to make the home atmosphere pleasant—and let the air out of the tires.   —Dorothy Parker

Keep in mind that dashes are most effective if they are used only when material needs particular emphasis. Too many dashes can interfere with the flow and clarity of your writing.

P-6c Parentheses

Use parentheses to enclose supplemental details and digressions.

▶ When I was a child, attending grade school in Washington, DC, we took classroom time to study manners. Not only the magic words "please" and "thank you" but more complicated etiquette questions, like how to answer the telephone ("Carter residence, Stephen speaking") and how to set the table (we were quizzed on whether knife blades point in or out).   —Stephen L. Carter, "Just Be Nice"

▶ In their apartments they have the material possessions that indicate success (a VCR, a color television), even if it means that they do without necessities and plunge into debt to buy these items.
—Diana George, "Changing the Face of Poverty"

▶ Before participating in the trials, Seeta and Ratna (not their real names) knew nothing about H.I.V.
—Dara Mayers, "Our Bodies, Our Lives"

P-6d Brackets

Put brackets around words that you insert or change in a QUOTATION.

▶ As Senator Reid explained, "She [Nancy Pelosi] realizes that you cannot make everyone happy."

If you are quoting a source that contains an error, put the Latin word *sic* in brackets after the error to indicate that the mistake is in the original source.

▶ Warehouse has been around for 30 years and has 263 stores, suggesting a large fan base. The chain sums up its appeal thus: "styley [*sic*], confident, sexy, glamorous, edgy, clean and individual, with it's [*sic*] finger on the fashion pulse."
—Anne Ashworth, "Chain Reaction: Warehouse"

P-6e Ellipses

Ellipses are three spaced dots that indicate an omission or a pause. Use ellipses to show that you have omitted words within a QUOTATION. If you omit a complete sentence or more in the middle of a quoted passage, put a period before the three dots.

ORIGINAL

▶ The Lux ad's visual content, like Resinol's, supports its verbal message. Several demure views of Irene Dunne emphasize her "pearly-smooth skin," the top one framed by a large heart shape. In all the photos, Dunne wears a feathery, feminine collar, giving her a birdlike appearance: she is a bird of paradise or an ornament. At the bottom of the ad, we see a happy Dunne being cuddled and admired by a man.

WITH OMISSIONS

▶ The Lux ad's visual content . . . supports its verbal message. Several demure views of Irene Dunne emphasize her "pearly-smooth skin," the top one framed by a large heart shape. . . . At the bottom of the ad, we see a happy Dunne being cuddled and admired by a man.

—Doug Lantry, " 'Stay Sweet As You Are' "

P-6f Slashes

When you quote two or three lines of poetry and run them into the rest of your text, use slashes to show where one line ends and the next begins. Put a space before and after each slash.

▶ In the opening lines of the poem, he warns the reader to "Lift not the painted veil which those who live / Call Life" (1–2).

—Stephanie Huff, "Metaphor and Society in Shelley's 'Sonnet'"

P-7   Hyphens

If your mother gives you much needed advice, has she given you a great deal of advice that you needed, or advice that you needed badly? What about a psychiatry experiment that used thirty five year old subjects: were there thirty-five subjects who were a year old? Thirty subjects who were five years old? Or an unspecified number of thirty-five-year-old subjects? Hyphens could clear up the confusion. This chapter provides tips for when to use hyphens and when to omit them.

P-7a Compound Words

Compound words can be two words (*ground zero*), hyphenated (*self-esteem*), or one word (*outsource*). Check a dictionary, and if a compound is not there, assume that it is two words.

Compound adjectives

A compound adjective is made up of two or more words. Most compound adjectives take a hyphen before a noun.

▶ a little-known trombonist

▶ a foul-smelling river

Do not use a hyphen to connect an -ly adverb and an adjective.

▶ a carefully executed plan

A compound adjective after a noun is usually easy to read without a hyphen; add a hyphen only if the compound is unclear without it.

▶ The river has become foul smelling in recent years.

Prefixes and suffixes

A hyphen usually isn't needed after a prefix or before a suffix (*preschool, antislavery, counterattack, catlike, citywide*). However, hyphens are necessary in the following situations.

WITH *GREAT-, SELF-, -ELECT* great-aunt, self-hatred, president-elect

WITH CAPITAL LETTERS anti-American, post-Soviet literature

WITH NUMBERS post-9/11, the mid-1960s

TO AVOID DOUBLE AND TRIPLE LETTERS anti-intellectualism, ball-like

FOR CLARTIY re-cover (cover again) *but* recover (get well)

Numbers

Hyphenate fractions and compound numbers from twenty-one to ninety-nine.

▶ three-quarters of their income

▶ thirty-five subjects

P-7b At the End of a Line

Use a hyphen to divide a multisyllabic word that does not fit on one line. (A one-syllable word is never hyphenated.) Divide words between syllables as shown in a dictionary, after a prefix, or before a suffix. Divide compound words between the parts of the compound if possible. Do not leave only one letter at the end or the beginning of a line.

> op-er-a-tion   knot-ty   main-stream

Dividing Internet addresses

Do not insert a hyphen in a URL that you break at the end of a line. Each **DOCUMENTATION** style has specific guidelines on URLs that you'll find in the chapters on **MLA**, **APA**, *Chicago*, and **CSE**; MLA style suggests that you divide an Internet address only after a slash.

P-8   Capitalization

Capital letters are an important signal, either that a new sentence is beginning or that a specific person, place, or brand is being discussed. Capitalize *Carol*, and it's clear that you're referring to a person; write *carol*, and readers will know you're writing about a song sung at Christmas. This section offers guidelines to help you know what to capitalize and when.

P-8a Proper Nouns and Common Nouns

Capitalize proper nouns, those naming specific people, places, and things. All other nouns are common nouns and should not be capitalized.

PROPER NOUNS	COMMON NOUNS
Sanjay Gupta	a doctor
Senator Schumer	a U.S. senator
Uncle Daniel	my uncle
France	a republic
the Mississippi River	a river
the West Coast	a coast
Christianity	a religion
Allah	a god
the Torah	a sacred text
Central Intelligence Agency	an agency
U.S. Congress	the U.S. government
Ohio University	a university
Composition 101	a writing course
World War II	a war
July	summer
the Middle Ages	the fourteenth century
Kleenex	tissues

Adjectives derived from proper nouns, especially the names of people and places, are usually capitalized: *Shakespearean, Swedish, Chicagoan*. There are exceptions to this rule, however, such as *french fries, roman numeral*, and *congressional*. Consult your dictionary if you are unsure whether an adjective should be capitalized.

Many dictionaries capitalize the terms *Internet, Net*, and *World Wide Web*, but you'll see variations such as *Website* and *website*. Whether you capitalize or not, be consistent throughout a paper.

P-8b Titles before a Person's Name

A professional title is capitalized when it appears before a person's name but not when it appears after a proper noun or alone.

Senator Dianne Feinstein   Dianne Feinstein, the California senator

P-8c The First Word of a Sentence

Capitalize the first word of a sentence. The first word of a quoted sentence should be capitalized, but not the first word of a quoted phrase.

▶ Speaking about acting, Clint Eastwood notes, "You can show a lot with a look.... It's punctuation."

▶ Sherry Turkle argues that we're living in "techno-enthusiastic times" and that we're inclined "to celebrate our gadgets."

Interrupted quotations

Capitalize the second part of an interrupted quotation only if it begins a new sentence.

▶ "It was just as nice," she sobbed, "as I hoped and dreamed it would be."   —Joan Didion, "Marrying Absurd"

▶ "On the newsstand, the cover is acting as a poster, an ad for what's inside," she said. "The loyal reader is looking for what makes the magazine exceptional."
                    —Katharine Q. Seelye, "Lurid Numbers on Glossy Pages!"

P-8d Titles and Subtitles

Capitalize the first and last words and all other important words of a title and subtitle. Do not capitalize less important words such as ARTICLES, COORDINATING CONJUNCTIONS, and PREPOSITIONS.

"Give Peace a Chance"
Pride and Prejudice
The Shallows: What the Internet Is Doing to Our Brains

Each documentation style has guidelines for formatting titles in notes and bibliographies. You'll find more on titles and subtitles in MLA-c, APA-c, CMS-b, and CSE-b.

P-9 Italics

Italic type tells us to read words a certain way. Think of the difference between the office and *The Office*, or between time and *Time*. In each case, the italicized version tells us it's a specific television show or magazine. This chapter provides guidelines on using italics in your writing.

P-9a Titles of Long Works

Titles and subtitles of long works should appear in italics (or underlined). A notable exception is sacred writing such as the Qur'an or the Old Testament.

BOOKS   *The Norton Field Guide to Writing*, *War and Peace*

PERIODICALS   *Newsweek*, *Teen Vogue*, *College English*

NEWSPAPERS   *Los Angeles Times*

PLAYS   *Medea*, *Six Degrees of Separation*

LONG POEMS   *The Odyssey*, *Paradise Lost*

FILMS AND VIDEOS   *Up in the Air*, *Baseball*

MUSICAL WORKS OR ALBUMS   *The Four Seasons*, *Rubber Soul*

RADIO AND TV SERIES   *Fresh Air*, *Glee*

PAINTINGS, SCULPTURES   the *Mona Lisa*, Michelangelo's *David*

DANCES BY A CHOREOGRAPHER   Mark Morris's *Gloria*

SOFTWARE   *Adobe Acrobat 9 Standard*

SHIPS, SPACECRAFT   *Queen Mary*, *Challenger*

WEBSITES   *Salon*, *Etsy*, *IMDb*

A short work, such as a short story, an article, an episode of a series, or a song, takes quotation marks.

P-9b Words as Words

Italicize a word you are discussing as a word. The same practice applies to numbers as numbers, letters as letters, and symbols as symbols.

▶ In those 236 words, you will hear the word *dedicate* five times.
—William Safire, "A Spirit Reborn"

▶ Most American dictionaries call for one *t* in the word *benefited*.

▶ All computer codes consist of some combination of *0*'s and *1*'s.

Some writers use quotation marks rather than italics to signal words discussed as words.

▶ I would learn, when I asked some people who didn't show up the next day, that "definitely attending" on Facebook means "maybe" and "maybe attending" means "likely not."
—Hal Niedzviecki, "Facebook in a Crowd"

P-9c Non-English Words

Use italics for an unfamiliar word or phrase in a language other than English. Do not italicize proper nouns.

▶ *Verstehen*, a concept often associated with Max Weber, is the sociologist's attempt to understand human actions from the actor's point of view.

If the word or phrase has become part of everyday English or has an entry in English-language dictionaries, it does not need italics.

▶ An ad hoc committee should be formed to assess the university's use of fossil fuels and ways to incorporate alternative energy sources.

▶ The plot of *Jane Eyre* follows the conventions of a bildungsroman, or a coming-of-age story.

P-9d For Emphasis

You can use italics occasionally to lend emphasis to a word or phrase, but do not overuse them.

▶ It is, perhaps, as much what Shakespeare did *not* write as what he did that seems to indicate something seriously wrong with his marriage.
—Stephen Greenblatt, "Shakespeare on Marriage"

▶ Despite a physical beauty that had . . . hordes of teenage girls (and a few boys) dreaming of touching his hair *just once*, Depp escaped from the Hollywood star machine.
—Sean Smith, "Johnny Depp: Unlikely Superstar"

P-10   Abbreviations

MTV. USA. OC. DNA. fwiw. D.I.Y. These are some common abbreviations, shortcuts to longer words and phrases. This section will help you use abbreviations appropriately in academic writing.

You can use common abbreviations if you are sure your readers will recognize them. If your readers might not be familiar with an abbreviation, include the full version the first time with the abbreviation in parentheses immediately after. Throughout the rest of the paper, you can use the abbreviation alone.

▶ In a recent press release, officials from the international organization Médicins Sans Frontières (MSF) stressed the need for more effective tuberculosis drugs.

Periods are generally used in personal titles that precede a name and in Latin abbreviations such as *e.g.* or *etc.* They are not needed for state abbreviations such as *CA*, *NY*, or *TX*, or for organizations that use initials, like *AP* or *YMCA*. In some cases, periods are optional (*BCE* or *B.C.E.*). Be sure to use them or omit them consistently. If you're not sure about a particular abbreviation, check a dictionary.

P-10a With Names

Most titles are abbreviated when they come before or after a name.

Mr. Ed Stanford	Ed Stanford Jr.
Dr. Ralph Lopez	Ralph Lopez, MD
Prof. Susan Miller	Susan Miller, PhD

Do not abbreviate job titles that are not attached to a name.

▶ The ~~RN~~ *nurse* who worked with trauma victims specialized in cardiac care.

P-10b With Numbers

The following abbreviations can be used with numbers.

632 BC ("before Christ")

344 BCE ("before the common era")

AD 800 (*"anno Domini"*)

800 CE ("common era")

10:30 AM (*or* a.m.)

7:00 PM (*or* p.m.)

Notice that BC, BCE, and CE follow the date, while AD precedes the date. Remember that these abbreviations cannot be used without a date or time.

▶ By early ~~p.m.,~~ *afternoon,* all prospective subjects for the experiment had checked in.

P-10c In Notes and Documentation

Abbreviations such as *etc.*, *i.e.*, and *et al.* are not appropriate in the body of a paper but are acceptable in footnotes or endnotes, in-text documentation, and bibliographies.

P-11   Numbers

Numbers may be written with numerals (97) or words (ninety-seven). This section presents general guidelines for when to use numerals and when to spell numbers out.

Spell out numbers and fractions that you can write in one or two words (*thirteen, thirty-seven, thirty thousand, two-thirds*). Any number at the beginning of a sentence should be spelled out as well.

▶ Yohji Yamamoto designed ~~75~~ *seventy-five* pieces for his first Paris collection.

▶ The number of reporters there approached ten thousand.

▶ *A collection of* 110 pieces ~~for a collection~~ struck the fashion editors as excessive.

Use numerals if you cannot express a number in one or two words.

▶ He designed ~~one hundred ten~~ *110* pieces for his first Paris collection.

For very large numbers that include a fraction or decimal, use a combination of numerals and words.

▶ One of the larger retailers had sold more than 4.5 million of its basic T-shirts the previous year.

In addition, numerals are generally used in the following situations.

ADDRESSES   500 Broadway, 107 175th Street

DATES   December 26, 2012; 632 BCE; the 1990s

DECIMALS AND FRACTIONS   59.5, 59½

PARTS OF WRITTEN WORKS   volume 2; chapter 5; page 82; act 3, scene 3

PERCENTAGES   66 percent (*or* 66%)

RATIOS   16:1 (*or* 16 to 1)

STATISTICS   a median age of 32

TIMES OF DAY   6:20 AM (*or* a.m.)

Credits

Glossary/Index

argument, 32–37 A writing GENRE and STRATEGY that uses REASONS and EVIDENCE to support a CLAIM or position. Key Elements: clear and arguable position • necessary background • good reasons • convincing support for each reason • appeal to readers' values • trustworthy TONE • careful consideration of other positions

article, 277–79 The word *a*, *an*, or *the*, used to indicate that a NOUN is indefinite (*a* writer, *an* author) or definite (*the* author).

audience, 2–3, 9, 81 Those to whom a text is directed—the people who read, listen to, or view the text.

collective noun, 248, 251–52 A NOUN —such as *committee, crowd, family, herd,* or *team*—that refers to a group.

comma splice, 235–37 Two or more IN-DEPENDENT CLAUSES joined with only a comma: *I came, I saw, I conquered.*

common ground, 279–81 Shared values. Writers build common ground with AUDIENCES by acknowledging others' points of view, seeking areas of compromise, and using language that includes, rather than excludes, those they aim to reach.

comparison and contrast, 18–19 A STRATEGY that highlights the points of similarity and difference between items. Using the *block method* of comparison-contrast, a writer discusses all the points about one item and then all the same points about the next item; using the *point-by-point method,* a writer discusses one point for both items before going on to discuss the next point for both items, and so on. Sometimes comparison and / or contrast serves as the organizing principle for a paragraph or whole text.

complement, 232, 233 A NOUN, noun phrase, PRONOUN, or ADJECTIVE that modifies either the SUBJECT or the direct OBJECT of a sentence. A *subject* *complement* follows a LINKING VERB and tells more about the subject: She is a *good speaker*. She is *eloquent*. An *object complement* describes or renames the direct object: Critics called the movie a *masterpiece*. We found the movie *enjoyable*.

contrast See comparison and contrast

coordinating conjunction, 236, 256–57, 259, 282, 287, 288 One of these words—*and, but, or, nor, so, for,* or *yet*—used to join two elements in a way that gives equal weight to each one (bacon *and* eggs; pay up *or* get out).

correlative conjunction, 256–57, 259–60 A pair of words used to connect two equal elements: *either . . . or, neither . . . nor, not only . . . but also, just as . . . so,* and *whether . . . or.*

counterargument, 37 In ARGUMENT, an alternative position or objection to the writer's position. The writer of an argument should not only acknowledge counterarguments but also, if at all possible, accept, accommodate, or refute each counterargument.

count noun, 227 A word that names something that can be counted (*one book, two books*). *See also* noncount noun

dominant impression The overall effect created through specific details when a writer DESCRIBES something.

E

edit, 10–12 To fine-tune a text by examining each word, PHRASE, sentence, and paragraph to be sure that the text is correct and precise and says exactly what the writer intends.

effect *See* cause and effect

essential element, 284–85 A word,

PHRASE, or CLAUSE with information that is necessary for understanding the meaning of a sentence: French is the only language *that I can speak.*

et al., 310
etc., 268, 310

evaluation A GENRE of writing that makes a judgment about something—a source, poem, film, restaurant, whatever—based on certain criteria. Key Elements: description of the subject • clearly defined criteria • knowledgeable discussion of the subject • balanced and fair assessment

evaluative annotations, 54–55, 57
even, 276
everybody, 248
everyday, 269
every day, 269
everyone, 248–49, 251, 296
everything, 248
"Eviction: The Day They Came for Addie Polk's House," 286

evidence, 8, 9, 33, 36 In ARGUMENT, the data you present to support your REASONS. Such data may include statistics, calculations, examples, AN-ECDOTES, quotations, case studies, or anything else that will convince your readers that your reasons are compelling. Evidence should be sufficient (enough to show that the reasons have merit) and relevant (appropriate to the argument you're making).

anecdotes, 36
arguments and, 65
case studies, 36
facts, 36
literary analyses and, 52
observation, 36
revising and, 10
scenarios, 36
sources of information and, 77, 79
statistics, 36
testimony, 36
textual evidence, 36

examples, transitions to show, 24
examples, using, 22
except, 267
exceptions, transitions to show, 24
exclamation points, 287, 290, 294
experts, interviewing, 75–76

explanation of a process, 20–21 A STRATEGY for telling how something is done or how to do something. An explanation of a process can serve as the organizing principle for a paragraph or whole text.

expletive, 231, 272 The words *it* or *there* used to introduce information provided later in a sentence: *It* was difficult to drive on the icy road. *There* is plenty of food in the refrigerator.

F

"Facebook in a Crowd," 232, 308
facts, 26, 36, 244–45

fallacy, 65 Faulty reasoning that can

mislead an AUDIENCE. Fallacies include *ad hominem*, bandwagon appeal, begging the question, either-or argument (also called false dilemma), false analogy, faulty causality (also called *post hoc, ergo propter hoc*), hasty generalization, and slippery slope.

field research, 75–76 The collection of firsthand data through observation, interviews, and questionnaires or surveys.

flow *See* coherence

formal writing Writing intended to be evaluated by someone such as an instructor or read by an AUDIENCE expecting academic or businesslike argument and presentation. Formal writing should be carefully REVISED, EDITED, and PROOFREAD. *See also* informal writing

fragment, sentence. *See* sentence fragments

freewriting, 6, 34, 43 A process for GENERATING IDEAS AND TEXT by writing continuously for several minutes without pausing to read what has been written.

fused sentence, 235–37 Two or more INDEPENDENT CLAUSES with no punctuation between them: *I came I saw I conquered.*

linking verb A VERB that expresses a state of being (for example, *appear, be, feel, seem*).

literary analysis, 50–53 A writing GENRE that examines a literary text (most often fiction, poetry, or drama) and argues for a particular INTERPRETATION of the text. Key Elements: arguable THESIS • careful attention to the language of the text • attention to patterns or themes • clear interpretation • MLA STYLE

looping, 6, 43, 47 A process for GENERATING IDEAS AND TEXT in which a writer writes about a subject quickly for several minutes and summarizes the most important or interesting idea in a sentence, which becomes the beginning of another round of writing and summarizing, and so on, until finding an angle for a paper.

M

counted or made plural with certain modifiers or units: *information, rice.*

nonessential element, 284–85 A word, PHRASE, or CLAUSE that gives additional information but that is not necessary for understanding the basic meaning of a sentence: I learned French, *which is a Romance language,* online. Nonessential elements should be set off by commas.

nonrestrictive element *See* nonessential element

noun, 230 A word that names a person, place, thing, or idea (*teacher,* *Zadie Smith, forest, Amazon River, notebook, democracy*).

O

object, 232, 233 A word or phrase that follows a PREPOSITION or that receives the action of a VERB. In the sentence I handed *him* the mail that was on the table, *him* is an *indirect object,* and *mail* is a *direct object* of the verb *handed; table* is an *object of the preposition* on.

group of words that tells about the relationship between a NOUN or PRO-NOUN and another word in the sentence. Some common prepositions are *after, at, before, behind, between, by, for, from, in, of, on, to, under, until, with,* and *without.*

present participle, 232 A VERB form used with a HELPING VERB to create progressive TENSES (is *writing*) or used alone as an ADJECTIVE (a *living* will). The present participle of a verb always ends in *-ing.*

present perfect, 89, 239 A TENSE used to indicate actions that took place at no specific time in the past or that began in the past and continue into the present: I *have* often *wondered* about my love of language. He *has cried* every day since his companion of fifty years died.

primary source, 70–71 A source such as a literary work, historical document, work of art, or performance that a researcher examines first-hand. Primary sources also include experiments and FIELD RESEARCH. In writing about the Revolutionary War, a researcher would likely consider the Declaration of Independence a primary source and a textbook's description of the writing of the document a SECONDARY SOURCE.

pronoun, 230, 250–55 A word that takes the place of a NOUN, such as *she, anyone, whoever.*

proposal A GENRE that argues for a solution to a problem or suggests some action. Key Elements: well-defined problem • recommended solution • answers to anticipated questions • call to action • appropriate TONE

purpose, 2, 81 A writer's goal: to explore, to express oneself, to entertain, to demonstrate learning, to report, to persuade, and so on.

Q

questioning, 6, 47 A process of GENERATING IDEAS AND TEXT about a TOPIC—asking, for example, *What? Who? When? Where? How?* and *Why?* or other questions.

relative pronoun, 249 A PRONOUN such as *that, which, who, whoever, whom,* and *whomever* that introduces a SUBORDINATE CLAUSE: The professor *who* gave the lecture is my adviser.

report, 42–45 A writing GENRE that presents information to inform or influence readers on a subject. Key Elements: tightly focused TOPIC • accurate, well-researched information • various writing STRATEGIES • clear DEFINITIONS • appropriate DESIGN

synthesis, 80–82 A process of bringing together ideas and information from multiple sources, exploring patterns and perspectives in order to discover new insights and perspectives.

T

tense, 88–89, 241 A characteristic of VERBS that indicates the time when action occurs or expresses a state of being. The three main tenses are the present (*I play*), the past (*I played*), and the future (*I will play*). Each tense has perfect (*I have played*), progressive (*I am playing*), and perfect progressive (*I have been playing*) forms.

textual analysis, 38–42 A writing GENRE in which a writer looks at what a text says and how it says it. Key Elements: summary of the text • attention to context • clear INTERPRETATION or judgment • reasonable support for conclusions

Revision Symbols

abbr	abbreviation **309**		∧	insert	
adj	adjective **273**		*i/p*	interesting point	
adv	adverb **273**		*ital*	italics **307**	
agr	agreement **246, 251**		*jarg*	jargon **263**	
⌄	apostrophe **295**		*lc*	lowercase letter **304**	
no ⌄	unnecessary apostrophe **298**		*mm*	misplaced modifier **275**	
			nice	well done!	
art	article **277**		*num*	number **311**	
awk	awkward		¶	new paragraph	
cap	capitalization **304**		//	parallelism **256**	
case	pronoun case **253**		*pass*	passive voice **243**	
cliché	cliché **263**		*ref*	pronoun reference **252**	
⌒	close up space		*run-on*	comma splice or fused sentence **235**	
∧	comma needed **282**				
no ∧	unnecessary comma **287**		*sexist*	sexist language **280**	
cs	comma splice **235**		*shift*	confusing shift **260**	
def	define **19**		*sl*	slang **262**	
dm	dangling modifier **276**		#	insert space	
doc	documentation **93–228**		*sp*	spelling	
emph	emphasis **260**		*trans*	transition **23**	
frag	sentence fragment **233**		*vb*	verb **237**	
fs	fused sentence **235**		*wrdy*	wordy **272**	
hyph	hyphen **302**		*ww*	wrong word **267**	

MLA Documentation Directory

APA Documentation Directory

Chicago Documentation Directory

CSE Documentation Directory

Detailed Menu